CHICANAS AND CHICANOS IN CONTEMPORARY SOCIETY

Edited by
Roberto M. De Anda
Trinity University
San Antonio, Texas

Allyn and Bacon
Boston • London • Toronto • Sydney • Tokyo • Singapore

In memory of César Chávez
(1927–1993)

 Copyright © 1996 by Allyn & Bacon
A Simon & Schuster Company
Needham Heights, MA 02194

Executive Editor: Karen Hanson
Vice President, Publisher: Susan Badger
Editorial Assistant: Sarah L. Dunbar
Editorial-Production Service: Walsh Associates
Cover Administrator: Suzanne Harbison
Manufacturing Buyer: Aloka Rathnam

Library of Congress Cataloging-in-Publication Data
Chicanas and Chicanos in contemporary society / edited by Roberto M.
De Anda
    p.   cm.
    Includes bibliographical references and index.
    ISBN 0-02-327982-6
    1. Mexican Americans—Social conditions.   I. De Anda, Roberto
Moreno.
E184.M5C43   1995
305.868'72073—dc20   94-48278
                                                                               CIP

Printed in the United States of America
10 9 8 7 6 5 4   99 98 97

PREFACE

This book is about social issues confronting Chicanas and Chicanos in today's society. It grew out of my concern about the shortage of anthologies dealing with this increasingly important population. The idea for this book was strongly supported by colleagues and friends who teach courses on the Chicana/o experience. Through their suggestions, they helped shape this book. This anthology covers a broad range of topics; it provides the reader with a better understanding of the current socioeconomic situation of Chicanas and Chicanos and of their continuing struggle for cultural survival and full participation in society.

This book is designed to offer the reader an interdisciplinary overview of the most pressing issues confronting Chicanas and Chicanos. The studies report original research and use a variety of research methods, including survey research, ethnography, discourse analysis, and archival research. Regardless of methodology used, the presentation of findings is straightforward.

Chicanas and Chicanos in Contemporary Society begins with a general introduction followed by four major parts. Part I provides a demographic profile of the Mexican-origin population in the United States. It also includes two chapters that examine economic inequality at different stages of the lifecycle: workers entering the labor market and mature workers.

Part II examines the Chicano family. The selections discuss the cultural strategies used by Chicano and Mexican immigrant families to confront issues of assimilation, urban poverty, and gender inequality. These studies stress the forms of cultural resistance that Chicanas and Chicanos have developed to shield themselves from the encroachment of the dominant society.

The central theme of Part III is the Chicano challenge to mainstream social institutions. The first selection describes how Chicanas and Chicanos are attempting to transform the Catholic Church to reflect their needs and interests. The second study analyzes the relationship between early Chicano *corridos* and recent *pinto* poetry. The next chapter explores the conscious and unconscious struggle for ethnic identity and cultural maintenance of Chicanos vis-à-vis mass media. The last chapter challenges the media stereotype of the Chicano gang member as a hard-core, psychopathic killer.

The last part of the book discusses issues related to ethnic identity and politics. The first study deals with the politics of bilingual education in the context of shifts in ethnic identity. The next chapter in this section argues that middle-class Mexican American politicians are ambivalent about their ethnic identification. The last chapter seeks to define the so-called Hispanic political and social agenda. Overall, these studies seek to contribute to our understanding of the Chicano's continuing struggle for self-definition and full political participation.

ACKNOWLEDGMENTS

First and foremost, I would like to acknowledge that this book would not have been possible without the support and collaboration of colleagues who contributed chapters. In this sense, this volume is truly the result of a collective endeavor. Charley Trujillo helped motivate this project in its early stages. Although I did not always follow their advice, Eric Romero, Manuel Hidalgo, and an anonymous reviewer helped make this a better book. I thank the students enrolled in my courses, for their comments on an early version of this volume. I am indebted to Pat Cummins who diligently prepared the manuscript for publication. I also thank Kathy Whittier for making this anthology more readable. I am also grateful to Trinity University for a Faculty Fellowship that provided support for two summers while I edited this book. Finally, I would like to thank my compañera, Hilda Munoz, for her unwavering support throughout.

CONTENTS

Preface   **iii**
Contributors   **xi**

1   **Introduction**   **1**
by Roberto M. De Anda
The Chicano Population and the Economy   1
Continuity and Change: The Chicano Family   2
Challenging Social Institutions   3
Chicano Identity and Politics   4

PART I   *The Chicano Population and the Economy*   7

2   **The Demography of Chicanos**   **9**
by Rogelio Saenz and Clyde S. Greenlees
Historical Demographic Content   10
Data Source for Analysis   12
The Demography of Chicanos in the United States and the Five
    Regions   12
Conclusions   22

3   **Economic Restructuring and Young Latino Workers in the
    1980s**   **25**
by Manuel Avalos
Theoretical Explanations for Income Inequality   26
Data Source   28
Young Latino and Anglo Workers in 1979   29
Structural Reform for a More Democratic Economy   36

4   Falling Back: Mexican-Origin Men and Women in the U.S. Economy   41
by Roberto M. De Anda
Labor Force Integration   42
Labor Force Participation   42
The Effect of Marginality on Income   48
Conclusions   48

PART II   *Continuity and Change: The Chicano Family   51*

5   Familism and Assimilation among Mexican-Origin and Anglo High School Adolescents   53
by Angela Valenzuela and Sanford M. Dornbusch
Sources of Data   55
Measures Used in the Analysis   55
Procedures   57
Empirical Results   57
Conclusions   60

6   Chicano Families and Urban Poverty: Familial Strategies of Cultural Retention   63
by Elsa O. Valdez
Theoretical Framework   64
Profile of the Latino Family   65
The Significance of Cultural Adaptation in Urban Areas   66
Characteristics of the Area of Study   67
Data Collection Method   67
Characteristics of the Sample   68
Measures of Familial Strategies   68
Findings   69
Conclusion   73

7   *Juntos y Separados:* Cultural Complexity in U.S. Mexican Households   75
by Javier Tapia
The Enculturation Process   76
The Households and the Household Cluster   77
The Setting   78
Methodology   78
The Renteria Household   79
The Morales Household   82
Discussion and Conclusions   84

**8 Independent Living among Mexican American Elderly:
The Need for Social Services Support   87**
by Diana J. Torrez
Social Support Theory   88
Data Source and Methods   89
Results   90
Conclusions   92

PART III   *Challenging Social Institutions   97*

**9 Liberation Theology and Social Change: Chicanas and
Chicanos in the Catholic Church   99**
by Gilbert R. Cadena and Lara Medina
*Demographic Overview of Chicanas and Chicanos in the Catholic
Church   100*
Religion as Source of Social Change   102
Liberation Theology   103
Calpulli: A Model for Social Change   106
Discussion and Conclusion   109

**10 Of *Corridos* and Convicts: *Gringo* (In)Justice in Early Border
Ballads and Contemporary *Pinto* Poetry   113**
by Raúl Homero Villa
*Intercultural Conflict: The Historical Context of Border Balladry and Critical
Pinto Poetry   114*
From la penitencia *to* la pinta: *Traditional Visions and Critical Revisions of the
Prison Experience   117*

11 Chicano Cultural Resistance with Mass Media   127
by Diana I. Ríos
Functions of Communication: Media Uses and Gratifications   129
Audience-Centered Functions   129
Data Source and Methods   130
Findings from the Field   131
Concluding Remarks   140

12 Ganging up on the Gang   143
by Raúl Tovares
Literature Review   144
Methodology   148
Findings   149
Discussion   150
Conclusion   152

PART IV   *Chicano Identity and Politics   155*

13 Bilingual/Bicultural Education and Politics in Crystal City, Texas: 1969–1989   157
by Armando L. Trujillo
The Winter Garden Region and Crystal City   158
Bilingual Education and Politics in Crystal City during the 1970s   161
National and State Policy Directives in the 1980s and Bilingual Program   Restructuring   167
Conclusion   173

14 Situational Identity of Suburban Mexican American Politicians in a Multiethnic Community   179
by José Zapata Calderón
Demographics   180
Perspectives on Situational Identity   181
Situational Character of Identity   182
Social Class and Assimilation   183
Discussion   185
Conclusions   187

15 Backwards from Aztlán: Politics in the Age of Hispanics   191
by Ignacio García
The Hispanic Political and Social Agenda   192
The Mexican American Generation   194
The Chicano Movement Generation   195
The Mexican American/Hispanic Generation   197
The Future   201

Index   205

CONTRIBUTORS

MANUEL AVALOS is Assistant Professor of Political Science at Arizona State University-West. He teaches research methods, public policy, and ethnic politics. He recently published "The Impact of the Latino Vote in the 1992 Presidential Elections in Arizona," *Harvard Journal of Hispanic Policy*. His current research focuses on a longitudinal study of inequality among Latinas from 1940–1990.

GILBERT R. CADENA is Assistant Professor of Sociology and Chicano Studies at Pomona College. His research interests are Chicanas/os and the Catholic Church, liberation theology, and race and ethnic relations. His articles include, "Religious Organic Intellectuals: Priests and Sisters in the Chicano/a Community."

JOSÉ ZAPATA CALDERÓN is Assistant Professor of Sociology and Chicano Studies at Pitzer College in Claremont, California. His publications include the following: "How the English Only Movement Was Passed in California," in *Estudios Chicanos and the Politics of Community*; and, "Hispanic and Latino: The Viability of Categories for Panethnic Unity," *Latin American Perspectives*.

ROBERTO M. DE ANDA is Assistant Professor of Sociology at Trinity University in San Antonio, Texas, where he teaches courses on the Chicano experience and racial/ethnic stratification. He has published on Chicana/o underemployment. Presently, he continues to study socioeconomic inequality among Mexican-origin workers.

SANFORD M. DORNBUSCH has been Professor at Stanford University since 1959. His research interests include the study of families and schools. He is the author of numerous articles and the author or editor of six books.

IGNACIO GARCÍA is Assistant Professor of History at Texas A&M University in Corpus Christi. He is the author of *United We Win: The Rise and Fall of the Raza Unida Party*. He is currently doing research on the decade of the 1950s to understand the social climate that led to the Chicano Movement in the 1960s. Additionally, he is studying the Viva Kennedy Club movement.

CLYDE S. GREENLEES is a Ph.D. student in the Department of Rural Sociology at Texas A&M University. His research interests include the demography of Latinos and race and ethnic relations. His current research deals with the changing industrial structure of the Chicano labor force and Mexican immigration patterns.

LARA MEDINA is Instructor of Chicano and Chicana Studies at the University of California, Los Angeles and California State University, Northridge. Her areas of instruction are religion and social change, liberation theology, and Latina feminist theology. She is currently a graduate student in the History Department at the Claremont Graduate School.

DIANA I. RÍOS is Assistant Professor at the University of New Mexico where she teaches intercultural communication. Her research interests are in mass communication research on Chicano audiences, ethnic studies, women's studies, and field research methodologies.

ROGELIO SAENZ is Associate Professor in the Departments of Rural Sociology and Sociology at Texas A&M University. His research interests include the demography of Latinos, race and ethnic relations, and rural sociology. His current research focuses on the migration patterns of Latinos and the self-employment patterns of Chicanos in the Southwest. His recent publications have appeared in *Demography*, *International Migration Review*, *Rural Sociology*, *Social Science Quarterly*, and *Sociological Perspectives*.

JAVIER TAPIA is Assistant Professor in the Graduate School of Education at the University of Pennsylvania. He recently co-authored "Living Knowledge: The Social Distribution of Cultural Resources for Thinking" in *Distributed Cognitions*. His research interests include the process of social and cultural reproduction in Latino communities.

DIANA TORREZ is Assistant Professor in the Sociology Department at the University of North Texas. She does research in the areas of birth outcomes, health, aging, and social health service delivery to Latino populations. She is presently examining the effect of the availability of informal services on the utilization of formal services.

RAÚL TOVARES is a Ph.D. candidate in the Department of Radio-Television-Film at the University of Texas at Austin. His major areas of interest are mass communication theory, minorities and mass communication, and film theory. He is currently working on how teenagers from different ethnic groups read television.

ARMANDO L. TRUJILLO is Assistant Professor in the Division of Bicultural-Bilingual Studies at the University of Texas at San Antonio. His research interests are in educational anthropology, Chicano studies, and bilingual education. Recent publications include: "Ethnoterritorial Politics and the Institutionalization of Bilingual Education at the Grass-roots Level," in *Critical Perspectives on Bilingual Education Research*.

ELSA O. VALDEZ is Assistant Professor of Sociology at California State University, San Bernardino. She co-authored "Work, Family, and the Chicana: Power, Perception, and Equity," in *Employed Mothers in the Family Context*. Currently, she is studying changes in attitudes within the Latino population toward Catholicism, sexuality, work/family roles, and cultural identity.

ANGELA VALENZUELA is Assistant Professor of Sociology at Rice University in Houston, Texas. Her research interests are in the area of Chicana/o youth in public and private schools. A recent publication is "Liberal Gender Role Attitudes and Academic Achievement among Mexican-Origin Adolescents in Two Houston Inner-City Schools," *Hispanic Journal of Behavioral Sciences*.

RAÚL HOMERO VILLA is Assistant Professor in the Department of English and Comparative Literary Studies at Occidental College in Los Angeles, California. His research and teaching interests are in contemporary Chicano literature and popular culture, U.S. minority literature, and cultural studies.

1

INTRODUCTION

ROBERTO M. DE ANDA

The studies presented in *Chicanas and Chicanos in Contemporary Society* cover a broad range of issues challenging this group. Two main themes bring the studies together: social inequalities—cultural, economic, and political—and the struggles carried on by Chicanas and Chicanos to eradicate them. The studies in this book seek to integrate both themes and give a current view of the complex experiences of Chicanas and Chicanos in U.S. society.

The book is divided into four major parts. The first part includes selections that focus on the causes of socioeconomic inequality, and the rest of the book highlights the struggle for equal participation in society. A common thread running through these chapters is that the struggle relies heavily on culture, regardless of the strategies used.

THE CHICANO POPULATION AND THE ECONOMY

In a few decades, Latinos will become the largest minority group in the United States, surpassing African Americans. The term *Latino* refers to persons who live in the United States and can trace their ancestry back to Latin American countries. The most sizable Latino subgroup is the population of Mexican descent, or Chicanos. Although there is no agreement about the origin of the term *Chicano*, it probably stems from the Nahuatl word, *mexica* (pronounced "meshica"), the Aztec name for the native peoples of central Mexico. In this book, contributors interchangeably use the terms Chicano or Mexican American to refer to the Mexican-origin population in the United States.

The Chicano population is rapidly growing. This demographic change raises a critical question: How will this population change influence relations between Chicanos and the majority population? Equally important is the issue of how this change will affect Chicanos themselves. Part I discusses the Chicano population and its participation in the economic system.

Chapter 2 provides an overview of the demographic characteristics of the Mexican-origin population in the United States. Saenz and Greenlees, drawing data from the 1990 Census, answer the following questions about the Mexican-origin population: How large is the group? How is it distributed throughout the country? What is its age composition? And, what is its family structure? The authors also provide information on Chicanos outside the Southwest.

Saenz and Greenlees found that between 1980 and 1990 the Chicano population grew at a rate more than five times faster than the U.S. population. The authors also found that there were twice as many female-headed households among Chicanos compared to whites. Another finding is that nearly one-third of the population of Mexican origin is younger than 15, compared with less than one-fifth of the non-Chicano population. Needless to say, these statistics have implications for the well-being of Chicanas and Chicanos. For instance, how do families with absent fathers cope? How well do Chicano youth fare in U.S. society?

To understand the socioeconomic situation of Chicanos, it is important to know their position in the economic system. In other words, a person's position in the economic system—for instance, whether he or she is employed or unemployed—affects his or her social well-being. A person's participation in the economy determines, to a large extent, the type of opportunities available; for example, where he or she lives, the quality of schools his or her children attend, where he or she worships, how well he or she can provide for family, his or her access to social services, and so on.

Chapter 3, by Avalos, provides an empirical analysis of the labor-market experiences of young men and women. Using a large national survey, he evaluates the effect of economic restructuring on the occupational distribution and incomes of young Latinas and Latinos. Avalos raises an intriguing question: Does restructuring offer an opportunity to increase the level of democratic participation at the workplace? His study also suggests an important question—namely, to what extent do the work experiences of young people affect their later careers? In other words, it is possible that young workers with poor participation in the labor market become trapped in lifelong low-paying, dead-end jobs.

Chapter 4 examines the labor force activity of Mexican-origin men and women. De Anda evaluates the quality of work available to Mexican workers compared to that for white workers. His focus is on the growth of inadequate employment or underemployment. De Anda's study reveals that Mexican men and women have been losing ground in the labor force, with deleterious economic consequences.

CONTINUITY AND CHANGE: THE CHICANO FAMILY

Part II deals with a key social institution in the Chicano community: the family. The culture of a group is transmitted by the family. The family also regulates the behavior of its members. The selections included in this section deal with issues of cultural maintenance and change. Just like any other social institution, the family is not immune to changes in the larger society. Among the factors that have affected the Chicano family are economic changes, the continuing increase in the number of households headed by women, changes in sex role expectations, and pressures to assimilate.

The assimilation model predicts that as Mexicans acculturate—that is, adopt the dominant group's culture—they will lose their traditional ways. Valenzuela and Dornbusch (Chapter 5) test this prediction by examining the prevalence of familism among Mexican-origin families. Their study examines the relation of socioeconomic mobility and generational change to familism. The authors find that familism, as an integral part of Mexican culture, is successfully resisting assimilation.

In Chapter 6, Elsa Valdez has a two-pronged approach to studying families headed by women. The first approach explores how female-headed families use various strategies to retain their culture. The second focuses on how this "cultural retention" helps Chicanos deal with their impoverished conditions. Although Chicano families face extremely difficult and harsh living conditions, Valdez reports high levels of familism and religiosity. Her results suggest that familism and religiosity shield inner-city families from the dominant society's oppression.

Chapter 7, by Tapia, examines survival strategies of Mexican immigrant households in the United States. He stresses how immigrant households do not operate independently of the socioeconomic environment; rather, the activities of households are heavily influenced by the larger economic system. His study focuses on the formation of household clusters, which help maintain and reproduce the family. The cluster provides each household with economic and social benefits. He also evaluates the unequal distribution of power, based on gender, among household members.

This section fittingly closes with a study of Mexican American elderly (Chapter 8). Diana Torrez questions the myth that the Chicano family is able to take care of its elderly. Due to economic and demographic changes, the number of extended families has been shrinking. In the absence of family support, she examines the obstacles encountered by many Mexican American elderly who want to live independently—mainly, the need for adequate social services.

The studies in this section try to present a balanced view of *la familia Chicana*. The Chicano family demonstrates its flexibility in accommodating social and cultural change. Overall, *la familia* seems to provide a safe harbor for Chicanos in an otherwise hostile society.

CHALLENGING SOCIAL INSTITUTIONS

Social institutions have generally been unresponsive to the needs of Chicanas and Chicanos. Part III includes four case studies where Chicanas and Chicanos question the status quo. Chapter 9 challenges the Catholic Church to hear the voice of its followers. Chapter 10 questions the moral precepts of the criminal justice system, and Chapters 11 and 12 critically examine the mass media.

While the Catholic Church has exercised dominance in the Chicano community, there is a growing discontent within the church for its leader's rigidity and unwillingness to bring about much needed social change. In their chapter, Cadena and Medina discuss how a Chicana- and Chicano-based theology of liberation is gaining momentum. This emerging theology of liberation, with its emphasis on social action, is challenging the church's power.

The criminal justice system has historically treated Chicanos unfairly. This unfair treatment has been documented in *corridos* or ballads. Villa's study links the tradition of *corridos* to contemporary *pinto* poetry. In both types of narratives, the protagonists, who are seen as the criminals, are exonerated and the Anglo system is exposed as the real culprit. The study shows a continuum of how basic ideas have been used and improved upon by recent *pinto* poets to challenge the dominant power, rather than passively accept violated rights.

The mass media have done much to distort the image of Chicanas and Chicanos over time. Although one does not see the negative stereotypes of yesterday, there is an almost complete absence of positive images portrayed of Chicanos. When they are portrayed, however, their presentation is less than flattering. These negative images fuel the stereotypical images present in the majority's collective mind. Chapters 11 and 12 explore some of these issues.

In her chapter, Diana Rios documents the struggle for ethnic identity and cultural maintenance of Chicanas and Chicanos vis-à-vis mass media. Chicanos experience a constant battle for positive affirmation during their everyday use of and exposure to popular media such as television, radio, and newspapers and magazines. This battle can be otherwise understood as cultural resistance to the acculturation process demanded by U.S. society. There is a generalized belief that violent youth gangs have some cities under siege. To a large extent, the media have been responsible for creating an image of drive-by shootings and street warfare. Just like any business, the media's main goal is to be profitable; sensational stories, such as those about gang violence, are effective in attracting audiences and making profits. Challenging the media's objectivity in presenting gangs, Raul Tovares examines gang-related stories in two city newspapers in Texas. He concludes that youth gangs are distorted, not examined, by these newspapers.

CHICANO IDENTITY AND POLITICS

Chicanos appear to be gaining ground in the political landscape. The number of Chicanas and Chicanos elected to office has substantially increased in the last decade. On the surface, this seems to point to greater political integration. The central question that emerges from this phenomenon is: Whose interests do these politicians represent? Part IV includes two community studies and a synthetic essay that address this important question.

In Chapter 13, Armando Trujillo analyzes the case of a South Texas community where Chicanos achieved political power through La Raza Unida Party. Based on extensive field work, the author focuses on the shift in ethnic identity from the cultural nationalism generated by the Chicano Movement to the assimilationist goals of Hispanics. Trujillo employs this sociopolitical backdrop to analyze concomitant changes in educational policy.

The study by Calderón (Chapter 14) examines the attitudes of Mexican American politicians toward their ethnic identification. In his study, Calderón attempts to determine: 1) whether Mexican American politicians have a common ethnic identity, 2) whether ethnicity plays a role in their political perspectives, and 3) whether they are unified politically as an ethnic group. He is also concerned with the role that class and ethnic factors play in the politics of Mexican American leaders. He found that middle-class Mexican American politicians were ambivalent about their ethnic identity; they used their ethnicity to meet their class interest, not the community's cultural goals.

The book appropriately ends with a study that analyzes the Chicano's struggle for political power. García points out in Chapter 15 that the last decade witnessed the largest number of Chicanas and Chicanos elected to public office. García poses two critical questions to evaluate this phenomenon: (1) What is the political agenda of these elected officials? and, (2) Where do they derive their political ethos? The author concludes that the so-called "Hispanic Agenda" is a far cry from self-determination advocated by the Chicano Movement.

PART I

THE CHICANO POPULATION AND THE ECONOMY

2

THE DEMOGRAPHY OF CHICANOS

ROGELIO SAENZ   CLYDE S. GREENLEES

The Chicano population represents one of the most dynamic ethnic groups in the United States. Perhaps no other ethnic group in this country has grown as rapidly as the Chicano population during the twentieth century. Indeed, while the country's total population more than doubled from 92 million in 1910 to 248.7 million in 1990, the Chicano population has grown almost 37-fold from 367,500 in 1910 to 13.5 million in 1990. This dramatic growth is even witnessed today, as evidenced by the fact that the Chicano population increased about 5.5 times faster (55.4 percent) than the U.S. total population (9.8 percent) between 1980 and 1990. Few other ethnic groups in the nation can match this contemporary growth pattern. Today, Chicanos represent the second largest minority group in the nation, trailing only African Americans.

Demographically, the blossoming growth of the Chicano population has been due to three factors. First, Chicanos tend to be relatively young compared to other groups in the United States. This youthfulness among Chicanos represents the potential for growth, since low proportions of group members are in age groups with high death rates, but high proportions are in the younger age groups that are associated with the childbearing and family-formation years. Second, Chicanos have traditionally had higher fertility rates compared to other groups. The addition of younger people to the population provides an impetus for further growth. Third, the Chicano population has been supplemented by large flows of immigrants compared to other groups. The flows of Mexican immigrants coming to the United States through both legal and illegal means have been major, especially since the 1960s. It has been suggested that immigration accounted for approximately half of the growth in the Latino population during the 1980s.[1] The newcomers not only stimulate growth in the Chicano population by their presence, but they also tend to be relatively young, which suggests that they represent a potential for further growth in the ethnic group.

9

Historically, the Chicano population has not been widely distributed across the United States. Rather, the group has been disproportionately located in five states—Arizona, California, Colorado, New Mexico, Texas—commonly referred to as the Southwest. Although this regional concentration has changed during the century (e.g., 95 percent of Chicanos lived in these states in 1910), approximately four-fifths (83.3 percent) of the country's Chicanos were found in the Southwest in 1990. Unfortunately, much of our knowledge of the Chicano population has been based solely on the Southwest.

This chapter seeks to provide an indepth overview of the demographic characteristics of the Chicano population in the United States and in five regions of the country—Southwest, Midwest, West, South, Northeast. The regional analysis will begin to fill the knowledge gap on the non-Southwest Chicanos and will serve to further illustrate the diverse nature of the population. For comparative purposes, data for the entire U.S. population are presented so that readers can observe the differences and similarities between the Chicano and U.S. populations. Before undertaking the analysis, however, a historical demographic context has to be established.

HISTORICAL DEMOGRAPHIC CONTEXT

The Chicano population represents one ethnic group with a long history in this country. The ancestors of today's Chicanos explored and established settlements in parts of the Southwest long before the arrival of Anglo immigrants to Plymouth Rock.[2] The incorporation of Chicanos into the United States came about through conflict between the United States and Mexico, first with the annexation of Texas in 1845 following the independence of Texas from Mexico, and later with the signing of the Treaty of Guadalupe Hidalgo in 1848 at the conclusion of the Mexican-American War. The Chicano population has grown significantly since the initial cohort of Chicanos who became U.S. citizens during this period. Unfortunately, there is a major dearth of historical demographic statistics enumerating the Chicano population. Indeed, historically, specific data for Chicanos have been either completely absent or have been plagued by inconsistent operational definitions of a "Chicano" or a "person of Mexican origin."[3] For example, the definition of persons of Mexican origin has varied over time from Mexicans being treated as a racial category, to the presence of a Spanish surname, to the use of the Spanish language. Fortunately, since the 1980 Census, people have been allowed to identify themselves with respect to whether they are of Hispanic origin and the specific Hispanic subgroup to which they belong.

While historical information on the population size of Chicanos is lacking, we do know that much of the growth in this population has been due to immigration. According to the U.S. Immigration and Naturalization Service,[4] approximately 2.5 million Mexicans have emigrated to the United States legally between 1820 and 1984, placing Mexico as the eighth largest sender of immigrants during the period.

However, this figure does not include the large numbers that have come to the United States as undocumented immigrants. Yet, large-scale Mexican emigration to the United States is very much of a twentieth-century phenomenon. Indeed, of the approximately 2.5 million Mexicans who have emigrated to the United States legally from 1820 to 1984, only a trickle (1.1 percent, or about 28,000) emigrated between 1820 and 1900. The first major wave of Mexican immigration to the United States occurred in the decades of the 1910s and 1920s, as many Mexicans fled the Mexican Revolution. Mexican immigrants coming to the United States through legal means during these two decades accounted for more than one-fourth (27 percent, or about 678,000) of all the legal Mexican immigrants between 1820 and 1984. The flow of immigrants coming to this country during the period, however, continued to be primarily dominated by Europeans.

The ethnic composition of immigrants has changed dramatically since the 1960s. For the 1961–1984 period, Mexico has been the major sender of immigrants to the United States with nearly 1.4 million (or 55 percent of all Mexicans that have entered legally between 1820 and 1984) Mexicans emigrating legally to the United States during the period. Again, the actual number of immigrants is much greater due to the untold numbers entering the United States without proper documentation. The heavy flow of Mexican immigration during the period has been due, in part, to the Immigration Act of 1965 and its emphasis on "family reunification," whereby permanent U.S. residents were allowed to petition to have close relatives enter the United States.

More recent legislation has also affected Mexican immigration. In 1986, the signing of the Immigration Reform and Control Act (IRCA) provided amnesty and a vehicle for legalization to large numbers of undocumented immigrants falling into two categories—"regular undocumented immigrants" and "special agricultural workers," or SAWs. In order to receive amnesty, regular immigrants had to prove they had lived in the United States on a continual basis since January 1, 1982, while agricultural workers were required to have worked at least ninety days in agriculture in the United States between May 1985 and May 1986.[5] Nearly 1.8 million people applied for legalization under the regular IRCA amnesty program, and an additional 1.3 million applied under the SAW program.[6] The large majority of IRCA applicants were Mexican, comprising about 70 percent of the regular applicants and nearly 82 percent of the SAW applicants. In 1991 alone, approximately 893,000 Mexicans who had applied for amnesty were granted permanent resident status.[7] Mexicans receiving permanent status are likely to add significant numbers to the Chicano population, for even if they were in the United States prior to 1982, they would not likely have been counted in the 1980 Census.

This historical demographic perspective illustrates the unique position of the Chicano population. This population is one that has a long, well-established presence in this country, but it also accounts for the majority of recent immigrants. This combination of new and old immigrants, along with the group's manner of initial incorporation into this country, is largely responsible for the diverse nature of the Chicano population. Indeed, the Chicano population contains people who trace their presence in this country back to the mid-1840s as well as those that have recently crossed the border into the United States. The continual flow of Mexican immigrants serves to rejuvenate not only the Chicano population but also the group's culture.

DATA SOURCE FOR ANALYSIS

The data used in the analysis come from the 1990 Census. In particular, the data were obtained from the 1990 General Population Characteristics for each of the states and the District of Columbia.[8] The data for Chicanos are based on the population indicating that they were of Hispanic origin and that they were of Mexican origin in particular. The comparative data for the total population represent the entire population, regardless of race or ethnicity. Part of the data presented below come from the 1980 General Population Characteristics and the 1990 Summary Tape File 1C (STF1C).[9]

The demographic variables included in the analysis represent various demographic domains: population and geographic distribution, residence, age structure, and marriage and family characteristics. The actual variables within each of these domains will be described and presented in the next section. The demographic analysis will present data for the U.S. Chicano population and for the five regions. The Southwest region includes Arizona, California, Colorado, New Mexico, and Texas.[10] Although the Census Bureau categorizes the U.S. states and the District of Columbia into four regions (Midwest, South, West, and Northeast), in our analysis, we develop a separate region, the Southwest, because of the concentration of the Chicano population in the five states comprising the region. The reader should keep in mind that the West region as used here does not contain Arizona, California, Colorado, and New Mexico, while the South region does not contain Texas.

THE DEMOGRAPHY OF CHICANOS IN THE UNITED STATES AND THE FIVE REGIONS

In this section, we will present a demographic profile of the Chicano population in the United States and in the five regions delineated above. Data for the entire United States are also presented for comparative purposes. We begin the demographic analysis with a discussion of the population and geographic patterns of the Chicano population.

Population and Geographic Characteristics

According to the 1990 Census, there were approximately 13.5 million Chicanos living in the United States in 1990 (Table 2–1). Thus, in absolute numbers the Chicano population increased by nearly 4.8 million between 1980 and 1990, with

TABLE 2–1 Population Characteristics for the Chicano and U.S. Population by Region, 1980 and 1990

Region	Chicano		U.S. Total	
	1980	**1990**	**1980**	**1990**
Population Size:				
Southwest	7,227,339	11,237,325	44,808,166	55,221,222
Midwest	820,218	1,153,296	58,865,670	59,668,632
West	260,801	477,618	12,593,515	14,551,370
South	344,305	452,703	61,143,171	68,459,420
Northeast	87,776	174,996	49,135,283	50,809,229
Total	8,740,439	13,495,938	226,545,805	248,709,873
Pct. Distribution:				
Southwest	82.7%	83.3%	19.8%	22.2%
Midwest	9.4%	8.5%	26.0%	24.0%
West	3.0%	3.5%	5.5%	4.9%
South	3.9%	3.4%	27.0%	27.5%
Northeast	1.0%	1.3%	21.7%	20.4%
Total	100.0%	100.0%	100.0%	100.0%
Pct. of Region's Population				
Southwest	16.0%	20.4%	–	–
Midwest	1.4%	1.9%	–	–
West	2.0%	3.3%	–	–
South	0.5%	0.7%	–	–
Northeast	0.2%	0.3%	–	–
Total	3.9%	5.4%	–	–

Source: U.S. Bureau of the Census, *1980* and *1990 General Population Characteristics.*

approximately 84 percent (or 4.0 million) of this growth centered in the Southwest region. During the same period, the entire U.S. population increased by almost 22.2 million. This suggests that although Chicanos accounted for a relatively small share of the nation's population in 1990 (5.4 percent), the growth in the Chicano population accounted for more than one-fourth of the total U.S. population growth during the decade of the 1980s.

This large-scale growth in the Chicano population during the 1980s can be further illustrated by examining the relative growth (percentage change) during the decade (Figure 2–1). Overall, the Chicano population increased at a rate (54.4 percent) that was 5.5 times faster than that of the U.S. population (9.8 percent) between 1980 and 1990. The rapid growth of the Chicano population relative to

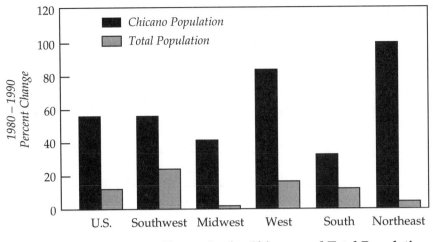

FIGURE 2–1   Percentage Change in the Chicano and Total Population between 1980 and 1990

Source: U.S. Bureau of the Census, *1980* and *1990 General Population Characteristics.*

the total population is also apparent across the different regions. The Chicano population grew the most rapidly in the Northeast region (99.4 percent), where the number of Chicanos essentially doubled, and the West region (83.1 percent) during the decade. In contrast, the Chicano population grew the most slowly in the South (31.5 percent) and Midwest (40.6 percent), although the growth was much more rapid than each region's overall population growth (South, 12.0 percent; Midwest, 1.4 percent). The Southwest Chicano population increased by about 56 percent between 1980 and 1990.

The Chicano population continues to be predominantly located in the Southwest region, with 83.3 percent of all Chicanos making their home in the region in 1990 (Table 2–1). Close to 9 percent of Chicanos live in the Midwest, while less than 4 percent are found in the West and in the South regions. Relatively few (1.3 percent or 175,000) Chicanos live in the Northeast. A quick glance at the regional distribution patterns of the total U.S. population reveals the extent to which Chicanos are concentrated in the Southwest, as the regional distribution patterns of the total population are much more even. In fact, proportionately speaking, Chicanos are four times more likely to be located in the Southwest compared to the total population.

A close examination of the different states, however, indicates that approximately three-fourths (74.2 percent) of Chicanos are located in California and Texas alone (Table 2–2). As such, three of every four Chicanos in the United States make their homes in these two states. The top ten most populous states with respect to Chicanos include California (6,118,996), Texas (3,890,820), Illinois (623,688), Arizona (616,195), New Mexico (328,836), Colorado (282,478), Florida (161,499), Washington (155,864), Michigan (138,312), and New York (93,244). As can be seen from this list, despite the fact that the large majority of Chicanos live in California

TABLE 2–2   Total and Chicano Population by State, 1990

State	Total Pop.	Chicano Pop.	State	Total Pop.	Chicano Pop.
Alabama	4,040,587	9,509	Montana	799,065	8,362
Alaska	550,043	9,321	Nebraska	1,578,385	29,665
Arizona	3,665,228	616,195	Nevada	1,201,833	85,287
Arkansas	2,350,725	12,496	New Hampshire	1,109,252	2,362
California	29,760,021	6,118,996	New Jersey	7,730,188	28,759
Colorado	3,294,394	282,478	New Mexico	1,515,069	328,836
Connecticut	3,287,116	8,393	New York	17,990,455	93,244
Delaware	666,168	3,083	North Carolina	6,628,637	32,670
Dist. of Col.	606,900	2,981	North Dakota	638,800	2,878
Florida	12,937,926	161,499	Ohio	10,847,115	57,815
Georgia	6,478,216	49,182	Oklahoma	3,145,585	63,226
Hawaii	1,108,229	14,367	Oregon	2,842,321	85,632
Idaho	1,006,749	43,213	Pennsylvania	11,881,643	24,220
Illinois	11,430,602	623,688	Rhode Island	1,003,464	2,437
Indiana	5,544,159	66,736	South Carolina	3,486,703	11,028
Iowa	2,776,755	24,386	South Dakota	696,004	3,438
Kansas	2,477,574	75,798	Tennessee	4,877,185	13,879
Kentucky	3,685,296	8,692	Texas	16,986,510	3,890,820
Louisiana	4,219,973	23,452	Utah	1,772,850	56,842
Maine	1,227,928	2,153	Vermont	562,758	725
Maryland	4,781,468	18,434	Virginia	6,187,358	33,044
Massachusetts	6,016,425	12,703	Washington	4,866,692	155,864
Michigan	9,295,297	138,312	West Virginia	1,793,477	2,810
Minnesota	4,375,099	34,691	Wisconsin	4,891,769	57,615
Mississippi	2,573,216	6,718	Wyoming	453,588	18,730
Missouri	5,117,073	38,274			

Source: U.S. Bureau of the Census, *1990 Census of Population and Housing Summary Tape 1C.*

and Texas, each of the five regions contains at least one state in the ranks of the top ten most populous Chicano states.

The large presence of Chicanos in the Southwest can also be illustrated through the examination of the top twenty cities with respect to the absolute and relative size of the Chicano population. Data from the Summary Tape File 1C (STF1C) are used to conduct this part of the analysis.[11] This data set contains data for the nation, states, counties, and places having at least 10,000 inhabitants. For our task at hand, we use data for places with at least 10,000 residents.

The lefthand portion of Table 2–3 contains a list of the twenty most populous places with respect to the Chicano population, which, overall, account for nearly one-third of the nation's Chicano population. All but one (Chicago) of the places is located in the Southwest; of the remainder most are located in Texas (9) and California (7). The ten places with the largest Chicano population include Los Angeles (936,507), San Antonio (478,409), Houston (358,503), Chicago (352,560), El Paso (338,844), San Diego (194,400), Dallas (185,096), Phoenix (176,139), San Jose

TABLE 2–3   Top Twenty Places in the United States with the Largest Absolute and Relative Chicano Populations, 1990

	Largest Chicano Population		Highest Pct. of Chicanos	
Rank	City	Chicano Population	City	Pct. Chicano
1	Los Angeles, CA	936,507	Socorro, TX	93.0%
2	San Antonio, TX	478,409	Calexico, CA	92.9%
3	Houston, TX	358,503	Eagle Pass, TX	91.9%
4	Chicago, IL	352,560	Coachella, CA	91.6%
5	El Paso, TX	338,844	Laredo, TX	89.3%
6	San Diego, CA	194,400	Nogales, AZ	87.7%
7	Dallas, TX	185,096	East Los Angeles, CA	87.5%
8	Phoenix, AZ	176,139	San Juan, TX	87.2%
9	San Jose, CA	173,803	Mercedes, TX	86.8%
10	Santa Ana, CA	173,776	Robstown, TX	85.7%
11	Corpus Christi, TX	118,713	Brownsville, TX	85.3%
12	East Los Angeles, CA	110,581	Pharr, TX	84.5%
13	Laredo, TX	109,796	Donna, TX	84.1%
14	Tucson, AZ	107,416	San Benito, TX	83.2%
15	Fresno, CA	95,229	Commerce, CA	83.0%
16	Austin, TX	93,323	Edinburg, TX	81.2%
17	Brownsville, TX	84,448	Douglas, AZ	78.2%
18	Long Beach, CA	80,523	South El Monte, CA	77.9%
19	Fort Worth, TX	79,443	Maywood, CA	77.7%
20	Denver, CO	74,629	Mission, TX	76.3%

Source: U.S. Bureau of the Census, *1990 Census of Population and Housing Summary Tape 1C.*

(173,803), and Santa Ana (173,776). It should be noted here that the populations of these places are for the city itself rather than also including the population of surrounding communities that comprise the Metropolitan Statistical Area (MSA). Thus, the populations of the MSAs of the places listed here would be substantially larger than the populations of the places.

At the national level, the Chicano population represented 5.4 percent of the total U.S. population in 1990 (see Table 2–1). However, this level of demographic representation is four times as great in the Southwest, where one in five inhabitants is Chicano. The Chicano population accounts for the greatest portion of the state population in Texas (22.9 percent), New Mexico (21.7 percent), and California (20.6 percent) (Table 2–2). The West region (3.3 percent) trails the Southwest considerably as the next region where Chicanos have the highest demographic representation. Chicanos account for less than 1 percent of the populations of the South and Northeast regions.

There are numerous places in the Southwest where Chicanos account for the largest majority of the population (Table 2–3). The righthand portion of Table 2–3 contains the top twenty places having the highest levels of Chicano proportional representation. Chicanos comprise at least 76.3 percent of the populations of these places. All the places are located in Texas, California, and Arizona. However, the top-twenty list is dominated by valley towns along the southernmost part of Texas, with eight of the twenty places located in Hidalgo or Cameron County in Texas. The top ten places where Chicanos account for the highest proportion of the population include Socorro, TX (93.0 percent), Calexico, CA (92.9 percent), Eagle Pass, TX (91.9 percent), Coachella, CA (91.6 percent), Laredo, TX (89.3 percent), Nogales, AZ (87.7 percent), East Los Angeles, CA (87.5 percent), San Juan, TX (87.2 percent), Mercedes, TX (86.8 percent), and Robstown, TX (85.7 percent).

Residence Patterns

The remainder of the data presented in this chapter are solely for 1990 and include information on residence patterns, age structure, and marriage and family characteristics. The statistics for Chicanos appear in Table 2–4, while those for the total population appear in Table 2–5.

TABLE 2–4   **Residence, Age, and Marriage and Family Characteristics of Chicanos by Region, 1990**

Selected Characteristics	Total	Southwest	Midwest	West	South	Northeast
Residence:						
Pct. in Metro Areas	88.0%	89.5%	86.1%	67.5%	73.5%	94.4%
Pct. in Nonmetro Areas	12.0%	10.5%	13.9%	32.5%	26.5%	5.6%
Age:						
Pct. < 15 Yrs. of Age	32.0%	31.9%	33.4%	35.5%	30.6%	25.1%
Pct. 65 Yrs. of Age or Older	4.2%	4.4%	3.6%	2.7%	3.2%	3.6%
Marriage and Family:						
Pct. of Family Households Headed by Women, No Husband Present	18.8%	19.3%	17.7%	16.7%	13.5%	17.3%
Pct. Males 15+ Currently Married	50.9%	51.3%	49.6%	49.6%	49.4%	43.3%
Pct. Females 15+ Currently Married	52.2%	51.9%	52.0%	55.1%	57.6%	50.8%

Source: U.S. Bureau of the Census, *1990 General Population Characteristics.*

TABLE 2–5   Residence, Age, and Marriage and Family Characteristics of the Total Population by Region, 1990

Selected Characteristics	Total	Southwest	Midwest	West	South	Northeast
Residence:						
Pct. in Metro Areas	77.5%	88.2%	71.5%	67.7%	68.3%	88.2%
Pct. in Nonmetro Areas	22.5%	11.8%	28.5%	32.3%	31.7%	11.8%
Age:						
Pct. < 15 Yrs. of Age	21.5%	22.9%	22.0%	23.6%	21.0%	19.7%
Pct. 65 Yrs. of Age or Older	12.6%	10.6%	13.0%	11.5%	13.2%	13.8%
Marriage and Family:						
Pct. of Family Households Headed by Women, No Husband Present	10.8%	11.1%	10.3%	9.5%	11.6%	10.5%
Pct. Males 15+ Currently Married	57.3%	55.3%	58.8%	58.5%	58.8%	55.6%
Pct. Females 15+ Currently Married	52.5%	52.5%	53.5%	56.6%	52.9%	49.5%

Source: U.S. Bureau of the Census, *1990 General Population Characteristics.*

The Chicano population tends to be overwhelmingly located in metropolitan areas. Metropolitan areas (MAs) include entire counties (or cities and towns in the case of the six New England states) and "contain either a city with at least 50,000 inhabitants or an urbanized area delineated by the Census Bureau; in the latter case, the MA must contain at least 100,000 people (75,000 in New England)."[12] Nonmetropolitan areas include all other areas not defined as metropolitan areas. Overall, 88 percent of Chicanos make their homes in metropolitan areas (Table 2–4), compared to 77.5 percent of the nation's entire population (Table 2–5). In general, within metropolitan areas, Chicanos tend to be concentrated in the central cities while the total population is more likely to be located in suburban areas. This geographic pattern has implications for employment. Social scientists focusing on labor markets have noted the "mismatch" pattern between labor supply and labor demand, when new jobs are disproportionately located in the suburbs while the unemployed minority poor reside in the central cities.[13] Across the regions, Chicanos exhibit the highest degree of metropolitan residence in the Northeast (94.4 percent) and Southwest (89.5 percent). By way of contrast, nearly one-third of Chicanos in the West (32.5 percent) and slightly more than one-fourth of those in the South (26.5 percent) are located in nonmetropolitan areas.

Age Structure

Given the unique demographic patterns of Chicanos, the age structure of the Chicano population differs significantly from that of the national population. The Chicano population is a young population. Indeed, approximately one of every three Chicanos in the United States was under fifteen years of age in 1990 (Table 2–4). In contrast, the U.S. population only had slightly more than one of five (21.5 percent) persons in this age category (Table 2–5). Young Chicanos under the age of fifteen account for the largest portion of the Chicano population in the West region with 35.5 percent of the region's population. Chicanos younger than fifteen are the least represented in the Northeast Chicano population (25.1 percent). On the other hand, elderly persons sixty-five years of age and older account for a relatively small portion (4.2 percent) of the entire Chicano population. The older age structure of the nation is evident in that about 13 percent of the total U.S. population is sixty-five or older.

The age composition of the Chicano population can be illustrated graphically with the age/sex pyramid. The age/sex pyramid is a bar graph containing bars for successive age categories from the youngest at the base to the oldest at the top, with males represented on the left side of the graph and females on the right side. The width of each bar indicates the percentage of the entire population comprised of a given age/sex group according to the percentage scale on the horizontal axis.

Figure 2–2 shows the age/sex pyramid for the Chicano population in the nation (bottom pyramid) and the U.S. total population (top pyramid). The shape of the two pyramids differs significantly, reflecting major differences in the age/sex structure of the two populations. The youthfulness of the Chicano population is evident by the wide bars at the base. Indeed, males and females less than five years of age each account for approximately 6 percent of the entire Chicano population. The immigration influence can also be observed in the wide bars associated with the 20–24 and 25–29 age groups. In fact, males in these age groups represent a significantly larger proportion of the entire population (about 12 percent) compared to their female counterparts, who comprise approximately 9 percent of the population. The pointed top of the pyramid reflects the relative scarcity of elderly in the Chicano population.

Marriage and Family

The marriage and family characteristics of Chicanos also tend to be unique compared to those of the general population. Overall, in the United States 18.8 percent of Chicano families have female householders without a husband present (Table 2–4). The householder is defined as "the person, or one of the persons, in whose

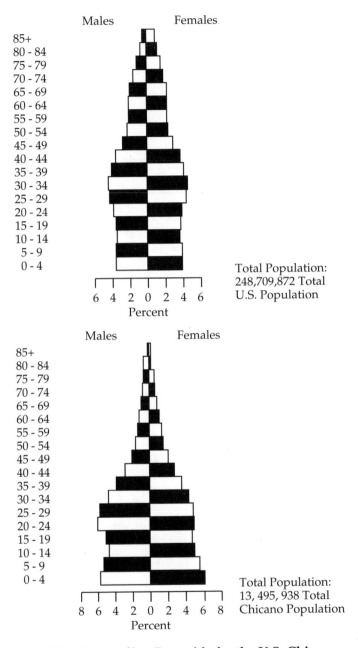

**FIGURE 2–2   Age/Sex Pyramids for the U.S. Chicano
and Total Population, 1990**

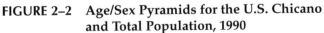

Source: U.S. Bureau of the Census, *1990 General Population
Characteristics.*

name the home is owned, being bought, or rented. . . ."[14] In contrast, approximately 11 percent (10.8 percent) of all of the families in the nation are headed by women without a husband (Table 2–5). Unfortunately, because the data are in aggregate form, we are unable to break down the marital statuses (currently married, divorced, separated, widowed, never married, etc.) of the female householders. The observed difference between Chicano and U.S. families challenges the long-held notion of marital stability in the Chicano family. Yet, even using 1980 Census data, Bean and Tienda noted only relatively minor differences in marital stability between Chicanas and Anglo women between the ages of 15 and 64.[15] One of the characteristics commonly associated with poverty is families with female householders without a husband.[16] This pattern is probably due to the combination of the gender discrimination that women encounter in the workplace as well as the high prevalence of a sole income earner in such families.

The different regions do not vary greatly with respect to their levels of female-headed households among Chicanos. The Southwest region tends to have the highest level of such households, with nearly one-fifth of families having female householders without a husband. In contrast, Chicano families in the South tend to have the lowest (13.5 percent) prevalence of families headed by females. The relatively larger presence of such families among Chicanos compared to the total families holds across the five regions. Yet, the difference is the most minor in the South, where 13.5 percent of Chicano families are headed by females without a husband present compared to 11.6 percent of all families in the region. However, part of this difference may be due to the relatively heavier presence of African Americans, the ethnic group that tends to have the highest levels of female-headed households, in the South.

Table 2–4 also contains information on the percentage of Chicanos fifteen and older who are currently married. Overall, in the United States approximately half of Chicanos (50.9 percent) and Chicanas (52.2 percent) fifteen and older were currently married in 1990. Compared to persons fifteen and older in the nation, Chicanas do not differ significantly from their counterparts (see Tables 2–4 and 2–5). However, males fifteen and older in the national population (57.3 percent) are significantly more likely to be married than Chicanos in the same age group (50.9 percent). This difference is likely due to two demographic factors. First, the fact that Chicanos represent a younger population suggests that Chicanos are likely to be disproportionately in the lower ages (15–20 or so) that tend to have relatively low marriage rates. Second, the low marriage percentage among Chicano males is also likely to reflect the relatively high presence of undocumented males, a group that is likely to have low marriage rates due to their unstable situation. The comparable percentages among Chicanas and U.S. females is probably also due to the age structure difference since the U.S. population tends to have a higher presence of widows than the Chicano population, thus lowering the percentage of females in the nation who are currently married. Unfortunately, data are not available at this time to standardize, or adjust, the marriage percentages for the different age structures.

The marriage percentages among Chicanos are relatively similar across the five regions. Two cases stand out, however. Chicano males fifteen and older in the Northeast are the least likely to be married, with only 43.3 percent currently married. In contrast, approximately 58 percent of Chicanas in the South region are currently married. The differences between Chicanos and the total population at the national level also hold across the five regions.

CONCLUSIONS

The task of this chapter has been to present an overview of the demography of Chicanos in the United States. The analysis conducted here suggests that the Chicano population has grown tremendously during the twentieth century. Today, this population continues to grow at a rapid rate, outpacing the growth exhibited by most other ethnic groups in the country. In fact, while Chicanos accounted for only about 5.4 percent of the total U.S. population in 1990, they were responsible for approximately one-fourth of the total growth in the U.S. population during the 1980s.

The large-scale growth of the Chicano population is likely to continue through the twenty-first century given the group's young age structure, high fertility rates, and continued emigration from Mexico. Under this realistic scenario, the Chicano population is likely to continue to account for major portions of the future growth in the national population. In addition, the group's proportional share of the U.S. population is likely to rise as well. People in both the public and private sectors will have to pay increasing attention to the Chicano population because of the tremendous growth of this group. We call on policymakers in particular to begin devoting more attention to the plight of Chicanos in such areas as education, training, and employment. The combination of a young age structure combined with a low educational level requires immediate attention to the problems of this group. Failure to address the problems of the Chicano population today will result in massive social and economic problems in the future, as Chicanos would be ill-prepared to compete effectively in an increasingly technological workforce in the near future. This failure would have severe economic ramifications for the larger society, for ill-prepared Chicano workers would be unable to heed the call to provide the tax base to support an increasingly elderly U.S. population, comprised predominantly of Anglos.

The analysis presented in this chapter has also shown the diverse nature of the Chicano population. It is still true that Chicanos continue to be disproportionately located in the Southwest, with about 83 percent making their homes in this region in 1990. However, Chicanos are found in all states of the country. Unfortunately, we have had only limited information on Chicanos outside of the Southwest. The analysis of the population has indicated that Chicanos in the five different regions vary to a certain extent on the different characteristics examined here. Therefore, the Chicano population cannot be characterized as a monolithic one, but rather one that is quite diverse. It is the hope that this chapter provides the reader with a demographic knowledge base for better understanding the more substantive aspects of the Chicano population presented in the remainder of this book.

NOTES

1. William P. O'Hare, "America's Minorities— The Demographics of Diversity," *Population Bulletin*, 47 (1992): 1–46.
2. Rogelio Saenz, "Exploring the Regional Diversity of Chicanos," in Y.I. Song and E.C. Kim (eds.), *American Mosaic: Selected Readings on America's Multicultural Heritage*, (Englewood Cliffs, NJ: Prentice-Hall, 1993), 117–129.
3. Marta Tienda and Vilma Ortiz, "Hispanicity and the 1980 Census," *Social Science Quarterly*, 67 (1986): 3–20.
4. U.S. Immigration and Naturalization Service, *Statistical Yearbook of the Immigration and Naturalization Service* (Washington, DC: U.S. Department of Justice, 1984).
5. Leon F. Bouvier and Robert W. Gardner, "Immigration to the U.S.: The Unfinished Story," *Population Bulletin*, 41 (1986): 1–50.
6. Frank D. Bean, Barry Edmonston, and Jeffrey S. Passel (eds.), *Undocumented Migration to the United States: IRCA and the Experience of the 1980s* (Washington, DC: The Urban Institute Press, 1990). U.S. Immigration and Naturalization Service, *Immigration Statistics: Fiscal Year 1991 (Advanced Report)* (Washington DC: U.S. Department of Justice, 1992).
7. U.S. Immigration and Naturalization Service, *Immigration Statistics: Fiscal Year 1991 (Advanced Report)*.
8. U.S. Bureau of the Census, *1990 Census of Population and Housing Summary Population and Housing Characteristics* (Washington, DC: U.S. Government Printing Office, 1991).
9. U.S. Bureau of the Census, *1980 General Population Characteristics* (Washington, DC: U.S. Government Printing Office, 1981). U.S. Bureau of the Census, *1990 Census of Population and Housing Summary Tape File 1 Technical Documentation* (Washington, DC: U.S. Government Printing Office, 1991).
10. The Midwest region contains Illinois, Indiana, Iowa, Kansas, Michigan, Minnesota, Missouri, Nebraska, North Dakota, Ohio, South Dakota, and Wisconsin. The West region is made up of Alaska, Hawaii, Idaho, Montana, Nevada, Oregon, Utah, Washington, and Wyoming. The South region is comprised of Alabama, Arkansas, Delaware, the District of Columbia, Florida, Georgia, Kentucky, Louisiana, Maryland, Mississippi, North Carolina, Oklahoma, South Carolina, Tennessee, Virginia, and West Virginia. The Northeast region includes Connecticut, Maine, Massachusetts, New Hampshire, New Jersey, New York, Pennsylvania, Rhode Island, and Vermont.
11. U.S. Bureau of the Census, *1990 Census of Population and Housing Summary Tape File 1 Technical Documentation*.
12. U.S. Bureau of the Census, *1990 Census of Population and Housing Summary Tape File 1 Technical Documentation*, A–9.
13. Kevin M. Fitzpatrick and Sean-Shong Hwang, "The Effects of Occupational Sex Segregation and the Spatial Distribution of Jobs on Commuting Patterns," *Social Science Quarterly*, 73 (1992): 550–564.
14. U.S. Bureau of the Census, *1990 Census of Population and Housing Summary Tape File 1 Technical Documentation*, B–8.
15. Frank D. Bean and Marta Tienda, *The Hispanic Population of the United States* (New York: Russell Sage Foundation, 1987).
16. Reynolds Farley and Suzanne M. Bianchi, "Social Class Polarization: Is it Occurring Among Blacks?" *Research on Race and Ethnic Relations*, 4 (1985): 1–31. Gertrude S. Goldberg and Eleanor Kremen (eds.), *The Feminization of Poverty: Only in America?* (New York: Praeger, 1990). Rogelio Saenz and John K. Thomas, "Minority Poverty in Nonmetropolitan Texas," *Rural Sociology*, 56 (1991): 204–223.

3

ECONOMIC RESTRUCTURING AND YOUNG LATINO WORKERS IN THE 1980s

MANUEL AVALOS

Since the mid-1970s, the United States has undergone an extended period of economic disturbance that has ultimately led to a radical corporate restructuring of work and production in the economy. These changes have benefited some workers but certainly not all. Adapting to the new economic climate has not been easy or painless, particularly for labor. Increased global competition from emerging industrialized Asian countries slowed productivity and economic growth in the United States. Consequently, the economy has not been able to sustain the income and wage growth of earlier decades. The impact of this slowdown has been particularly evident within the Latino workforce during the last two decades.

A recent longitudinal study of Latino income and earnings from 1950 to 1980 by DeFreitas indicates that while Latinos have made impressive progress in educational attainment and occupational mobility since the 1950s, they have also experienced a decline in their relative earning levels since the early 1970s. Analysis of Current Population Survey (CPS) data from 1973–87 indicates that the Latino-to-Anglo earnings ratio has declined among part-time as well as full-time, year-round workers. This gap in wages and salary between Latinos and Anglos has been widening at a rate of 0.4 to 0.5 percent per year over the period 1973–87.[1]

In the next decade, as the Latino population increases in numbers (estimated to reach 36 million by the year 2000), the gap in earnings between Latinos and Anglos may become a national rather than a regional problem. Public policymakers need greater understanding of the causes of income inequality between Latinos and Anglos in order to combat these inequalities of income and occupational distribution as we enter the twenty-first century. This chapter reviews the causes of income inequality and occupational distribution between young Latino and Anglo workers during the 1980s. Using survey data from the 1979–1990 National

Longitudinal Surveys of Youth (NLSY) we ask the question, Did structural changes in the economy during the 1980s produce a redistribution across occupations and economic sectors that altered previous income inequality between majority and minority groups? Before examining data on earnings and occupational distribution among young Latino and Anglo workers, we will first consider the various theoretical explanations developed by scholars studying income inequality during the last three decades.

THEORETICAL EXPLANATIONS FOR INCOME INEQUALITY

In the last thirty years, there have been numerous attempts to understand the chronic labor market problem of earnings inequality. Economists' and sociologists' interest in wage inequities generated in economics and sociology can be traced back to studies of black ghetto unemployment in the 1960s that identified significant income inequalities between black and white workers. These income inequalities were not confined to the period of the 1960s, but were historically characteristic of the post-industrial labor market.[2]

Most empirical studies of earnings inequality have utilized the human capital approach.[3] Human capital theory focuses on individual factors (e.g., native ability, formal education, vocational education, on-the-job training, and on-the-job experience) that affect workers' productivity before they enter the labor market. Studies using this approach explain earnings differences between majority and minority workers as a function of the variation in human capital skills among them.[4]

Other models that have been developed to explain earnings inequalities between minority and majority groups emphasize class and/or structural variables rather than individual characteristics of workers. These class/structural models include the dual labor market theory, the segmented labor market theory, and the ethnic enclave theory.[5] From a class/structuralist point of view, income inequality does not derive entirely from differences in individual skills, but is more likely to be a function of structural inequalities (e.g., labor market discrimination and economic restructuring).

In the decade of the 1980s, much of the research on social inequality and the decline in workers' earnings in the United States focused on the impact of corporate restructuring over the last three decades and how this process affected the labor market outcomes of the working class.[6] The following two sections summarize this literature.

Structural Theories and Labor Market Inequalities

Research utilizing class/structural theories has focused on the ways in which corporate restructuring in the United States has affected the labor market. Instead of comparing individual characteristics of workers, structural theorists focus on macro changes in the United States economy, such as the oil crisis of the 1970s, the development of a more competitive international market, and the restructuring of the workforce for a predominantly service-oriented economy.

The energy crisis was the first shock to the American economy in the 1970s, but a more fundamental transformation in the international economy had begun years before. Since the late 1960s, foreign competition in American markets has increased, particularly from Asian firms. What were once considered less developed nations have since become dynamic industrial nations (Japan being the classic example) whose growth is based primarily on exports, predominantly to the United States. During the 1970s, over one-third of the country's rising trade deficit came from Japan. By the next decade, four other countries, South Korea, Hong Kong, Taiwan, and Singapore had become major players in international industrial trade. By the mid-1980s, these four Asian countries and Japan accounted for over half of the United States trade deficit.[7]

The United States' increasing trade deficit with these new industrialized Asian nations has made it less competitive in the international market. Three factors have made the United States less competitive (and affected our balance of trade with foreign nations) in the new global economy: the higher cost of labor, aging capital, and the buildup of the federal debt under the Reagan administration. In an attempt to curtail the rising fiscal deficit in the 1980s, the Reagan administration financed that deficit by encouraging foreign investment rather than cutting expenditures or raising taxes.

To attract these foreign funds, the United States kept (real) interest rates high, which created a strong dollar overseas. From 1980 to 1985, the exchange rate of foreign currency for American dollars rose by 56 percent, which made American exports more expensive and foreign imports cheaper, thereby hurting American manufacturers (such as the automobile industry) severely. The competitiveness of the Asian economies and the favorable exchange rate to foreign firms created a United States trade deficit of well over $100 billion by the mid-1980s.

The increases in oil prices and in foreign competition disrupted the American economy and placed enormous pressure on businesses to become more efficient. In order to remain competitive, U.S. firms have been forced to restructure. This restructuring left many firms bankrupt, and shifted investments to regions in the country with less costly energy and labor, such as the Sunbelt. It also accelerated the adoption of new technology in industries such as telecommunications where job deskilling[8] is taking place; deskilling leads to wage cuts. Highly centralized U.S. companies with well defined internal career paths are being replaced by small companies that offer employees fewer long-term career opportunities in order to remain competitive with foreign firms.

In the 1980s the federal government facilitated these processes by pursuing a laissez-faire economic policy. The tendency has been to let market forces guide the restructuring process, as evidenced by the government's reluctance to protect industries under stress (e.g., automobile and steel industries), its efforts to deregulate other industries, and its promotion of free trade. The consequences of international competition and laissez-faire economic policies are evident in the shift away from an economy dominated by manufacturing to a service-oriented economy in which workers, predominantly women and minorities, are worse off economically than their counterparts in the manufacturing sector.

The Impact of Restructuring on Workers

In the 1970s, the most critical factor affecting Latino earnings was corporate restructuring. In an increasingly stagnant and low productive economy, an American household must contribute more labor hours to increase its per capita income. Among minorities this has necessitated an increase in the percentage of women in the labor force. The increase in labor force participation of minority women has occurred, however, in the involuntary part-time labor[9] market where corporate restructuring increased part-time employment at the expense of full-time jobs.

Due to corporate restructuring, many firms converted full-time jobs into part-time jobs to increase market flexibility. Informal estimates suggest that there has been an increase of ten million part-time workers since 1980.[10] This trend adversely affected the incomes of Latino workers, particularly female. Part-time workers are paid lower hourly wages than full-time workers and are not usually covered by health insurance and pension plans.[11] Economic restructuring affected the earnings of the working class more than any other class in the United States labor market. Harrison and Bluestone have argued that economic restructuring in the 1970s led to an increase in low wage (service) employment and a reduction in blue-collar manufacturing jobs. Much of the decline in working class incomes came at the expense of organized labor, which in the 1950s and 1960s had been effective in raising the wages of blue-collar workers in the smokestack industries, but was unable to protect these gains during the restructuring of the 1970s.[12] While manufacturing jobs declined, lower-paying service sector jobs increased rapidly. Between 1973 and 1979, the service sector created about one-fifth of all new employment in the United States. Consequently, annual wages and salaries in 1979 were lower than 1973 median wages by about $7,400 (in 1986 dollars). By 1985, over 40 percent of all new employment occurred in the service sector—a sector in which workers were seven times more likely to earn wages below the poverty line than were workers in the manufacturing sector.[13] Economic restructuring produced an economy dominated by low productivity jobs, low wages, and greater income inequality. This is the economy in which most Latino workers must now compete for scarce full-time jobs.

DATA SOURCE

Data from the National Longitudinal Study of Youth[14] (NLSY) is the basis of the following analysis. The NLSY is a nationally representative sample of 12,686 young people. It is stratified by gender in order to yield approximately equal numbers of men and women born between the calendar years of 1957 and 1964 (aged 14-21 on January 1, 1979). The Latino and white probability samples have been included in this analysis.

The NLSY cohort contains 2,002 civilian Latino[15] youth, 1000 males, and 1002 females. Over the course of thirteen annual interviews conducted since 1979, these young people have achieved economic independence. They moved out of parental homes; made decisions about continued education and training; entered the labor market; married, and started families. For the purposes of this analysis, only data from the 1979 and 1990 NLSY were analyzed. All comparisons are made between ethnic (Latino and Anglo) and within gender groups.

YOUNG LATINO AND ANGLO WORKERS IN 1979

As mentioned previously, Latinos' earnings levels stagnated throughout the decade of the 1970s. Analysis of CPS data during the 1970s indicated that the Latino-Anglo earnings ratio was in decline throughout the decade, even among full-time year-round male workers. The gap in income widened during this period.

An examination of NLSY data allows us to see if this trend in income inequality affected a new young Latino(a) cohort in the 1980s. For the most part, young Anglo and Latino male and female groups in 1979 resembled each other demographically with few exceptions. The majority of Anglo and Latino youths had not yet entered the labor force in 1979. The most significant difference between these two groups was the percentage of youth living with families in poverty. Latino males (34 percent) were almost twice as likely to be living in impoverished households than Anglo males (18 percent). Almost 36 percent of Latinas were living with families in poverty compared to about 23 percent of Anglo females.

Table 3–1 provides comparative characteristics of employed Anglo and Latino male and females in 1979. These two groups' work experiences were similar. Only about one-third of Anglo and Latino males were working full-time[16] in 1979. They averaged less than thirty hours of work per week, most were single with no children, and they earned less than $5,300 per year.

Anglo and Latino females were also very similar demographically. The major difference between female groups was in the percentage of full-time workers. Almost 47 percent of Latinas were working full-time compared to only 34 percent of Anglo female workers. Most Latina and Anglo female workers worked less than thirty hours per week and earned less than $3,500 per year.

Earnings Differentials and Labor Market Structure

Table 3–2 examines structural dimensions that affected earnings outcomes among Anglo and Latino male and female workers in 1979: occupations and economic sectors. Human capital theorists have argued that human capital characteristics (returns to education, work experience) and social origins determine occupational and earnings differences.[17] The data in Table 3–2 show that gender influences occupational options. Those occupations that are female dominated generally pay less.[18] Occupational gender typing limits the range of women's employment opportunities.

TABLE 3–1   Selected Demographic Characteristics of Latino and Anglo, Male and Female Workers

	Anglo Male (N=1764)	Latino Male (N=436)	Anglo Female (N=1685)	Latina Female (N=338)
% Married	9.4	14.0	13.8	16.9
% In Poverty	16.1	26.2	20.2	24.6
% Full Time Worker	36.2	32.7	34.2	46.8
Mean Years Education Completed	10.9	10.4	11.4	10.8
Mean Hours Work per Week	29.6	29.7	25.1	28.8*
Mean Age (Years)	18.3	18.5	18.4	18.5
Mean Income	$5,258	$4,869	$3,478	$3,430
Mean No. of Children	0.4	0.5	0.5	0.5

Source: National Longitudinal Surveys of Youth, 1979.
* p < .01 between race within gender groups, two-tailed test.

Earnings returns are also determined by structural divisions in the economy. Structural theorists have defined a tripartite economy consisting of monopoly, competitive, and state sectors.[19] These sectors are differentiated from one another by economic scale, internal labor markets,[20] rates of employee turnover, and industry-wide levels of unionization. Using these sector classifications, researchers have found that differences in job opportunities, earnings, and job stability can all be directly related to the sector in which one is employed.[21]

The competitive sector consists of firms where the capital-to-labor ratio and output per worker are low. This sector includes, for example, restaurants, drug and grocery stores, services (wholesale, medical, repair, eating and drinking, legal), textiles and manufacturing industries. Small-scale production is characteristic of these firms, and they operate primarily in unstable local or regional labor markets. Due to the low rates of capital to productivity, employment in the competitive sector tends to be poorly paid, and work tends to be temporary or seasonal. O'Connor estimated that one-third of the U.S. labor force in the 1970s was located in the competitive sector, in predominantly service and distribution occupations.[22] Today the competitive sector is the most rapidly growing sector in the United States economy. Workers who want but are unable to find full-time, year-round employment in the monopoly or state sectors usually accept employment in the competitive sector. The competitive sector has been dominated by women and minority workers who have historically been locked out of high-wage union

TABLE 3–2 Occupation and Sector Distributions: Latino and Anglo Male and Female Workers

Occupation	Anglo Male (N=1764)	Latino Male (N=436)	Anglo Female (N=1685)	Latina Female (N=338)
Prof'l, Technical	3.6%	2.3%	4.1%	2.1%
Manager/ Farm Manager	2.8%	2.7%	2.2%	0.9%
Sales & Clerical	13.4%	11.1%	40.2%	48.1%
Craftsmen	13.9%	15.1%	1.5%	0.9%
Operative	20.3%	22.6%	7.5%	13.2%
Laborer	25.3%	22.2%	3.9%	5.3%
Service Workers & Private Household	20.5%	23.7%	40.5%	29.6%
Sector				
Competitive	65.4%	63.1%	71.1%	67.1%
Monopoly	24.5%	26.9%	8.3%	11.8%
State	10.1%	9.9%	20.5%	21.2%

Source: NLSY, 1979

industries in the monopoly sector. Working conditions in competitive industries tend to be poor and unemployment is high.

In contrast to the competitive sector, the monopoly sector depends on a rapid growth in the capital-to-labor ratio and high output per worker (physical productivity). Within the monopoly sector growth of production depends less on the growth of employment than on increases in physical capital per worker and technological advances. Firms in the monopoly sector include those producing capital goods such as steel, copper, aluminum, machinery, and consumer goods such as automobiles, appliances, and various food products. The largest proportion of firms in this sector are in manufacturing and mining. Production within the monopoly sector is typically large scale and markets are national or international in scope. Wages are relatively high in monopoly firms. Due to increased foreign competition in the production of capital goods, the growth of firms in the monopoly sector has diminished in the United States.

The state sector of the economy consists of two categories: production of goods and services organized by the state itself, and production organized by industries under contract with the state. Examples of the first category are the U.S. Postal Service, public education, public health, other social services, and the military. Examples of the second category are the production of military equipment and supplies, capital construction, and highway construction. O'Connor estimated that only about 12 percent of the U.S. labor force worked in the state sector in the 1970s.[23] In the state-organized activities within this sector, the ratios of capital to labor and productivity are relatively low, and production growth depends mainly on increased employment. In the second category, the ratio of capital to labor is relatively high and production growth depends on capital investment, improvements in technology, and the number of workers employed.

The demand for labor in the state sector, although relatively stable, is subject to political shifts that affect budgetary priorities. In general, subsidization of production insures job stability. Anglo males have generally monopolized the better-paying state sector positions. However, political norms that govern hiring, promotion, and other personnel decisions (e.g., equality of opportunity, upward mobility programs) have forced state sector employers and contractors since the 1960s to open their doors to minorities and women.

In summary, structural theorists argue that income inequality within population groups is determined in part by how groups are distributed (or redistributed) across occupations, classes, and sectors. Differences in the rates at which earnings change are a function of where an individual is structurally located within occupations and economic sectors of the economy.

Did structural changes in the economy during the 1980s produce a redistribution across occupations and economic sectors that altered previous income inequality between majority and minority groups? Using the NLSY samples, we can respond to this question. As noted earlier, in 1979 there were no statistical differences in earnings within our race-gender groups. This is not surprising due to the fact that the majority of these youth were just entering the labor market in 1979 and were working in mostly part-time jobs. The kinds of occupations available to youth with relatively few skills, little training, and little or no labor market experience are generally quite limited and pay close to the minimum wage. Table 3–2 shows the occupation and economic sector[24] distributions of Latino and Anglo male and female workers in 1979.

The data in Table 3–2 reveal that in 1979 Latino and Anglo males were distributed quite similarly across occupation and economic sectors. Seventy-four percent of Anglo and 77 percent of Latino males jobs were situated in four low-paying occupational classifications: craftsmen, operatives, non-farm laborer, and service. Almost 88 percent of these occupations were within private companies, and approximately 65 percent were located in the competitive sector of the economy.

In 1979, Latino and Anglo females were also distributed within a narrow range of low-paying occupational classifications. More than three-fourths (80.7 percent) of all Anglo female workers were in four low-paying occupations: clerical and sales (40.2 percent), service and private household (40.5 percent). Over ninety percent (90.9 percent) of Latinas were working in clerical and sales occupations (48.1 percent), as operatives (13.2 percent), or in service and household occupations (29.6 percent). Like their male counterparts, over 80 percent of females were employed by private companies, and over 65 percent of female jobs were in the competitive sector of the economy.

TABLE 3–3 Selected Demographic Characteristics of Latino and Anglo Male and Female Full-Time Workers

	Angle Male (N=1764)	Latino Male (N=600)	Anglo Female (N=1462)	Latina Female (N=405)
% Married	60.0	57.8	56.0	53.1
% In Poverty	3.8	11.6	6.3	8.9
% Full Time Worker	84.3	82.6	66.3	75.8
Mean Years Education Completed	15.0	14.3	14.6	14.6
Mean Hours Work Per Week	48.2	47.3	43.8	43.2
Mean Age (Years)	29.1	28.9	29.1	29.1
Mean Income	25,639	$20,842*	18,057	16,126*
Mean No. of Children	0.9	1.2*	0.9	1.3*

Source: NLSY, 1990
* p < .01 between race within gender groups, two-tailed test.

By 1990 the average age of our male and female samples was 29 years, more than 50 percent had married, and most had full-time jobs and averaged over 43 hours of work per week (see Table 3–3). Their occupational and economic distributions changed over the eleven-year period between 1979 and 1990. Table 3–4 compares the occupational distributions between male and female groups. Approximately one-third of full-time Anglo males (33.5 percent) were employed in high-paying professional, technical, or managerial occupations compared to only 24.5 percent of Latino males. Despite the growth of white collar employment, the majority of Latino males (56.9 percent) were still employed in the low-paying competitive sector in 1990.

A comparison of Anglo and Latino female groups reveals the same occupational distribution. In 1990, over 37 percent of all full-time employed Anglo females worked in higher-paying professional, technical, or managerial jobs compared to only 26.8 percent of Latinas. As was the case for Latino males, a majority of Latino females (61.5 percent) were still employed in low-paying clerical and sales (47 percent) and service and private household (14.5 percent) occupations. Forty-seven percent of Anglo females were employed in these occupational categories (31.6 percent clerical and sales; 15.4 service and household).

Table 3–5 shows the effect of occupations and economic sector on earnings[25] in 1990. Research shows that the expansion of white-collar employment increased earnings in professional and managerial occupations,[26] a fact reconfirmed by com-

TABLE 3–4   Occupation and Sector Distributions: Latino and Anglo Male and Female Full-Time Workers

Occupation	Anglo Male (N=2147)	Latino Male (N=600)	Anglo Female (N=1462)	Latina Female (N=405)
Prof'l Technical	15.8%	11.9%	21.6%	14.9%
Manager	17.7%	17.6%	15.4%	12.3%
Sales & Clerical	12.2%	10.4%	34.6%	47.0%
Craftsmen	22.2%	21.6%	2.1%	3.7%
Operative	16.6%	19.1%	9.6%	6.4%
Laborer	7.7%	12.2%	1.3%	1.5%
Service Workers and Private Houshold	7.8%	12.4%	15.4%	14.5%
Sector				
Competitive	49.3%	56.9%	55.2%	55.1%
Monopoly	38.5%	29.4%	16.1%	13.3%
State	12.3%	13.8%	28.6%	31.6%

Source: NLSY, 1990

parisons between Anglo and Latino female earnings within white-collar occupations. Female incomes are highest in professional, technical, and managerial occupations. The fact that there is no statistically significant difference in earnings within these three occupational classifications would lend support to the conclusion that restructuring has benefited women (regardless of ethnicity) in high-growth white-collar occupations where demand for labor is high. Workers in these occupations thus enjoy greater flexibility in acquiring better-paying jobs.

However, it is also the case that restructuring has had a negative impact on some women (Latina more than Anglo) in clerical and service occupations located in the relatively low-wage-paying competitive sector. Although both Anglo and Latino females fared better in the state sector (compared to the competitive sector), several studies pointed out that jobs in this sector are on the decline due to the fiscal crises of state and local governments that have forced layoffs.[27]

In short, the data in Table 3–5 indicate that industrial restructuring in the 1980s promoted earnings inequality by further polarizing or bifurcating the female labor force across occupations. Restructuring escalated employment growth in the competitive rather than monopoly sector and possibly decreased government agency work opportunities at the state and local level. It is likely that industrial restructuring slightly increased the number of opportunities for women in high-paying professional and managerial jobs, but at the same time also

TABLE 3–5   Full-Time Mean Earnings by Occupation and Sector: Latino and Anglo Males and Females

Occupation	Anglo Male (N=2147)	Latino Male (N=600)	Anglo Female (N=1462)	Latina Female (N=405)
Prof'l, Technical	$33,375	$26,390*	$24,446	$23,136
Manager	31,638	24,601*	22,591	19,475
Sales	36,997	17,632*	21,339	18,385
Clerical	22,136	19,579	16,120	15,694
Craftsmen	22,682	22,825	17,298	13,860
Operative	20,683	18,249**	12,996	9,750*
Laborer Non-Farm	19,076	17,248	NR	NR
Service Worker	18,494	18,303	11,507	11,201
Sector				
Competitive	25,320	20,336*	16,977	15,568*
Monopoly	25,726	20,676*	20,470	17,564*
State	27,016	22,569*	18,670	16,480**

Source: NLSY, 1990
NR - Too few cases to report mean earnings.
* p < .01 between race within gender groups, two-tailed test.
** p < .05 between race within gender groups, two-tailed test.

increased their concentration in jobs with lower earnings. The occupational polarization of the female work force has negatively affected minority women more than Anglo women. Our analysis shows that statistically significant earnings inequalities exist between Anglo and Latino females, particularly in the competitive sector where Latinas are disproportionately employed.

Economic restructuring also appears to have increased income inequalities between Latino and Anglo males within white-collar occupations, as well as within sectors. Table 3–5 shows that white-collar professional, technical, and managerial occupations paid the highest wages in 1990. For both occupational groups the earnings differential ($7,000) was about the same between Anglo and Latino males. Previous studies employing a human capital model have argued that wage gaps within white-collar occupations are likely due to differences in educational attainment of workers; however, data in Table 3–3 indicate no significant differences in educational attainment between Latino males (14.3 years) compared to Anglo males (15.0 years). The difference in wages between Latino and Anglo males within white-collar occupations may be due to labor market discrimination. However, confirming that hypothesis requires an empirical testing, using a model of structural and individual variables to determine the relative impact of these factors on earnings differences.

To some extent, it appears that economic restructuring also polarized or bifurcated the male labor force across occupations and sectors. While Anglo and Latino males have greater opportunities to enter white-collar occupations than their female counterparts, Anglo males have benefited most from this advantage. Less than 25 percent of the Latino males in our samples were working in white-collar jobs in 1990. Anglo males were employed in greater proportion in professional, technical, or managerial occupations (over 32 percent).

In summary, we can see that economic restructuring benefited (albeit unequally) Anglo male workers and Anglo and Latina workers in white-collar occupations, but it also caused a polarization of Latino male and Anglo and Latino female labor across occupations, sectors, and classes. This polarization has created wage inequalities for women (both Latina and Anglo) and Latino males because they are more likely to be employed in greater numbers in low-paying occupations in the competitive sector rather than in the more stable monopoly sector. Restructuring has also led to a decline in state sector jobs during the 1980s, a trend that had the greatest impact on Latinas' earnings.

STRUCTURAL REFORM FOR A MORE DEMOCRATIC ECONOMY

Our analysis seems to indicate that earnings inequalities among our sample of young workers were not created by the low productivity of workers (as suggested by human capital theory), but created by the low productivity of jobs in the competitive sector during the 1980s. The rise in productivity jobs (and income inequalities) is structural in nature. Millions of workers labor in modern firms (e.g., fast food chains) where prices must remain low because their products are minimally valued in the marketplace. In these occupations it is not workers' level of productivity but rather their low productivity jobs that explain their low wages.

Nevertheless, these firms can survive because labor market competition, high unemployment, and historic patterns of discrimination allow them to keep the wages of many of their workers low. These firms can continue to survive by exploiting cheap sources of labor (predominantly women and minorities). Such low-wage employment persists in both large and small industries, young and old firms (e.g., McDonald's, one of the largest employers of low-wage labor, is also young and very large).

Breaking this low-wage, low-productivity trend requires addressing structural problems on two fronts. First, capital investment must be readily available to both low and high productivity sectors.[28] Second, the federal government must further intervene in the labor market to make occupational roles more gender neutral and to also raise the floor on worker's wages. Without such intervention the historical forces that have generated labor market job segregation, competition, and discrimination will continue to sustain unproductive and inefficient firms. Such a comprehensive national policy must raise the wages of low-wage workers more rapidly than the wages of high-wage workers to provide greater wage parity across occupations.

Federal intervention in the economy to correct abnormal or unhealthy structural defects is not unprecedented. The New Deal of the 1930s, and more recently the bailout of the savings and loan industry, are two examples of this kind of crisis intervention. The federal government has not recognized persistent earnings inequalities as an economic crisis. Yet the government's long-standing toleration of the structural problem that sustains genuine wage inequalities has permitted an employment structure that falls far short of the democratic ideal.

NOTES

1. Gregory DeFreitas, *Inequality at Work* (New York: Oxford University Press, 1991), 57–59.

2. B. Bergmann, "The Effects on White Incomes of Discrimination in Employment," *Journal of Political Economy* 79 (1971): 294–333; Michael Reich, "The Economies of Racism," in David M. Gordon (ed.), *Problems in Political Economy, An Urban Perspective* (Lexington, MA: D.C. Heath, 1971); Michael Brown and Steven P. Erie, "Blacks and the Legacy of the Great Society," *Public Policy*, 2 (1981): 33–45; David Gordon, Richard Edwards, and Michael Reich, *Segmented Work, Divided Workers* (London: Cambridge University Press, 1982).

3. Gary S. Becker, *Human Capital: A Theoretical and Empirical Analysis with Special Reference to Education*, 2nd edition (New York: National Bureau of Economic Research, 1975); James Smith, "Race and Human Capital," *The American Economic Review*, 74 (1984): 685–698.

4. Cordelia W. Reimers, "A Comparative Analysis of the Wages of Hispanics, Blacks and Non-Hispanic Whites," in George J. Borjas and Marta Tienda (eds.), *Hispanics in the U.S. Economy* (New York: Academic Press, 1985); Leonard A. Carlson and Caroline Swartz, "The Earnings of Women and Ethnic Minorities, 1959–79," *Industrial and Labor Relations Review*, 41 (1988): 530–45.

5. Randy Hodson, "Labor in the Monopoly, Competitive and State Sectors of Production," *Politics and Society*, 8 (1978): 429–480;

Charles Tolbert, Patrick M. Horan, and E. M. Beck, "The Structure of Economic Segmentation: A Dual Economy Approach," *American Journal of Sociology*, 85 (1980): 1095–1116; Alejandro Portes and Robert Bach, *Latin Journey: Cuban and Mexican Immigrants in the United States* (Berkeley: University of California Press, 1985).

6. Barry Bluestone and Bennett Harrison, *The Deindustrialization of America* (New York: Basic Books, 1982); Bennett Harrison and Barry Bluestone, *The Great U-Turn: Corporate Restructuring, Laissez-Faire and the Challenge to America's High Wage Society* (New York: Basic Books, 1988).

7. Colin Bradford and William H. Branson, *Trade and Structural Change in Pacific Asia* (Chicago: University of Chicago Press, 1987); Martin Feldstein (ed.), *The United States in the World Economy* (Chicago: University of Chicago Press, 1988).

8. Job deskilling is the process by which new technologies have often replaced highly skilled workers in some industries with less skilled workers, usually through automation or other new changes in work production that require less skilled workers.

9. Researchers studying employment distinguish between voluntary and involuntary part-time work. Persons who by choice work less than 35 hours per week are called voluntary part-time workers. Involuntary part-time

workers, on the other hand, would like to work a standard workweek but cannot due to slack work. For recent trends of involuntary part-time work among Chicano workers, see De Anda, "Falling Back: Mexican-Origin Men and Women in the U.S. Economy" (Chapter 4, this volume).

10. Rodolfo D. Torres and Adela de la Torre, "Latinos, Class and the U.S. Political Economy: Income Inequality and Policy Alternatives," in Edwin Melendez, Clara Rodriquez, and Barry Figueroa (eds.) *Hispanics in the Labor Force* (New York: Plenum Press, 1991).

11. Ronald Ehrenberg, Pamela Rosenberg, and Jeanne Li, "Part-time Employment in the United States," in Robert Hart (ed.), *Employment, Unemployment and Hours of Work* (London: George Allen and Unwin, 1991).

12. Bennett Harrison and Barry Bluestone, *The Great U-Turn: Corporate Restructuring, Laissez-Faire and the Challenge to America's High Wage Society*.

13. Bennett Harrison, "The Impact of Corporate Restructuring on Labor Income," *Social Policy*, 18 (1987): 6–11.

14. The NLSY is sponsored by the Bureau of Labor Statistics, U.S. Department of Labor, and conducted by the U.S. Bureau of the Census for the Center for Human Resources (CHR) at Ohio State University. CHR maintains and distributes the data.

15. The Latino sample in 1979 consisted of 60 percent Mexican origin respondents, 17 percent Puerto Rican respondents, 6 percent Cuban respondents, and 16 percent who identified themselves as "Other Spanish" or "Other Latino."

16. Full-time workers are defined as working 35 or more hours per week for 50 or more weeks during the year.

17. Peter Blau and Otis Dudley Duncan, *The American Occupational Structure* (New York: Wiley, 1967); Otis Dudley Duncan, David Featherman, and Beverly Duncan, *Socioeconomic Background and Achievement* (New York: Seminar Press, 1972).

18. Donald Treiman and Heidi I. Hartmann, *Women, Work and Wages: Equal Pay for Jobs of Equal Value* (Washington DC: National Academy Press, 1981).

19. James O'Connor, *The Fiscal Crisis of the State* (New York: St. Martin's Press, 1973); "The Structure of Economic Segmentation," 1095–1116.

20. Doeringer and Piore make a distinction between internal and external labor markets. Internal labor markets are characterized by industries that have stable employment patterns (low job worker turnover); where pay is usually salaried rather than hourly wage structured, which usually include employee health benefits and paid vacations; and provide job ladder avenues for advancement in the firm. External labor markets are characterized by firms that hire workers at an hourly wage rate, offer few if any benefits (retirement, health insurance, pension plans), and have a high turnover in employees (low job stability). Workers who are employed in internal labor markets generally receive higher incomes than workers employed in external labor markets. Peter B. Doeringer and Michael Piore, *Internal Labor Markets and Manpower Analysis* (Lexington, MA: Lexington Press, 1971).

21. Doeringer and Piore, *Internal Labor Markets and Manpower Analysis*; David Gordon, Richard Edwards, and Michael Reich, *Segmented Work, Divided Workers* (London: Cambridge University Press, 1982).

22. James O'Connor, *The Fiscal Crisis of the State* (New York: St. Martin's Press, 1973).

23. O'Connor, *The Fiscal Crisis of the State*, p. 17.

24. Economic sectors were operationalized by first classifying 3-digit census industry codes into the categories listed below following Singlemann and Browning; Joachim Singlemann and Harley Browning, "Industrial Transformation and Occupational Change in the U.S.," *Social Forces*, 59 (1980): 246–264. These categories were then collapsed into competitive, monopoly, or state economic sectors based on O'Connor's description. This operationalization of economic sectors closely parallels that of Cummings and Smith; Scott Cummings, "Vulnerability to the Effects of Recession: Minority Female Workers," *Social*

Forces, 65 (1987): 834–857; Shelley A. Smith, "Sources of Earnings Inequality in the Black and White Female Labor Forces," *The Sociological Quarterly*, 32 (1991): 117–138.

Competitive

Agriculture
Textiles
Transportation
Wholesale
Retail
Banking
Insurance
Real Estate
Engineering
Accounting
Miscellaneous Production
Legal Services
Medical Services
Non-Profit
Domestic Services
Hotels

Monopoly

Mining
Construction
Food

Metal
Machinery
Chemical
Miscellaneous Manufacturing
Communications

State

Utilities
Hospitals
Education
Welfare
Postal
Public Administration
Miscellaneous Social Services

25. Earnings were measured as full-time year round dollar earnings.
26. Peter Henle and Paul Ryscavage, "The Distribution of Earned Income among Men and Women, 1958–1977," *Monthly Labor Review*, 103 (1980): 3–10.
27. Bluestone and Harrison, *The Deindustrialization of America*.
28. Samuel Bowles, David Gordon, and Thomas Weisskopf, *Beyond the Wasteland* (New York: Anchor Press, 1983), 329–337.

4

FALLING BACK: MEXICAN-ORIGIN MEN AND WOMEN IN THE U.S. ECONOMY

ROBERTO M. DE ANDA

The socioeconomic integration of the Mexican-origin population traces its beginnings to World War II. Labor shortages created by the war opened opportunities in the labor market, although very often Mexican-origin participation was limited to the least desirable positions. After the war, Mexicans[1] continued to struggle for more labor-market opportunities and greater equality in the workplace. For the first time, the number of individuals of Mexican descent attending college increased, and there was a growing professional middle class. Significant inroads were also made into skilled and unionized occupations.[2]

Despite this era of postwar prosperity, improvement in the socioeconomic standing of Mexicans was limited. While some Mexicans experienced upward social mobility, others continued to do poorly in the labor market, as can be seen in their concentration in low-status jobs and persistently lower incomes than whites. Moreover, it is evident that today Mexicans continue to experience marginal participation in the economy despite their educational and civil rights gains since the 1940s. For example, in the last few years the number of "good" jobs available to them has decreased. This is clearly seen in the higher level of marginal jobs among Mexican workers compared to white workers. For example, the jobless rate continues to be higher for Mexicans than for whites, and the number of part-time and irregular jobs has been increasing.[3] The Mexican workers' disadvantaged position in the labor market makes little sense in light of their socioeconomic advancements.

This chapter analyzes the level of economic integration of Mexican-origin workers from the mid-1970s to the early 1990s. The first section defines labor force integration; the next section discusses labor force participation, followed by an analysis of occupational distribution, and a section comparing joblessness and underemployment. This chapter concludes with a discussion of the effect of labor force marginality on income.

LABOR FORCE INTEGRATION

Generally speaking, economic integration refers to the degree to which members of a particular minority group are distributed in a pattern similar to that of the population as a whole in the economic system. The discussion here will be limited to labor force integration. For example, the degree of labor force integration can be evaluated by comparing the workforce participation of a minority group to that of the dominant population. Similarly, the minority group's occupational distribution is also an indicator of economic integration.

Another dimension of labor force integration, and the focus of this chapter, is the evaluation of the quality of jobs of persons active in the labor force. That is, the quality of the job indicates whether a person is fully integrated into the labor force or has marginal participation in it. Obviously, being without a job indicates marginal participation. But having a job does not guarantee full participation in the labor force. For example, persons having part-time or irregular jobs also show inadequate participation. Similarly, those with full-time jobs who do not earn enough to cover their basic needs are also marginal participants in the labor force.

To be sure, full labor force integration of Mexican workers would mean that labor force participation rates would be similar, and the occupational and income distribution of the minority group would match those of the whole society. And, most importantly, both groups of workers would have equal access to stable jobs.

LABOR FORCE PARTICIPATION

The labor force is a useful concept to gauge a group's level of economic activity. By definition, a person is included in the labor force if he or she has a job or is actively looking for one. The labor force participation rate (LFPR) refers to the percentage of the population that is active in the economy.

For several decades, the LFPR for Mexicans has been comparable to that of whites.[4] In fact, the rate for Mexican men has been constantly higher than that of their white counterparts. But this has not been the case for women: Mexican women have had lower participation rates compared to their white peers. For example, in 1992 the LFPR for Mexican men was 80.5 percent versus 75.2 percent for whites. For women, on the other hand, Mexicans have a lower rate than whites: 51.6 percent and 58.0 percent, respectively.[5] As will be discussed in the following sections, the higher LFPR for Mexicans, however, does not translate into a higher percentage of "good" jobs or a lower jobless rate.

Occupational Distribution

Although there has been improvement in the occupational distribution of Mexican workers, there is still a significant gap between them and white workers. Table 4–1 presents data on the occupational distribution of these two groups of workers by gender. Mexicans are severely underrepresented in occupations requiring high levels of education and concentrated in those requiring less education. In 1992, for example, less than 10 percent of Mexican men were employed in managerial and professional specialty occupations (e.g., accountants and engineers), compared to nearly 30 percent for white men. Mexican women fared slightly better in this occupational category than their male counterparts, but they were still underrepresented relative to white women.

While Mexican workers tend to be underrepresented in the white-collar occupations, they are clustered in the blue-collar, services, and farming occupations. Fully three-fourths of Mexican-origin men and half of the women work in these types of occupations. Since these occupations typically require less formal schooling than white-collar occupations, they also tend to pay less.

It should not be overlooked, however, that there has been substantial improvement in the occupational distribution of Mexicans, that almost one-fourth of the men and one-half of the women hold white-collar jobs, and only a small

TABLE 4–1   **Percentage Distribution of Occupation for Mexican and White Workers by Gender: 1992**

Occupational Group	Male		Female	
	Mexican	White	Mexican	White
Managerial & Professional Specialty	9.3	28.6	14.0	29.7
Technical, Sales, & Admin. Support	14.0	21.9	39.3	45.6
Subtotal	(23.3)	(50.5)	(53.3)	(75.3)
Services	16.6	9.0	24.6	15.4
Farming, Forestry, & Fishing	10.9	3.7	2.8	0.9
Precision Production, Craft, & Repair	20.0	18.8	3.1	1.9
Operators, Fabricators & Laborers	29.2	18.0	16.2	6.5
Total Percent	100.0	100.0	100.0	100.0

Source: Adopted from *Current Population Reports*, Series P20-465RV, Tables 2 and 3.

fraction (one-tenth) are farm workers—all indications of substantially greater economic integration than was the case a generation ago. Nonetheless, this description of the Mexican occupational structure masks the fact many of these workers are increasingly found in unstable work positions.

Joblessness

Usually discussions about the labor market problems of Mexican workers focus on the jobless rate. This makes sense since joblessness indicates labor force marginality. In fact, during the last two decades the unemployment rate has been from 50 to 100 percent higher for Mexican than for white workers.[6] However, there are many people who are working but whose jobs are either part-time, temporary, or don't pay enough to make ends meet. This type of marginal employment is called underemployment.[7]

Underemployment

To measure the extent of labor force integration of Mexican-origin workers, the *Labor Utilization Framework* will be employed.[8] This approach focuses on the quality of work that society offers to its economically active population.

By definition, a person is considered adequately employed if he or she works a full workweek (i.e., over 35 hours per week) at a wage above the poverty level. Conversely, a person is said to be underemployed if he or she works fewer hours than a full workweek or his or her income is inadequate to meet basic needs.

Besides joblessness, the following three forms of underemployment are discussed:

1. *Involuntary part-time work.* Includes persons who work less than 35 hours per week due to economic reasons beyond their control (e.g., slack work).[9]
2. *Intermittent employment.* Refers to workers who experience three or more spells of joblessness, or were jobless for more than 15 weeks.
3. *Working poor.* Refers to full-time workers whose annual work-related income is less than 1.25 times the poverty level.[10]

In addition to joblessness, the sum of underemployment categories 1–3 provides a measure of total underemployment or marginal employment.

Figure 4–1 shows that underemployment for Mexican men has been rising between 1976 and 1987. The data also show dramatic differences in the underemployment level for Mexican and white workers. While the level of underemployment for Mexicans jumped from 32.2 percent in 1976 to 41.4 percent by 1987, white underemployment for the same period actually dropped, decreasing slightly from 21.7 percent to 20.8 percent. Thus, by 1987, there were twice as many underemployed Mexicans as whites.

Figure 4–2 displays the level of underemployment for women. Although the twelve-year period under consideration shows a drop in the level of underem-

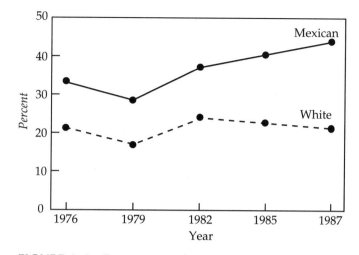

FIGURE 4–1   **Percentage of Underemployed Mexican-Origin and White Males, Aged 16–64: 1976–1987**

Source: *CPS,* 1976–1987.

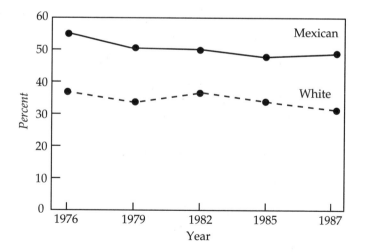

FIGURE 4–2   **Percentage of Underemployed Mexican-Origin and White Females, Aged 16–64: 1976–1987**

Source: *CPS,* 1976–1987.

ployment for women, it has remained higher than the men's level. In 1976, the underemployment level for Mexican women was 54.4 percent, whereas for white women it was 36.4 percent. By 1987, the level for Mexican women had dropped to 46.7 percent. Throughout the period under consideration, the gap between Mexican and white women remained about the same: 50 percent higher for Mexican women relative to their white counterparts.

Table 4–2 displays the components of underemployment for Mexican and white men and women. Although joblessness is a serious labor market problem, it accounts for less than one-third of total labor force marginality.

The widening gap between the Mexican and white levels of underemployment can be traced to the growth of part-time and low-income work. For example, in 1976 the Mexican-to-white part-time ratio was 1.8, whereas by 1987 it had

TABLE 4–2   Percentage Distribution of Underemployment among Mexican and White Workers by Gender

	Components*				
	UN	IPT	IN	LOW	Total
Males					
1976					
Mexican	11.2	5.5	6.0	9.5	32.2
White	7.5	3.0	5.3	5.8	21.7
Ratio	1.5	1.8	1.1	1.6	1.5
1987					
Mexican	12.5	8.8	6.5	13.6	41.4
White	6.8	3.5	4.0	6.5	20.8
Ratio	1.8	2.5	1.6	2.1	2.0
Females					
1976					
Mexican	17.0	9.8	6.7	21.0	54.4
White	10.1	5.2	4.0	17.1	36.4
Ratio	1.7	1.9	1.7	1.2	1.5
1987					
Mexican	13.4	10.8	3.9	18.7	46.7
White	6.7	5.9	2.9	14.8	30.2
Ratio	2.0	1.8	1.3	1.3	1.6

Sources: U.S. Bureau of the Census, *Current Population Survey (CPS), Annual Demographic Files* (ICPSR 7700), 1976. U.S. Bureau of the Census, *Current Population Survey, Annual Demographic Files* (ICPSR 8863), 1987.
*UN = unemployment; IPT = involuntary part-time work;
IN = intermittent employment; LOW = low income.
Total Underemployment = UN + IPT + IN + LOW.

increased to 2.5. In other words, in 1987 for every ten whites working part time twenty-five Mexicans were doing so.

The low income category was the second major contributor to the Mexican/white underemployment differential. Whereas this category increased for Mexicans by little over four percentage points between 1976 and 1987, the corresponding change for whites was less than one percentage point. In fact, by 1987 the working poor level surpassed the jobless level.

It is well known that women tend to have lower incomes than men. Not surprisingly, the working poor component is the largest for women. In 1976, over one-fifth of Mexican women were working but poor. This proportion slightly decreased by 1987 to 18.7 percent. Joblessness seems to be the second highest form of underemployment that women experience. It, too, dropped for the period under consideration. Involuntary part-time work, however, remained consistently high during this period. Although the data show that the Mexican male and female underemployment is converging, it must not be forgotten that the women's level is still over five percentage points higher.

Table 4–3 shows underemployment rates for Mexican and white workers who did not finish high school. Overall, the data indicate that poorly educated workers

TABLE 4–3   Underemployment among Mexicans and Whites with Less than Twelve Years of Schooling by Gender

	Components*				
	UN	IPT	IN	LOW	Total
Males					
1976					
Mexican	10.6	6.5	6.1	11.8	35.0
White	11.2	5.1	6.8	7.6	30.7
1987					
Mexican	12.6	11.0	7.9	17.7	49.2
White	14.3	6.2	5.6	9.4	35.5
Females					
1976					
Mexican	20.5	13.8	7.2	22.5	64.0
White	14.4	8.3	6.1	21.4	50.2
1987					
Mexican	18.4	11.9	4.7	24.3	59.3
White	15.0	10.3	3.5	23.4	52.2

Source: *CPS*, 1976 and 1987.
*UN = unemployment; IPT = involuntary part-time work;
IN = intermittent employment; LOW = low income.
Total Underemployment = UN + IPT + IN + LOW.

are more likely to be marginally employed. Moreover, comparing the underemployment levels between 1976 and 1987, it is clear that the situation for less-educated workers is getting worse. For Mexican males, the underemployment level was 35 percent in 1976, but it increased to almost 50 percent by 1987—an increase of fifteen percentage points. This suggests that education is essential for workers to be competitive in today's economy.

Lastly, while joblessness remained fairly constant for Mexicans with less than twelve years of schooling, much of the growth in their level of underemployment can be attributed to increases in the involuntary part-time work and working poor components.

THE EFFECT OF MARGINALITY ON INCOME

Income is an important indicator of how well a group is doing in the economy. The discussion that follows will focus on work-related income only, that is, wages and salary. The underemployment data reveal that more than two-fifths of Mexican men and almost half of Mexican women have marginal jobs. By and large, these are irregular, low-wage jobs. This suggests that the working poor have grown steadily as a proportion of the Mexican workforce.

Although underemployment measures current labor force marginality, it is possible to evaluate the labor-force experience of workers over the span of the a year. De Anda (1991) uses this approach to examine the effects of irregular and involuntary part-time employment on annual income.[11] He found that marginal employment has a powerful effect on earnings. For example, in 1986, workers who were marginally employed earned 37 percent less than their fully employed counterparts. This is a substantial difference considering that even fully employed Mexican workers earn less than white workers.

CONCLUSIONS

Data on the economic integration of Mexican-origin workers paint a mixed picture. Although the labor force participation rates of Mexican workers have been slightly higher than for non-Mexicans, this has not translated into adequate labor force integration. No doubt there has been some improvement in the occupational distribution of Mexicans, but there still remains a significant gap between them and white workers. Worse yet, the findings unequivocally show that marginal labor participation increased for Mexican workers during the 1980s. For this period, employment opportunities among Mexicans severely deteriorated, particularly among the poorly educated.

NOTES

1. In this chapter, the terms Mexican-origin and Mexican are used interchangeably, regardless of place of birth, to indicate Mexican descent.

2. Mario Barrea, *Race and Class in the Southwest: A Theory of Racial Inequality* (Notre Dame, IN: Notre Dame University Press, 1979).

3. Roberto M. De Anda, "Inequality at Work: A Comparison of Underemployment and Stratification between Mexican-Origin and White Workers," Unpublished Ph.D. dissertation, University of Arizona 1991.

4. Frank D. Bean and Marta Tienda, *The Hispanic Population of the United States* (New York: Russell Sage, 1987).

5. U.S. Bureau of the Census, "The Hispanic Population in the United States: March 1992," *Current Population Reports*, Series P-20 (Washington, DC: Government Printing Office, 1993).

6. Gregory DeFreitas, *Inequality at Work: Hispanics in the U.S. Labor Force* (New York: Oxford University Press, 1991).

7. Roberto M. De Anda, "Unemployment and Underemployment Among Mexican-Origin Workers," *Hispanic Journal of Behavioral Sciences*, 16 (1994): 163–175.

8. For full discussion of the Labor Utilization Framework, see Teresa Sullivan, *Marginal Workers, Marginal Jobs* (Austin: The University of Texas Press, 1978); also, Clifford Clogg, *Measuring Underemployment* (New York: Academic Press, 1979).

9. For an extended discussion of this form of underemployment, see Roberto M. De Anda, "Involuntary Part-Time Work among Chicanos: Its Causes and Consequences," in Tatcho Mindiola and Emilio Zamora (eds.), *Chicano Discourse: Selected Conference Proceedings of the National Association for Chicano Studies* (Houston: University of Houston, Mexican American Studies Program, 1992).

10. For example, the low income level for an individual worker in 1986 is calculated as follows: $5,909 × 1.25 = $7,386. For a detailed explanation of this technique, see Clifford Clogg and Teresa Sullivan, "Labor Force Composition and Underemployment Trends, 1969–1980," *Social Indicators Research*, 12 (1983): 117–152.

11. See De Anda, "Inequality at Work," Chapter 5.

PART II

CONTINUITY AND CHANGE:
THE CHICANO FAMILY

5

FAMILISM AND ASSIMILATION AMONG MEXICAN-ORIGIN AND ANGLO HIGH SCHOOL ADOLESCENTS

ANGELA VALENZUELA   SANFORD M. DORNBUSCH

At a general level, this study contributes to the debate over assimilation among Mexican Americans. We intend to show that the conventional theoretical framework in the assimilationist literature lacks explanatory value in the area of educational achievement. Contrary to the view of some scholars, key aspects of Mexican culture, such as a sense of familism, survive the acculturation process. This is especially evident when we associate key measures of acculturation with a refined definition of familism.

This study examines the relation of socioeconomic mobility and generational status to three dimensions of familism: attitudinal (or ideological), structural, and behavioral. As an ideology, familism attitudes express the collective orientation that the needs of individuals are subordinate to the needs of the family. The structural dimension refers to the number of geographically proximate kin, and the behavioral dimension reflects actual contact with relatives. We build on earlier research, which observes that Mexican-origin youth are not only more familistic than their Anglo counterparts, but that this orientation predicts the academic achievement of Mexican-origin youth if parents have at least a high school diploma.[1]

Scholars in the assimilationist tradition have suggested that once Mexican-origin persons acculturate into the mainstream of society, they will shed their "traditional" orientations.[2] Talcott Parsons, in particular, theorized that specific values are critical to those trying to become middle class. Accordingly, the need for mobility, individual achievement, and competition are said to overshadow more traditional or primordial orientations, both to one's family and one's original culture. Thus, a more individualistic orientation eventually replaces familism

53

because of its putative ability to confer greater success and mobility. Researchers, however, have demonstrated that the Mexican American family continues to contain protective and supportive qualities despite acculturation experiences.[3]

Two positions color the response to the assimilationist prediction, one pointing to the primacy of culture and the other to structure. Some scholars suggest that familism rests at the ideological core of U.S. Mexican culture, evident in its time-tested ability to withstand the forces of acculturation.[4] Others caution against romanticized depictions, arguing that familism is a key source of Chicanas' oppression because of the hierarchical and male-dominated structure of Mexican families.[5] This concern is echoed in gerontological research by scholars who fear that flattering portrayals of Mexican American families will deprive the elderly of services many of them need.[6]

Cross-cultural research underscores the structural basis of familism. Familism is used as a common coping strategy among poor and working class people throughout the world.[7] That Anglos are rarely described as familistic attests to their greater economic solvency relative to minority populations. Despite wide variations in measures used, comparative research consistently shows that Anglos are less familistic than U.S. Mexicans.[8] Whenever they are so characterized, structural factors like social class, discrimination, rural origins, and regional differences are used as explanations.[9]

Both cultural and structural positions have merit.[10] It is our contention that familism is both a core ideological construct in U.S. Mexican culture and a product of social structural factors. In reconciling the culture-structure debate, we must first conceptualize familism as having both cultural and structural attributes, and second, specify *which dimensions of familism reflect culture and which reflect social structural conditions.*

Our study draws heavily on research conducted by Keefe and colleagues, which documents the prevalence of familism among Mexican-origin adults. Keefe and colleagues used familistic dimensions very similar to the ones employed in this study, although they did not describe them in the same terms.[11]

Keefe and Padilla suggest that the attitudinal dimension of familism is an attribute of U.S. Mexican culture, whereas the structural and behavioral dimensions reflect social structural conditions. They note the general failure of assimilation theory to take into account the partial or incomplete assimilation of ostensibly traditional characteristics, including familism. Whereas many social and cultural traits, such as the Spanish language, the celebration of Mexican holidays, and the adherence to lifecycle rituals, are altered or lost in the process of mobility and acculturation, a sense of familism remains strong. That familistic ideology persists generationally even as social and structural factors change suggests that familism has special meaning for Mexican Americans.

To be sure, structural factors contribute to, but do not wholly determine, the retention of familism as an ideology. Were there a tighter correspondence, familism would plummet with the incidence of divorce and family separation. Instead, the opposite appears to be true.[12] Sometimes in defiance of objective reality, familistic ideology expresses the subjective wishes of a people to share life's experiences together and to leave behind memories of a rich and enduring past.

TABLE 5–1   Ethnic and Sex Composition of Matched Sample

Sample Characteristics		Number of Subjects	Percent of All Subjects
Ethnicity	Sex		
Mexicans	Males	313	9%
	Females	332	9%
	Subtotal	645	18%
Anglos	Males	1,412	40%
	Females	1,480	42%
	Subtotal	2,892	82%
	Total	3,537	100%

Our main hypothesis is that familism as an ideology will transcend socioeconomic and generational status and so persist as a cultural ideal. Structural and behavioral aspects of extended family relations are subject to change with mobility and across generations. Given that the concept of familism has only rarely been applied to Anglos, who tend to be characterized as more individualistic, they are less central to our study.[13] The data for Anglos nevertheless provides a much-needed comparative perspective for our findings among Mexicans.

SOURCES OF DATA

The data come from two sources: a fall 1987 survey of adolescents and a spring 1988 follow-up of many of these same adolescents. Each involved a questionnaire administered to all students present on a particular day in six urban and suburban high schools in the San Francisco Bay Area. Matched data from both surveys produced a sample of 3,537 students for the current analysis (see Table 5–1).

MEASURES USED IN THE ANALYSIS

Sex

Males and females in both groups were fairly evenly distributed, with 52.0 percent females among Mexicans and 51.2 percent females among Anglos.

Ethnicity

The ethnicity variable contrasts Mexicans to Anglos. The ethnic and gender composition of the sample appears in Table 5–1. Of the total sample, 645 Mexican-origin male and female subjects are available for analysis, indicating their under-representation in these schools.

Parental Education (Pared)

Parental education categories in the student questionnaire consisted of the following: (1) some grade school; (2) finished grade school; (3) some high school; (4) high school graduate; (5) some college or two-year degree; (6) four-year college graduate; (7) some school beyond college; and (8) professional or graduate degree. An average of the mother's and father's education was used and trichotomized into low, middle, and high categories. "Low Pared" parents attained a less than high school level of education; "Mid Pared" parents attained either a high school diploma and/or some college; and "High Pared" parents attained at least a four-year college degree. These categories conform to the distribution of education in the Mexican-origin sample with 33.5 percent, 38.8 percent, and 27.8 percent falling into the low, mid, and high categories, respectively. Among Anglos, 2.5 percent, 23.6 percent, and 74.0 percent fall into these categories, reflecting their rather high levels of educational attainment.

Generational Status (Gen)

Generations were separated using information on parent and student nativity. Students born abroad whose parents were born abroad were classified as first generation. Second-generation students were born in the United States but had parents born abroad. Students were classified as third generation if they and their parents were born in the United States. Generational status reflects the acculturative changes that families undergo with time in the United States. For this paper, generational differences only among Mexicans are examined.

Familism Attitudes (Attitudes)[14]

This ideological component of familism is measured on a 14-point scale derived from principal components analysis that asks students to rate how strongly they agree or disagree with the following four items about relatives. "I should keep in close contact with my relatives"; "Having many relatives nearby is good because I can always rely on them in times of need"; "One of the good things in life for me is to talk and have fun with my relatives"; and "It's best to go to a relative first, rather than a teacher or counselor when a person has an emotional problem and needs help."

Familism Structure (Structure)

This single item measures the number of adult relatives living within an hour's drive of the respondent's home and ranges on a 6-point scale from "none" to "20 or more."

asking how often students see or talk to relatives who do not live in household

Familistic Behavior (Contact) ✳

Contact is measured with a single variable that consists of a 6-point frequency scale asking <u>how often students see or talk on the telephone with adult relatives who do not live in their household.</u>

PROCEDURES

The central question that this study investigates is whether familism among youth declines with socioeconomic mobility and generational status as predicted in the assimilation literature. Familism is related to socioeconomic status, as measured by parents' educational attainment within both the Mexican and Anglo groups, whereas generational status is examined only within Mexicans. Ethnic comparisons according to each dimension of familism are followed by analyses of familism within low, middle, and high parental education categories. Results based on sex differences in dimensions of familism are not reported since no statistically significant differences were observed. Mean differences in dimensions of familism by generational status conclude the analysis. Multiple comparisons of familism dimensions by parents' educational attainment and by generational status are accomplished using Tukey's Studentized Range test procedure.[15]

EMPIRICAL RESULTS

In general, both Mexicans and Anglos are high on familistic attitudes (see Table 5–2). All youth also have available to them a kinship network with whom they are in frequent contact. The means for familism among Mexicans nevertheless differ

TABLE 5–2   **Ethnic Differences in Familistic Attitudes, Structure, and Contact among Mexican-Origin and Anglo High School Adolescents (Means)**

	Attitudes	Structure	Contact
Mexicans	12.52***	3.77***	3.47*
	2.6[a]	1.6	1.5
	(485)[b]	(552)	(544)
Anglos	11.90	2.83	3.31
	2.5	1.5	1.3
	(2373)	(2670)	(2692)

Note: * means are statistically significant at the .05 level, ** at the .01 level, and *** at the .001 level (one-tailed test). The statistical test is whether Mexican means are significantly different from those of Anglos.

[a] standard deviation

[b] sample size

from those of Anglos in every dimension. Mexicans not only register significantly higher familistic Attitudes, but they also report more Structure (adult relatives living within an hour's drive of their home) and greater Contact. Mexican-origin adolescents report having anywhere from six to ten adult relatives who are geographically proximate, compared to three and five among Anglos.

Before concluding that Mexicans were more behaviorally enmeshed in their extended kinship networks than were Anglos, we conducted additional analyses of Contact not reported here. We were concerned that greater contact with kin might simply reflect the number of potentially available relatives with whom to be in contact. After controlling for the number of adult kin available to youth in their networks, significant differences in levels of contact persisted. Even with equal numbers of geographically proximate kin, Mexicans are significantly more involved with their relatives than are Anglo youth.[16] These ethnic differences suggest that despite high levels of familism attitudes among both Mexicans and Anglos, their structural and behavioral worlds are markedly different. Moreover, differences in familistic attitudes, structure, and behavior are circumscribed more by ethnic than gender considerations.

In examining the relation of socioeconomic mobility to dimensions of familism (see Table 5–3), we find that familistic Attitudes among Mexicans are not significantly related to levels of parental educational attainment. In contrast, Anglos experience a decline at the high parental education level, differing significantly only from the middle parental education group. With respect to Structure, a gradual decline is evident among Mexicans, though no differences are statistically significant. Among Anglos, a precipitous decline in the number of geographically proximate kin is evident among youth whose parents have attained a high level of education. The number of available kin reported in this group differs significantly from both the low- and middle-parental-education groups.

Contact with extended kin among Mexicans is the only familism variable affected by social class. Contact has a curvilinear relation to parent education. Contact starts low, peaks at the middle-parental-education-level and then declines at high levels of parental education. The middle-parental-education group differs significantly from both the low and high groups, whereas the low and high groups do not differ significantly from each other. Hence, contact with extended family is not a linear function of educational attainment. Among Anglos, a similar curvilinear pattern is observed, but the differences are not statistically significant.

Socioeconomic mobility thus produces mixed results among Mexican-origin and Anglo youth, depending on the familism dimension in question. Only the behavioral dimension of familism among Mexicans appears to be affected by the parents' level of educational attainment, and the relation is not linear. Among Anglos, only the attitudinal and structural dimensions are affected by increases in parents' education.

Analyses of generational differences illuminate the relation of familism to acculturation among Mexicans (see Table 5–4). With respect to Attitudes, no statistically significant differences are obtained. A strong, positive identification to family thrives despite acculturation to mainstream society. Structure has a curvilinear relation to generation among Mexicans, with the second generation enjoying the

TABLE 5–3 Ethnic Differences in Familistic Attitudes, Structure, and Contact among Mexican-Origin and Anglo High School Adolescents (sample size in parentheses)

	Referent	Referent Mean	Comparison	Comparison Mean	Diff. between Means	Alpha ≤05
			Mexicans			
Attitudes	Low Pared	12.39 (152)	Mid Pared	12.51 (177)	−.12	
			High Pared	12.59 (121)	−.20	
	Mid Pared		High Pared		−.08	
Structure	Low Pared	3.91 (165)	Mid Pared	3.84 (192)	.07	
			High Pared	3.70 (132)	.21	
	Mid Pared		High Pared		.14	
Contact	Low Pared	3.25 (165)	Mid Pared	3.71 (190)	−.46	***
			High Pared	3.36 (132)	−.11	
	Mid Pared		High Pared		.35	***
			Anglos			
Attitudes	Low Pared	11.98 (49)	Mid Pared	12.14 (520)	−.16	
			High Pared	11.83 (1686)	.15	
	Mid Pared		High Pared		.31	***
Structure	Low Pared	3.10 (60)	Mid Pared	3.30 (572)	−.20	
			High Pared	2.68 (1905)	.42	***
	Mid Pared		High Pared		.62	***
Contact	Low Pared	3.17 (59)	Mid Pared	3.40 (574)	−.23	
			High Pared	3.28 (1925)	−.11	
	Mid Pared		High Pared		.12	

TABLE 5–4   Generational Differences in Family Attitudes, Structure, and Contact among Mexican-Origin High School Adolescents (sample size in parentheses)

Variable	Referent	Referent Mean	Generational Comparison	Generation Mean	Diff. between Means	Alpha ≤05
Attitudes	Gen1	12.52 (101)	Gen2	12.29 (143)	.23	
			Gen3	12.55 (205)	−.03	
	Gen2		Gen3		−.26	
Structure	Gen1	3.29 (107)	Gen2	4.23 (154)	−.94	***
			Gen3	3.83 (219)	−.54	***
	Gen2		Gen3		.40	***
Contact	Gen1	3.07 (99)	Gen2	3.24 (156)	−.17	
			Gen3	3.75 (217)	−.68	***
	Gen2		Gen3		−.51	***

greatest number of geographically proximate kin, followed by a decline in the third generation. The third generation, however, consists of significantly greater numbers of available kin than are available among first generation youth.

Mexican-origin youth report significantly higher levels of contact with extended kin in the third generation than in either the first or second generations. This finding, in combination with the previous finding of a decline in the number of available kin in the third generation, implies the prevalence of contact even when fewer relatives are available. There can be no stronger evidence of the continuing importance of kin as sources of support and recreation for more acculturated Mexican-American youth.

CONCLUSIONS

Taken together, these findings are consistent with the highly familistic images of Mexican-origin families in the literature on Mexican-American families. These findings also partially refute the assumptions in the assimilationist literature that extended family orientations decline either as families achieve greater socioeconomic success or as they increase their exposure to mainstream culture. Finally, we demonstrate the utility of employing a multidimensional framework to the study of familism. This multidimensional framework not only reveals different configurations of familism cross-ethnically, but it also locates disjunctions between the ideology of familism and the actual interaction among extended family members. These findings attest to the multidimensionality of familism, and yet lead to the conclusion that no dimension of familism is declining as Mexicans are exposed to greater acculturation through the generations or to greater success in American society. Familism is successfully resisting assimilation.

Acknowledgements: We would like to thank Amado Padilla for providing helpful comments on earlier drafts of this paper. The research was supported by a fellowship from the Woodrow Wilson Spencer Fellowship Foundation, a grant from the Business and Professional Women's Association to Angela Valenzuela, as well as a grant from the Carnegie Corporation to Sanford M. Dornbusch at the Stanford Center for the Study of Families, Children and Youth at Stanford University.

NOTES

1. Angela Valenzuela and Sanford M. Dornbusch, "Familism and Social Capital in the Academic Achievement of Mexican-Origin and Anglo Adolescents," *Social Science Quarterly*, 75 (1994).

2. Nathan Glazer and Daniel Patrick Moynihan (eds.), *Beyond the Melting Pot: The Negroes, Puerto Ricans, Jews, Italians and Irish of New York City* (Cambridge, MA: M.I.T. Press, 1963); Talcott Parsons, "The Kinship System of the Contemporary United States," *American Anthropologist*, 45 (1943): 22–38; William J. Goode, *World Revolution and Family Patterns* (New York: The Free Press, 1970). Many studies, however, have observed great heterogeneity in the composition of Mexican-origin households, weakening the proposition by the assimilationists that Mexican social organization may be characterized as traditional and at an early stage in development. Richard Griswold del Castillo, *La Familia: Chicano Families in the Urban Southwest, 1884 to the Present* (Notre Dame, IN: University of Notre Dame Press, 1984); Jaime Sena-Rivera, "Extended Kinship in the United States: Competing Models and the Case of La Familia Chicana," *Journal of Marriage and the Family*, 41 (1979): 121–129; Mario T. Garcia, "La Familia: The Mexican Immigrant Family, 1900–1930," in Mario Barrera, Albert Camarillo, and Francisco Hernandez (eds.), *Work, Family, Sex Roles and Language* (Berkeley, CA: Tonatiuh-Quinto Sol, International, 1980).

3. Susan E. Keefe, "Real and Ideal Extended Familism among Mexican Americans and Anglo Americans: On the Meaning of Close Family Ties," *Human Organization*, 43 (1984): 65–69; Susan E. Keefe, Amado M. Padilla, and Manuel L. Carlos, "The Mexican-American Extended Family as an Emotional Support System," *Human Organization*, 38 (1979): 144–152; M. Jean Gilbert, "Extended Family Integration among Second Generation Mexican Americans," In J. Manuel Casas and Susan E. Keefe (eds.), *Family and Mental Health in the Mexican American Community* (Los Angeles: Spanish Speaking Mental Health Research Center, UCLA, 1978); Fabio Sabogal, Gerardo Marín, Regina Otero-Sabogal, Barbara VanOss Marín, and Eliseo J. Pérez-Stable, "Hispanic Familism and Acculturation: What Changes and What Doesn't?" *Hispanic Journal of the Behavioral Sciences*, 9 (1987): 397–412; Carlos I. Velez-Ibañez and James B. Greenberg, "Formation and Transformation of Funds of Knowledge among U.S.-Mexican Households," *Anthropology and Education Quarterly*, 23 (1992): 313–335; Kyriakos S. Markides, Joanne S. Boldt, and Laura A. Ray, "Sources of Helping and Intergenerational Solidarity: A Three-Generations Study of Mexican Americans," *Journal of Gerontology*, 41 (1986): 506–511.

4. Oscar Ramirez and Carlos H. Arce, "The Contemporary Chicano Family: An Empirically Based Review," In Agustín Baron, Jr. (ed.), *Explorations in Chicano Psychology* (New York: Praeger Publishers, 1981), 3–28; Sabogal et al., "Hispanic Familism and Acculturation: What Changes and What Doesn't?"; Michael V. Miller, "Variations in Mexican American Family Life: A Review Synthesis of Empirical Research," *Aztlán*, 9 (1978): 209–231.

5. Maxine Baca Zinn, "Employment and Education of Mexican-American Women: The Interplay of Modernity and Ethnicity in Eight Families," *Harvard Educational Review*, 50 (1980): 47–62; Maxine Baca Zinn, "Mexican-American Women in the Social Sciences," *Signs: Journal of Women in Culture and Society*, 8 (1982): 259–272; Jennifer Pierce, "The Implications of Functionalism for Chicano Family Research," *Berkeley Journal of Sociology*, 29 (1984): 93–117; Denise Segura, "Labor Market Stratification: The Chicana Experience," *Berkeley Journal of Sociology*, 29 (1984): 57–91; Denise Segura and Beatriz M. Pesquera, "Beyond Indifference and Antipathy: The Chicana Movement and Chicana Feminist Discourse," *Aztlán*, 19 (1993): 69–92.

6. David Maldonado, "The Chicano Aged," *Social Work*, 20 (1975): 213–216.

7. Carol Stack, *All Our Kin* (New York: Harper, 1974); Edwin Eames and Judith Granich Goode, "Coping Strategies of the Urban Poor," in Edwin Eames and Judith Granich Goode (eds.), *Urban Poverty in Cross Cultural Context* (New York: The Free Press, 1973), 157–216.

8. Oscar Ramirez and Carlos H. Arce, "The Contemporary Chicano Family: An Empirically Based Review," in Baron, Jr. (ed.), *Explorations in Chicano Psychology*; Keefe, "Real and Ideal Extended Familism among Mexican Americans and Anglo Americans: On the Meaning of Close Family Ties"; Susan E. Keefe and Amado Padilla, *Chicano Ethnicity*. (Albuquerque, NM: University of New Mexico Press, 1987); Sabogal et al., "Hispanic Familism and Acculturation: What Changes and What Doesn't?"; Miller, "Variations in Mexican American Family Life: A Review Synthesis of Empirical Research."

9. Susan E. Keefe, Una Mae Lange Reck, and Gregory G. Reck, "Ethnicity and Education on Southern Appalachia: A Review," *Ethnic Groups*, 5 (1983): 199–225.

10. Maxine Baca Zinn, "Familism among Chicanos: A Theoretical Review," *Humboldt Journal of Social Relations*, 10 (1982/83): 224–38.

11. Keefe, "Real and Ideal Extended Familism among Mexican Americans and Anglo Americans: On the Meaning of Close Family Ties";

Keefe and Padilla, *Chicano Ethnicity*; Keefe et al., "The Mexican-American Extended Family as an Emotional Support System."

12. Keefe, "Real and Ideal Extended Familism among Mexican Americans and Anglo Americans: On the Meaning of Close Family Ties."

13. Janet T. Spence, "Achievement American Style: The Rewards and Costs of Individualism," *American Psychologist*, 40 (1985): 1285–1295.

14. This scale utilizes four of the original ten items used in Keefe's study of familistic attitudes among Mexican-origin adults. Principal components analysis based on the entire sample of 5,008 students was conducted, for we did not want to limit the analysis to a single ethnic group. This four-item scale formed the first of two factors of familism attitudes. It was selected on both empirical and conceptual grounds. Keefe, "Real and Ideal Extended Familism among Mexican Americans and Anglo Americans: On the Meaning of Close Family Ties," 66.

15. John W. Tukey, *The Problem of Multiple Comparisons* (Princeton, NJ: Princeton University, 1953). Tukey's multiple comparison procedure subtracts the smallest from the largest mean and divides by the square root of the number of observations in each sample minus 1, multiplied by the pooled estimate of the common population standard deviation. This test statistic is very similar to the more familiar t-tests of significance comparing two means, except that it does not have a *t* distribution, nor does it compare two sample means until the largest and smallest sample means have been observed, effectively reducing the chances of making a type 1 error (i.e., falsely rejecting the null hypothesis of equality in population means). The alpha level, set at less than or equal to .05 for all comparisons, signifies the probability of falsely declaring any pairwise comparison significant.

16. An adjusted measure of contact was devised. This measure calculates for each individual a standardized score on contact, with a mean of zero based on the typical level of contact for all adolescents in the sample at each level of structure.

6

CHICANO FAMILIES AND URBAN POVERTY: FAMILIAL STRATEGIES OF CULTURAL RETENTION

ELSA O. VALDEZ

This chapter examines two main topics: first, how inner-city Chicano families headed by single mothers use various familial strategies for the purpose of retaining their culture; and second, how this cultural retention enables the Chicano family to cope with persistent poverty conditions and pressure exerted by the dominant society to assimilate and conform to the "American way of life." It is proposed that although these families face extremely difficult and harsh living conditions, such as high rates of poverty, absence of a father figure, residential segregation, inferior education, drive-by shootings, unemployment, low-paying jobs, and high levels of stress, the mothers' emphasis on various familial strategies appears to be a significant factor in accounting for the Chicano family's survival in an urban jungle.

Familial strategies of cultural retention are viewed as stemming from two primary interrelated processes. The first process involves changes and modifications that have occurred in the Chicano family's structure (e.g., value system, work/family roles, mother-centered households, child-rearing practices and socialization) in response to historical and contemporary socioeconomic events. For example, institutional racism has historically excluded Chicanos and other minorities from equal participation in such major institutions as the economic, political, and legal systems. This historical discrimination and exclusion determines the position of Chicanos and other minorities in American society today, and this in turn affects the structure of the Chicano family. Second, familial strategies have also been shaped by inequalities based on race, class, and gender. These three components are thought to be interconnected and cannot be treated as separate factors, since for single female-headed households, race, class, and gender operate simultaneously and relegate Chicanas to the least desirable hierarchal positions in society.

The concept of familial strategies is partially derived from Tilly's (1978) "family strategies." According to Tilly, "Family strategies are conscious and unconscious solutions to the constraints imposed upon households by economic and social structures."[1] He argues that families develop various strategies for dealing with marriage, children, and work. The poor devise distinct strategies and support structures that differ from the rest of society in response to ingrained patterns of racial and class inequality. He concludes that the poor " . . . don't simply respond passively to material conditions, but rather they use their culture and their families to shape their own lives."[2] Subsequently, I will employ the concept of familial strategies to illustrate how these Chicano families have developed alternative structures to deal with social inequalities based on race, class, and gender, and how these familial strategies serve as a mechanism for cultural retention.

Rodman's (1963) study of the lower class in Coconut Village, Trinidad demonstrates how the "lower-class value stretch" is useful for explaining why the poor find it necessary to modify or "stretch" family structure and value systems.[3] According to Rodman, lower class members attempt to emulate the values of the larger society (e.g., achievement and success, moral orientation, progress, activity, and work). However, due to poverty conditions, the lower class must develop and combine a value system comprised of the larger socially accepted values, while retaining those values that have enabled previous generations to survive. Alternative family structures such as female-headed households, cohabitation, and out-of-wedlock children are related to enduring socioeconomic uncertainties rather than specific cultural forms. Furthermore, these alternative family structures are viewed as positive ways of coping since they enhance the lower-class family's health and sense of well being.

Similarly, Baca Zinn and Eitzen (1987)[4] and Williams (1990)[5] are critical of studies that explain family differences in terms of defective family/cultural values and faulty socialization. Baca Zinn and Eitzen advocate a conflict-structural approach that examines how many family patterns, labelled as culturally deficient, are actually responses that poor people develop in an effort to deal with the problems that emerge from structural inequalities based on race, class, and gender.[6] Williams relies on a symbolic interaction framework to illustrate how " . . .Mexican Americans are, in the context of rapid social change, redefining their roles within the extended and conjugal families."[7]

THEORETICAL FRAMEWORK

Whereas the conflict-structural perspective emphasizes the struggle for scarce resources by groups in a society, that is, how dominant elites use power to control the less powerful, the symbolic interaction perspective examines how people use symbols (e.g., language, ideas, and norms) to create meaning, cultivate their views of the world, and communicate with one another. In studying the family, conflict theorists examine inequality, power, competition, and exploitation, while the symbolic interactionists would focus on what the family members say and what they do. Since each theoretical model emphasizes different features of social life, and each one provides a different interpretation, both perspectives will be used to guide this analysis. By integrating the contributions of each approach, it is possible to gain a more comprehensive picture of both macro and micro processes of social life. In short, using a symbolic interactionist and conflict-structural framework, I will illustrate how the families in this study appear to have devised meaningful and strategic familial forms of cultural retention in response to structural inequalities.

To test strategies of cultural retention the following variables/concepts will be examined: (1) Spanish retention, (2) level of familism, (3) attitudes toward women's roles, (4) attitudes toward sexuality, (5) parental responsibilities, (6) children's responsibilities, (7) religiosity, (8) sense of self-worth, (9) child centerness, and (10) levels of mental well-being/depression. Several interrelated hypotheses are proposed. First, it is hypothesized that levels of religiosity, familism, child centerness, and Spanish retention will be fairly high since these are key components for transmitting cultural values. Second, it is hypothesized that attitudes toward sexuality and women's roles have been somewhat modified in response to larger structural changes. Third, it is proposed that parental and children's responsibilities are considered very important since Chicanos tend to be rather family oriented. And finally, it is hypothesized that sense of self-worth will be moderately high and depression will be fairly low, since the family is thought to provide a safe haven for its members. I will argue that these familial strategies are positive survival tactics developed by these urban families in response to dealing with social inequality based on race, class, and gender.

PROFILE OF THE LATINO FAMILY

Within the Latino family population there are significant differences in composition, size of families, family income, and levels of poverty. Since Latinos are often treated as a homogeneous group, the following discussion will provide a brief demographic overview to illustrate socioeconomic differences between Chicanos and other Latino families. The ensuing statistics are based on "The Hispanic Population in the United States: March 1991," as reported by the U.S. Bureau of the Census.[8] In 1991, there were 66 million families in the United States. Of these 66 million families, 8 percent were Latino with Chicanos constituting the largest group, 6 percent. About 74 percent of Chicano families were married-couple families, compared to about 52 percent of the Puerto Rican families, 76 percent of the Cuban families, and 66 percent of the Central and South American origin families.

Families maintained by a female householder with no husband present consisted of 19 percent of the Mexican-origin families, 43 percent of the Puerto Rican, 19 percent of the Cuban, and 26 percent of Central and South American origin.

There were also differences in family size. Chicanos had the highest proportion of families with five or more members, 34 percent; in comparison, Puerto Ricans had 20 percent, families of Cuban origin had 16 percent, and Central and South American families had 26 percent. Median family income also varied. In 1990, the median family income for Chicanos was $23,240, compared to $18,008 for Puerto Rican families, $31,439 for Cubans, and $23,445 for Central and South American families. Of those Latino families who lived below the poverty level, 25 percent were Mexican-origin families, 38 percent Puerto Rican, 14 percent Cuban, and 22 percent were Central and South American families. For female householders, husband absent, 46 percent of Chicanas lived below the poverty level, compared to 64 percent of Puerto-Rican females, and 39 percent of Central and South American origin women. Cuban-origin females were excluded due to insufficient cases.

THE SIGNIFICANCE OF CULTURAL ADAPTATION IN URBAN AREAS

Why is it important to examine how poor Chicano families are culturally adapting in urban areas? It is important because Chicano families are devising strategies to survive in U.S. society—economically and socially. Economically, Chicano/Latino families are disadvantaged relative to white families. For example, in 1990 the median income for all Mexican-origin families was $23,240[9] compared to $36,915 for all white families.[10] And where there is a female householder with no husband present, median income in 1990 for Latinas was $11,914; whereas for white women it was $19,528.[11] Additionally, Chicano families are more likely to live below the poverty level than white families. According to the U.S. Bureau of the Census, 25 percent of all Chicano families in 1990 lived below the poverty level,[12] while only 8 percent of all white families were impoverished.[13] And 46 percent of Chicana householders with husbands absent were likely to live below the poverty level,[14] compared to 27 percent white householders with no husbands present.[15] Given these adverse economic differences, Chicano families, and especially female-headed households, have had to devise familial strategies to deal with unfavorable economic conditions.

Additionally, this topic merits scholarly inquiry because Chicanos have not been fully integrated into mainstream society, due to socioeconomic discrimination; subsequently, they constitute a minority group. One of the characteristics of belonging to a minority group is that " . . . behavior and/or characteristics of minority group members are stereotyped and systematically condemned by the dominant or majority group."[16] To deal with negative stereotyping and its outcomes, Chicano families have developed strategies for retaining culture to protect its members—sociopsychologically. As one mother who was interviewed commented, "Siempre que hay algo en la television sobre Este Los Angeles, usualmente es de un 'gang shooting' o problemas con drogas. Nunca ven las cosas buenas que estan occurriendo, como las madres en esta comunidad que estan tratando de criar a sus hijos que sean buenos y que tengan respeto." (Anytime you see anything on television about East Los Angeles, it's usually about a gang shooting or drug problems. They never look at the good things that are going on, like how mothers in this community are trying to raise their children to be good and respectful.) And finally, this study is significant because people's attitudes toward the poor have changed very little over the years. Kluegel's (1987) public opinion survey found that most Americans believe people are poor because there is something wrong with them (e.g., deficient morals or lack of incentive/motivation).[17] Additionally, according to a recent poll by the New York Times (1989), many Americans feel that welfare benefits encourage the poor to remain impoverished.[18] These attitudes toward the poor are significant because policy makers tend to examine the causes of poverty and propose solutions based on a functional/cultural view. Therefore, if poverty is largely viewed as a product of cultural deficiencies, our current policies regarding the poor will continue to focus on fixing single female-headed families, rather than investigating how the government can provide inner-city families with the necessary resources (e.g., jobs, job training programs, and childcare) that will enable them to help themselves in a dignified, humane, and compassionate manner.

CHARACTERISTICS OF THE AREA OF STUDY

Dolores Mission, located in Boyle Heights in East Los Angeles, is one of the poorest parishes in the city of Los Angeles. The parish's pastor is the director of Proyecto Pastoral (Pastoral Project). He has been involved in the development of a women's cooperative, a low-cost daycare center, a leadership development project, a police monitoring group, gang outreach efforts, a shelter program for homeless Latino families, and an alternative high school for dropouts. This project is one of the few grassroots projects that has been very successful largely because the staff and community members view their work as a partnership rather than a top-down relationship. The families living in Pico Gardens and Pico-Aliso Extension housing projects have an average income of about $8,000. Half of the households are headed by single Latinas from Mexico and Central America who don't speak English. Very few have marketable urban job skills. For over fifty years this eastside neighborhood has been an unofficial port of entry for Latino immigrants.

DATA COLLECTION METHOD

Data for this study were collected by conducting multiple, separate in-depth interviews with nine Chicana mothers and their respective son or daughter, during the summer of 1992. The mothers and youths were contacted through Proyecto Pastoral at Dolores Mission. The adolescents in the sample are enrolled in the alternative high school program. Mothers preferred to be interviewed in Spanish while the adolescents chose to respond in English. The interviews took place in the respondents' homes in an effort to provide a nonthreatening, familiar environment and to encourage them to be fairly straightforward in their views and comments. It is acknowledged that the participants' responses to the religiosity questions may be biased since all of the families are receiving assistance from a church-based program. However, it is believed that the home in-depth interview method helped respondents to feel less intimidated.

Both the mothers and adolescents were quite candid during the interviewing process. Initially, the adolescents were reluctant to participate; they seemed to be suspicious, since they frequently get surprise visits from the county probation officers. However, after I explained how their responses would be a way for their voices to be heard by both the Latino and non-Latino community they became eager and willing participants. The mothers, on the other hand, commented that they were pleased to be part of this study. As one mother commented, "Yo pienso que una persona que habla mi idioma y es de mi cultura, entiende mejor lo que nosotros sufrimos en una sociedad que no piensa mucho de los Mexicanos. (I feel that someone who can speak my language and comes from my culture understands what we suffer in a society that does not think well of Mexicans.)

CHARACTERISTICS OF THE SAMPLE

All of the mothers report that they are either divorced or separated; they range in age from 31 to 52. Three are employed in service-type jobs and six receive Aid to Families with Dependent Children. Eight of the mothers are immigrants from Mexico, and one was born in the United States. The mothers who were born in Mexico have been in the United States for fifteen years or longer. Family size ranges from four to eight children, and at least five of the families have extended family members living with them (e.g., married sons/daughters), and all are Catholic.

The adolescents—five females and four males—range in age from fifteen to seventeen. They attend this alternative school because they have been suspended from the public high school. Apparently, most of them were expelled primarily due to disciplinary problems or gang-related activities. Two of the youths were born in Mexico and the rest were born in the United States. Of the nine teenagers, three males and two females currently belong to a gang, one male used to belong to a gang, and the other three females do not belong to a gang. Six of the adolescents work part-time in various low-wage jobs (e.g., janitor, clerical worker, housekeeper). The youths were placed in these jobs through the Proyecto Pastoral.

MEASURES OF FAMILIAL STRATEGIES

Familial strategies consist of ten variables that are used to determine whether the mothers and adolescents in this study are involved in "stretching" middle class values, relying on cultural values, and/or revising gender roles in response to dealing with adverse socioeconomic conditions. Subsequently, I will also assess whether any of the ten familial strategies constitute a form of cultural retention. To determine primary language spoken or Spanish retention, respondents were asked, "What is your primary language?" Parent/child orientation is used to assess whether the family is child-centered, and consists of ten questions that ask adolescents how often their mother does a variety of things with them, such as help them with their homework, discuss birth control, or other activities. And conversely, mothers are asked how often they do a variety of things with their children. Respondents are then categorized low, moderate, or high. Religiosity is based on the frequency of church attendance, and whether the respondent feels religion is important to herself or himself. Levels of religiosity can range from low to high.

For family orientation, two questions are asked for the purpose of examining how important family is to the individual and participants are either low, moderate, or high in family orientation. For moral attitudes toward sexuality, respondents are asked whether it is okay for unmarried people (18 years old or younger) to have sexual relations if they have strong feelings for each other, and if it is okay for an unmarried couple to live together as long as they have plans to marry. If the respondent sees this as not acceptable, he or she is considered traditional; if it is somewhat acceptable, he or she is categorized moderately traditional; and if it is acceptable, the respondent is considered nontraditional. Depression/mental well-being consists of ten questions that ask how respondents felt or behaved last week, and categories range from low to high levels of depression. The gender attitudes item consists of four questions about women's roles in U.S. society, and participants are either traditional, nontraditional, or transitional. The self-esteem category is made up of ten questions that ask how they feel about themselves (e.g., I feel I have a lot of good qualities). Respondents are either low, moderate, or high in self-esteem. For parent's responsibility, respondents had to select what they think are a parent's most important responsibilities to her children. And children's responsibility consists of participants choosing what they view are a child's most important responsibilities to his or her family. Both parent and children's responsibility can range from low to high.

FINDINGS

The results of the interviews show that indeed these families appear to be relying on a combination of "stretching" middle class values, cultural values, and revision of gender roles in an effort to deal with impoverished conditions and to retain their culture.

Language Spoken

Spanish retention appears to be high for both mothers and adolescents. While eight out of the nine mothers report speaking only Spanish, all nine of the teenagers say that they speak both English and Spanish. That is, these Chicana mothers have made sure that their children speak both languages, thereby ensuring cultural retention while embracing the language of the larger society—

English. Subsequently, this variable is considered both a middle-class value stretch and a cultural value. As noted by Cafferty (1988), "Language is a transmitter of culture; it is a mechanism by which individuals are socialized into society. The values, beliefs, and attitudes of society are communicated, and loyalty and allegiance to society are expressed."[19]

Parent/Child Orientation

Both mothers and children convey that there are moderate to high levels of parental involvement or child centerness in the home. While two mothers and five adolescents say that their home is moderately child-centered, seven mothers and four children report that it is high. This variable is classified lower-class value stretch because parental participation, which is typically thought to be a middle-class trait, appears to be important in these households as well. And it is considered a cultural value since numerous scholars such as Mirandé conclude that Chicano families tend to be matriarchal or mother-centered, and a mother's relationship with her sons and daughters is "characterized by warmth and affection."[20] Additionally, Coltrane and Valdez (1993) found that most Chicano mothers and fathers are rather involved in their children's activities, regardless of social class.[21]

Family Orientation

Both mothers and children see family as fairly important. Six mothers and five youths say it is moderately important; three parents and three teenagers say it is highly important. Only one of the children reports that it is not very important. This variable is classified a cultural and lower-class value stretch. It is cultural because Mirandé contends that "probably the most significant characteristic of the Chicano family is its strong emphasis on familism. While the impact of the family may have been ended somewhat by urbanization and acculturation, it is still a central institution for the individual."[22] It is class since " . . . recent research has found that the Chicano extended family has roots in racial and economic conditions of U.S. society."[23] Alvirez and Bean (1976) note that " . . . familism may be, at least in part, a response to historical conditions of economic deprivation."[24]

Moral Attitudes toward Sexuality

Mothers and children differ in their views of sexuality. All nine adolescents view premarital sex and cohabitation as somewhat acceptable, while all nine mothers say it is not acceptable. It is plausible that the adolescents are less traditional because gender roles have been changing, especially during their generation. In contrast, for mothers, instilling traditional values such as marriage and family may be a way to retain culture despite the marital shifting that has occurred in their own lives due to persistent socioeconomic problems. This being the case, the adolescent's moral attitudes toward sexuality are thought to be influenced by lower-class value stretching and revision of gender roles; while the mothers' moral attitudes are based on cultural values. Additionally, during the course of the interviews the majority of mothers and adolescents conveyed that religion is very important to them. Subsequently, it could be that mothers transmit Catholic teachings prohibiting premarital sex and cohabitation to their children, which then serves to get their children to conform; and this in turn works to retain culture.

Depression

When it comes to mental well-being, mothers and youths vary in reported levels of depression. Two adolescents and four mothers appear to be highly depressed; four children and one parent have moderate levels of depression; and three youths and four mothers fall in the low depression category. I expected to find that levels of depression would be fairly low for most of the respondents, since the family is thought to provide its members with sociopsychological support. However, these findings could result from the fact that regardless of how much support family members get at home, dealing with impoverished conditions on a daily basis takes its toll on a person's mental health. Although poverty weakens the family's ability to provide its members with high levels of mental well-being, retention of cultural values seems to shield respondents from even higher levels of depression.

Gender Attitudes

The views on women's roles in society tend to be rather nontraditional for all respondents. While four adolescents and three mothers hold traditional views toward women's roles, the rest hold nontraditional beliefs or are in transition. Since egalitarian notions of women's roles are typically associated with the middle class, this variable is classified a lower-class value stretch and revised gender roles. If these families are becoming less traditional toward women's roles, what does this mean for retention of their culture? Based on their previous responses (especially to moral attitudes toward sexuality and parent/child orientation), it appears that these families are both modern and traditional. That is, they are able to change when necessary (e.g., revise gender roles in response to larger societal changes), but at the same time, they instill numerous traditional values that enable the family to retain the most crucial aspects of their culture. (e.g., Spanish retention and familism).

Self-Esteem

Most mothers and adolescents report moderate to high levels of self-esteem. This variable is considered a cultural and lower-class value stretch. This concept is cultural because the family provides a supportive and nurturing environment against the socioeconomic and psychological battering that occurs to Chicanos in the broader society; it is a lower-class value stretch since high self-esteem is generally thought to be a middle-class trait. Consequently, high levels of self-esteem promote maintenance of culture by functioning as a buffer against the larger alienating institutions.

Parent's Responsibility

For this variable, all of the respondents agree that it is the parents' responsibility to provide for their children financially, love them, teach them right from wrong, and educate them. This concept is considered a cultural and lower-class value stretch. It is a cultural characteristic, because Chicano families tend to view parenting as very important, and a lower-class value stretch since educational/financial responsibility and moral development are usually considered middle-class values. This variable is thought to serve as a form of cultural retention because both children and parents view children's moral and socioeconomic needs as a parental/family responsibility, rather than a social responsibility.

Child's Responsibility

The responses for this variable indicate that most of the participants expect children to behave, be respectful, help out at home, be trustworthy, and do well in school. This variable is considered a cultural and lower-class value stretch. It is a cultural trait because within the Chicano culture, obedience and respect to the elders is a commonly accepted socialization practice that is held in high reverence because it indicates that an individual is "bien educado" (has good manners). And it is a lower-class value stretch because some of the responses, such as doing well in school and trust, are usually associated with middle-class values. This characteristic functions to retain culture since this is a widely accepted norm that cuts across class lines within the Chicano community.

Religiosity

And finally, religiosity was rated as rather important by the respondents. Three mothers and four youths report that religion is moderately important to them, while six mothers and four adolescents say it is very important. Only one teenager feels that it is not important. Religion is considered a cultural value because it has played a vital historical role for the Chicano family, and numerous researchers contend that there is a link between religion and culture. McCready (1988) observes that "people who have been socialized into a specific cultural system which has a strong integration between religion and culture, also derive considerable increments regarding their own personal sense of integration; a sense which can be most useful when confronting a new society and a different, unyielding culture."[25] As one adolescent gang member states, "I pray a lot because I don't know if I'm going to be alive tomorrow. None of the homeboys say they pray like I do, but I'm pretty sure they do 'cause our moms told us it's important and so we do it." In sum, religion serves as a familial form of cultural retention since it provides these families with a sense of purpose within their family, local community, and the larger society.

CONCLUSION

It appears that all of the hypotheses were confirmed, with the exception of that concerning depression or mental well-being. While the findings in this study cannot be generalized to the larger Chicano/Latino population, they nonetheless exemplify Rodman's concept of the lower-class value stretch, which refers to the idea that lower-class families also embrace the values of the larger society, but due to impoverishment they must make modifications to fit their needs. Tilly's family strategies look at how the poor consciously and unconsciously seek solutions to deal with problems; Baca Zinn and Eitzen's conflict-structural approach to the family examines family differences in terms of inequality based on race, class, and gender. And finally, William's symbolic interaction perspective emphasizes how Chicanos are in the process of redefining roles within the working and professional class families.

We have seen that the Chicano family has found constructive and meaningful ways to deal with an array of structurally oppressive actions directed at them by the dominant society, but they have endured partially due to their use of familial strategies. These familial strategies function as a buffer against continual encroachment both at the micro and macro level. And finally, while cultural retention appears to be crucial for protecting the family members, familial strategies are undergoing some fundamental changes in response to changes that have occurred in the larger society. The ability to be receptive to change while at the same time retaining traditional values that are useful makes these inner-city, single female-headed households an important topic of study, because the coming decade will bring with it an increasing number of female-headed households for all groups, and these households constitute the "new poor" in American society. According to Baca Zinn and Eitzen (1993), "This trend toward solo parenthood has two sources: the relatively high divorce rate and out-of-wedlock births, which currently are the highest ever recorded."[26]

By challenging pejorative and prejudiced assumptions about poor, urban minority families, perhaps we can begin to implement social policy aimed at examining the root causes of social inequality, rather than blaming the group for its own problems, such as failing to assimilate into mainstream society, an increasing number of female-headed households, rising poverty rates, greater gang and drug-related problems, and other culturally deficient notions. On the contrary, these mothers and adolescents appear to be culturally adapting to unfavorable socioeconomic conditions by learning how to stretch class values, modifying gender roles, and retaining key cultural practices.

NOTES

1. Cited in Maxine Baca Zinn and D. Stanley Eitzen, *Diversity in American Families* (New York: Harper and Row Publishers, 1987), 174.

2. Baca Zinn and Eitzen, *Diversity in American Families*, 174.

3. Baca Zinn and Eitzen, *Diversity in American Families*, 150.

4. Baca Zinn and Eitzen, *Diversity in American Families*, 139–140.

5. Norma Williams, *The Mexican-American Family: Tradition and Change* (New York: General Hall Inc., 1990), 1–2.

6. Baca Zinn and Eitzen, *Diversity in American Families*, 140.

7. Williams, *The Mexican-American Family*, 1.

8. U.S. Bureau of the Census, "The Hispanic Population in the United States: March 1991," *Current Population Reports*, Series P-20, No. 455 (Washington, DC: Government Printing Office, 1991), 1–8.

9. U.S. Bureau of the Census, "The Hispanic Population in the United States: March 1991," 18.

10. U.S. Bureau of the Census, "Money Income of Households, Families, and Persons in the United States: 1990," *Current Population Reports*, P-60, No. 174 (Washington, DC: Government Printing Office, 1991), 53.

11. U.S. Bureau of the Census, "Money Income of Households, Families and Persons in the United States: 1990," 53.

12. U.S. Bureau of the Census, "The Hispanic Population in the United States: March 1991," 18.

13. U.S. Bureau of the Census, "Poverty in the United States: 1991," *Current Population Reports*, Series P-60, No. 181 (Washington, DC: U.S. Government Printing Office, 1992), 7.

14. U.S. Bureau of the Census, "The Hispanic Population in the United States: March 1991," 18.

15. U. S. Bureau of the Census, "Poverty in the United States: 1991," 7.

16. D. Stanley Eitzen and Maxine Baca Zinn, *In Conflict and Order: Understanding Society* (Boston: Allyn and Bacon, 1993), 290.

17. Cited in Beth Hess, Elizabeth W. Markson, and Peter J. Stein, *Sociology* (New York: Macmillan, 1992), 186.

18. Hess et al., *Sociology*, 186.

19. Pastora San Juan Cafferty, "Language and Social Assimilation," in Pastora San Juan Cafferty and W.C. McCready (eds.), *Hispanics in the United States*, (New Brunswick, NJ: Transaction Books, 1988), 87.

20. Alfredo Mirandé, *The Chicano Experience* (Notre Dame, IN: University of Notre Dame Press, 1985), 157.

21. Scott Coltrane and Elsa O. Valdez, "Reluctant Compliance: Work-Family Role Allocation in Dual-Earner Families," in Jane Hood (ed.), *Men, Work, and Family* (Newbury Park, CA: Sage, 1993), 169.

22. Mirandé, *The Chicano Experience*, 153.

23. Baca Zinn and Eitzen, *Diversity in American Families*, 173.

24. Cited in Baca Zinn and Eitzen, *Diversity in American Families*, 173.

25. McCready, *Hispanics in the United States*, 52.

26. Baca Zinn and Eitzen, *Diversity in American Families*, 305.

7

JUNTOS Y SEPARADOS: CULTURAL COMPLEXITY IN U.S. MEXICAN HOUSEHOLDS

JAVIER TAPIA

Descriptions of Mexican households in the United States often highlight a familistic tendency.[1] These researchers mention the importance of the family in providing support to its members, and their tendency to spend much time in the company of each other. Another view of the family acknowledges its familistic orientation, but also points out that there are conflicts, contradictions, and inequalities within the family unit.[2] These perspectives on the family are not contrasting, but rather illustrate the complex nature of individuals' activities as household members.

The complex character of U.S. Mexican households can be ascertained by noting their operation within the larger process of cultural and social reproduction. These concepts refer to the reproduction of cultural practices through time and the maintenance of existing inequalities between and within social groups. This process is accomplished by the specific linkages between the households and the larger socioeconomic environment or system. The structure and organization of households are shaped and delimited by the larger system, but the latter is influenced in return by people's actual activities as they try to improve their living situations. In addition, household dynamics are organized by prior forms of composition and their forms of incorporation into the larger environment.

The process of social and cultural reproduction for a number of Mexican immigrant households in the United States is affected by their social and historical formation in Mexico (including relationships between households as part of a larger cluster), the conditions leading to migration, and their incorporation to a new social and economic setting. Thus, household members behave in culturally meaningful ways, and the transformation or maintenance of cultural practices results when they try to enact these activities in new contexts. These periods are characterized by conflict, ambiguity, and dissonance.

Cultural complexity in U.S. Mexican households is the result of the interplay of all the factors mentioned above. The role of culture and its complexity among U.S. Mexicans can be better understood by noting the activities of individuals as household members. The familistic aspect of the population and its conflicting characteristics can be explained by focusing on household members' activities as they try to improve their living conditions. Two case studies from the greater Los Angeles area are used to illustrate this issue. However, the households in these studies can be better understood by first reviewing briefly the enculturation process and the structure and organization of the household cluster. This section is followed by a description of the research setting and a brief note on methodology.

THE ENCULTURATION PROCESS

Enculturation, as part of social and cultural reproduction, is the process by which individuals learn and become competent members of their own social groups. Practice theory focuses on the activities enacted by individuals on a daily basis as the foundation for understanding this process.[3] This model centers on human practices in relation to a global entity referred to as "the system." The system is seen as an active entity affecting human practices while being influenced by these actions in return.

The reciprocal relationship between human agency and the system derives from the fact that the latter consists of several mutually influencing domains or parts. Thus, an event such as a wedding is not only a system of social and ceremonial relations, but also of economic arrangements, cultural categories, and values.[4] In addition, relations of inequality, asymmetry, and domination are present at the core of the system. These factors both shape and transform the system, thus providing it with a highly contradictory characteristic.[5]

The specific workings of the system in its relation to human agency result in specific patterns of regularized and repetitive practices. According to Bourdieu,[6] these patterns of behavior are principally created within the context of the household by the interplay of social and economic forces impinging on family relationships. Presently, the system is constituted by capitalist forms of production and exchange that regulate and constrain human action required for the maintenance and reproduction of social groups.

In a capitalist society, the household has been identified as the domain where human life and labor are maintained and reproduced.[7] This is accomplished by the practices of the household members to meet their material, social, and affective needs. Among other things, household reproduction includes the acquisition and/or production of food and its processing, household management, shelter, education, and psychological or affective provisioning.[8] Historically, household labor has been performed along gender lines, and women have been primarily responsible for the domestic domain (even if they also participate in wage labor).[9]

The household is also the domain where the essence of culture is mediated and translated into action.[10]

Individuals' activities are guided by a set of cultural models first learned within the domain of the household. Aside from being a residential locality, the household is also the locus for the demonstration of kinship, gender and age roles, socialization, economic cooperation, and the allocation of tasks. Thus, it is in this context where people learn to value and behave according to a number of principles that provide meaning to their actions.

From this perspective, the structure and organization of U.S. Mexican households is shaped and constrained by the larger socioeconomic, political, and cultural system. However, the specific configuration of the household is also affected by its previous composition and organization.[11] In addition and as will be shown in this chapter, individuals attempt to improve their living conditions by selecting the best possible options available to them. These options or avenues guiding behavior are culturally mediated, for people's actions have symbolic meaning. Thus, individuals' activities as household members often result in contradiction and conflict within the unit itself.

THE HOUSEHOLDS AND THE HOUSEHOLD CLUSTER

Specific aspects of the enculturation process for Mexicans in Los Angeles can be better understood by examining in detail the structure and operation of individual households. Material and affective needs of individuals are met, to a greater or lesser degree, by the activities of household members. However, as reported by Vélez-Ibáñez and by Tapia, Mexican households operate in relation to a larger household cluster.[12] A complete cluster consists of a core household of middle-aged individuals (grandparents) and a number of related but independent households (adult offspring and their children). The cluster is a characteristic of U.S. Mexicans, regardless of generational status and differences in socioeconomic background. However, economic or social features may be more common for some households than for others depending on the latter factor.

An important feature of the cluster is that the households are all interconnected in a series of economic and social exchanges. Frequent family visits, telephone calls, exchange of labor, and participation in social and ceremonial activities are important features of the cluster. Among other factors, the composition of the cluster is affected by geographic factors as well as by the lifecycle stage of individual households. Nevertheless, households belonging to partial clusters often come together to recreate many features of complete ones. They often do so by engaging in similar reciprocal relationships with fictive kin and/or friends.

Probably the best way to illustrate the structure and organization of households and their relationship to the larger cluster is by investigating the economic, social, recreational, and ceremonial activities of its members. The configuration of each unit along these domains impacts the nature of relationships among individuals from the same unit and also between those of related ones. An attempt is made to discuss separately these domains of activities, but their importance can only be gained by noting their overlapping characteristics.

THE SETTING

The site of investigation for this study is located in the southern part of the greater Los Angeles area. This is an area that has experienced ethnic and socioeconomic changes in the last twenty-five years. In 1968, the school district had an enrollment of 2,837 students, of which 81 percent were white. In 1988, the student population was close to 5,000, of which 88 percent were of Hispanic origin. Similarly for Latinos and Mexicans as a whole, the area consists primarily of working class, low-income households. About 75 percent of the population are of Mexican descent, primarily from the states of Jalisco and Michoacan.[13]

Several Mexican restaurants and fast-food places are located on the main street of this community. Mexican and Central American bakeries, Spanish music tape stores, beauty salons, markets, and other businesses are scattered throughout the streets of this district. Rows of apartment buildings and several residential areas provide housing for the population. Several parks are used by the people as well as by organized soccer clubs on Sundays.

At least two large hotels are located on the main street. These establishments, along with a number of the restaurants, cater to the large number of people who use the services of the Los Angeles International Airport. The lives of many of the residents in this community have been directly or indirectly affected by this large commercial enterprise. Many of them are working or have worked for the businesses catering to LAX or to enterprises that economically benefit from it.

METHODOLOGY

Most of the data for this study was collected over a seven-month period from January to June 1992. The households were visited fifteen and eleven times respectively. The duration of the visits ranged from one-and-one-half to three hours. Rapport and mutual trust developed quickly due to the background similarities between the informants and myself. The informants did not receive any monetary compensation, but I brought bread, candies, and ice cream for the families on several occasions. They reciprocated by inviting me to share meals with them.

Only one questionnaire was used in the study. Its principal purpose was to collect data on the composition of the household. Most of the information was gathered through open-ended questions and by pursuing selected topics (i.e., migratory history, labor history, household economics, and the division of labor) in greater detail. Information was collected from parents (together and separately) and children. I also collected data from relatives and friends whenever possible. Finally, I changed family names and places of birth to protect the informants' identities.

THE RENTERIA HOUSEHOLD

"En esta casa, soy la cabecera del hogar" (I am head of the household in this home). Mrs. Renteria made this statement on my first visit to the household. She told me that she was the only one working at the present moment because her husband had suffered an accident in his construction job in November 1991. I inquired if her husband's present situation was the reason for her statement. She replied that the main reason was because she was the one trying very hard to improve the situation of the family. I began to develop the impression that Mr. Renteria's status as a husband and father was precarious. On my third visit to the family, I was "informed" by Elsa (age 9 and the oldest of three offspring) that her father did not do much but play Nintendo.

The present economic situation of the household, and its members' views towards the unit and to each other can be better understood by reviewing its historical formation. Mrs. Renteria was born in Chihuahua, Mexico. She was twenty years old when she migrated to Los Angeles in 1980. She began to work at an early age, first in agriculture and then as a maid. After a temporary visit to a brother in New Mexico, she came to California to visit her sister and the latter's family. When the opportunity arose, she worked in a factory, but when it closed down, she found employment as a cleaning maid in a hotel. Mrs. Renteria has been working in this place since 1981, and she met her husband here as well.

Mr. Renteria was born in a small coastal town in Jalisco, Mexico in 1960. He first came to the United States in 1976 to work in the agricultural fields of California. At the end of the agricultural season, he returned to Mexico. However, since there was not much work available in his hometown, Mr. Renteria came back to California in 1978. He has lived in the same locality of Los Angeles since that time. He worked in several jobs, including construction, until 1980. The company that hired him went bankrupt, and a friend helped him get the job in the hotel where he met his wife.

In 1981 both of them left their own households and moved into a studio apartment. Their first child, Elsa, was born in this unit. The family moved later to a one-bedroom and then to a two-bedroom apartment. They needed more space because they had two other daughters (Sonia and Centella). Aside from their daughters, they often had relatives staying with them. Mrs. Renteria's mother came to Los Angeles for a number of months. The woman came to care for the children while Mrs. Renteria was at work. One of Mr. Renteria's brothers also lived with them for a number of years, and he contributed to the apartment's expenses.

Mrs. Renteria states that she started to think about buying a house after the girls were born. The apartment complex where they lived did not have a safe space for the children to play. She urged her husband to find a higher paying job so they could save money for a house. Mr. Renteria worked in construction from 1983 to 1991. They moved to their present house in the summer of 1991. Mrs. Renteria states that it was the ugliest house but the only one they could afford. Money for the downpayment of $11,000 came from their savings and from a car-accident settlement that Mrs. Renteria received.

Presently, the house mortgage and other expenses are Mrs. Renteria's principal concerns. She has problems with her husband when he does not want to give her extra money needed for the household. To better understand this aspect of household dynamics, I decided to take an economic profile of the unit. Mrs. Renteria's income from her hotel job is about $326 per two weeks (income varies with respect to her seniority and number of people staying in the hotel). She supplements this amount by selling cosmetic products and aluminum cans. Her average monthly income is $750. Mr. Renteria's average monthly income is $890. This is a combination of his disability check and auto repairs he performs on a part-time basis. The total monthly income for the household is $1,640.

On the average, monthly household expenditures amount to $1,928. The mortgage for the house is $1,100. Groceries ($360), electricity ($110), water ($88), and the furniture store ($114) make up the other major expenses. The telephone bill, clothing, and gasoline are expenses that fluctuate on a month-to-month basis. The discrepancy between total household income and expenditures does not illustrate deception or arithmetic ignorance, but rather the complexity of the survival strategies of the household.

Previous research has shown that many economic and social aspects of Mexican households occur in relation to a larger household cluster.[14] Exchange relations between the units provide security in conditions of poverty and uncertainty. For example, to augment their income, the Renterias converted the garage into two small apartments (a two- and a one-bedroom unit). Monthly rent from the units is $450 and $200, respectively. The one-bedroom apartment has been recently rented by the boyfriend of Mrs. Renteria's younger sister (Lupe, age 19). Mrs. Renteria receives an additional $200 from the rent of space for a trailer parked in the back patio. The trailer is owned by Mrs. Renteria's oldest brother and his family.

Aside from earnings and expenditures, there are other economic activities required for the maintenance and reproduction of the unit. Most household chores are carried out by Lupe and Mrs. Renteria. Lupe cooks and cleans the apartment when Mrs. Renteria is at work. She also takes the older girls to and from school. Lupe has been with the family for about eleven months. She came from Chihuahua to visit and help her sister with the children. Mrs. Renteria does most of the washing and cooking on her days off. She remarked that her husband does not help in these tasks.

Auto maintenance and house repairs are done by Mr. Renteria. He is often assisted by relatives in some of these activities. For example, major repairs were done to the roof and windows of the house in February and March of 1992. The repairs were financed with the Renteria's income tax refund. The heaviest and most difficult work was done over a period of two weeks. Mr. Renteria was assisted by two of his brothers and by Mrs. Renteria's oldest brother. No monetary compensation was given to these relatives, but Mrs. Renteria used money from the sale of aluminum cans to buy groceries for the food prepared for all the people who worked on weekends.

Economic activities are just one domain of household operation. Household members also engage in various practices of a more social and ceremonial nature. The specific character of these activities and the way they are enacted provide another example of the "familistic" characteristic of Mexicans depicted in the literature. The U.S. Mexican population's long history of survival in conditions of economic uncertainty has been mentioned as one of the major factors for individuals' heavy reliance on each other. However, as Vélez-Ibáñez points out, this familistic tendency is present even for economically better-off families.[15] For these households, social and emotive components may be more salient than economic ones.[16]

 not too much contact with family extended

In the Renteria household, the nature of family visits, birthday parties, and recreational activities are shaped by the lifecycle stage of the household and the geographic location of related households. In contrast to the households studied by Vélez-Ibáñez and by Tapia in Arizona,[17] the Renterias are part of a partial household cluster. Mrs. Renteria's parents and most siblings reside in Chihuahua and their contact is limited to monthly telephone conversations. Mrs. Renteria has a brother and a sister living in the Los Angeles Metropolitan area, but they visit her only once a month. Nonetheless, they talk to each other on the telephone at least once a week.

Mrs. Renteria is visited more frequently by her oldest brother, who is on permanent disability as a result of an injury suffered in a construction job. In order to help each other economically, he purchased a trailer and moved his family to Mrs. Renteria's back patio. He does many chores around the house and the property. Lupe, being a household member, is always around, and the fact that her boyfriend moved to one of the apartments in the back suggests that her relationship with Mrs. Renteria will continue for some time in the future.

Although Mr. Renteria's mother and several siblings live in the immediate vicinity, they do not visit each other with much frequency. Their households were more interconnected in the past. Presently, Mr. Renteria's relatives participate primarily in their own cluster. However, the specific relationships between households are not always visible to the participants who tend to view each other's practices from different perspectives. Mrs. Renteria states that her in-laws are very ungrateful. She said that she helped her husband save money to bring his relatives to Los Angeles but that they seem to forget this fact. As an example, she said that she lent a blender to one of her sisters-in-law and the woman broke the appliance. Mrs. Renteria received a blender of a lesser quality, and she had to buy another one. She was upset because she had been saving money to buy clothes for her daughters.

Nevertheless, on a few occasions, both Mrs. Renteria and her husband's relatives get together for birthday parties. For example, many people attended Sonia and Centella's birthday party. It was held on the same day because Mrs. Renteria did not have enough money for two events. The party was planned several weeks in advance by Mrs. Renteria and Lupe. Cake, ice cream, punch, and potato chips were served at the event. Lupe also helped in the preparation of the food and the cleanup afterwards. Children played and sang outdoors while many adults watched television indoors. The girls received gifts from women on both sides of the family. One of Mr. Renteria's sisters gave Barbie dolls to the girls, and Lupe gave a bicycle only to Centella because she did not have enough money to buy two.

Recreational activities are another important aspect of household dynamics. Mrs. Renteria states that since they do not have much money, they do not go out to eat, to see movies, or even to the park. Most household members like to watch television. Mrs. Renteria and Lupe watch Mexican soap operas in the evening. Mr. Renteria likes to see movies in both English and Spanish. He is also accused of playing too much with the Nintendo. The children watch cartoons and other programs on television. They have bicycles but Mrs. Renteria does not allow them to ride them much on the street because she is concerned about their safety. She is concerned about cars and gangs in the area. She wants to save money to buy a swing set so the girls can play on the back patio. The girls also have several dolls. Lupe is the only household member who goes out with any frequency. She goes with her boyfriend to the Wax Museum and other places, and she often brings one of her nieces along.

Economics is a very salient feature in this household. Mrs. Renteria said that she had separated from her husband once in the past, and that she was not sure if she would be able to put up with him much longer. She gets upset when he does not want to give her more money earned repairing cars. She added that he likes to drink and always has money for a bottle of wine. I was surprised to find out that Mrs. Renteria had been pregnant, and then after a period of three weeks lost the baby. Mr. Renteria was upset because he thought his wife had intentionally induced the abortion. Mrs. Renteria said that it had been a natural miscarriage.

Notwithstanding these problems, the Renterias try to improve their situation from their real and perceived options. On my last visit to the family, Mrs. Renteria stated that if they ever went back to Mexico, she wished her husband would open up an auto repair business because she was tired from working all her life and wanted to retire. Meanwhile in Los Angeles, Mr. Renteria was hoping that his lawyer would send him to an auto-mechanic school. He wanted to get a certificate in order to work in a job he liked so much.

THE MORALES HOUSEHOLD

There are five family members in the Morales household. Mr. Morales is thirty years old, and he has been residing in Los Angeles since 1985. He has two full-time jobs. He repairs cars in a used-car lot in the daytime, and he works in a restaurant in the evening. Mrs. Morales is twenty-seven years old, and she came with her two older daughters in 1986 to join her husband. She is a homemaker, but she occasionally babysits for friends and neighbors. Both of them are from the same town in Jalisco, Mexico. They have three children, Leticia (age 8) and Sol (age 7) were born in Mexico, Felipe (age 2) was born in Los Angeles.

The Morales live in a two-bedroom apartment in a complex of six units. Their residence is about ten blocks east of the Renteria's house. The apartment complex is adjacent to an elementary school, and it is farther away from the area's busiest streets. Each apartment has a small backyard, and the units are separated by a driveway along the middle of the complex. Two large garages are also present in the unit.

In contrast to the Renteria household, the Morales are more economically stable. This household characteristic has a very strong effect in the overall structure and organization of the unit. And as a feature of all systems, economic stability

Children hardly see father

have a good sense of familism in attitude

may also have a negative impact on several aspects of family life (social and affective needs). On one of my visits to the family, Mrs. Morales said that her husband worked too much and that neither she nor the children saw much of him. She added that it seemed as if the children only had a mother, and she told her husband to reduce his workload or she would go back to Mexico with her parents.

I was unable to obtain earnings data for the household. Mrs. Morales said that her husband put the money in the bank, and she only asked him for money to cover all household expenses. However, the nature of Mr. Morales' jobs and the household expenditures provides insights into this domain. Mr. Morales has held two jobs almost since his arrival to this area. He worked day shift in a factory and night shift in a restaurant from 1985 to 1989. He dropped the factory job in 1989 when he began working in a used-car lot. Presently, he works six days per week, and he used to earn additional money repairing cars on Sundays.

Although they fluctuate, the household's monthly expenditures are $1,370. Most of the major expenses are from the apartment's rent, $525 (it has been the same since 1987), food, $640 (husband spends $100/week at work; Mrs. Morales spends $60/week); and telephone, $80. Other utility bills make up the remaining expenses. Both Mrs. and Mr. Morales send money to their parents in Mexico. She usually sends $60/month, and he sends money on Mother's Day and Christmas. He sent $1,000 on one occasion. Besides these expenditures, the economic "power" of the household affects their participation in social, recreational, and ceremonial activities. These, in turn, are influenced by the family's relations to relatives and friends.

Similarly to the Renterias, the Morales are part of a partial household cluster. However, many of their activities revolve around a number of households from the same apartment complex. Both Mrs. Morales and her husband have relatives in the area and in some other suburbs of Los Angeles, but most of their relatives, including their parents, live in Jalisco, Mexico. Mrs. Morales has been back only once to visit her relatives because it is very expensive. This is due to her undocumented immigrant status. Mr. Morales has two cousins, but they do not see them very often because they live some distance away. Mrs. Morales is visited by one of her husband's sisters once every two weeks. Her brother and his wife live a few blocks away, but she does not see them with much frequency because she does not get along with the wife.

Mrs. Morales visits and is visited frequently by some of her neighbors in the apartment complex. She has not thought about moving to a house or to another apartment because she likes the price and the people in this complex. The apartment owners and three other families are from the same town in Jalisco. Mrs. Morales said that she has the most "trusting" relationship with her front-door neighbor. She takes care of her neighbor's young daughter when the latter is at work. They also exchange food and visit each other frequently. This friendship is now stronger because the neighbor's oldest daughter served as a godmother for one of Mrs. Morales' daughters. Mrs. Morales also interacts with other neighbors, especially for birthday parties and other celebrations.

Many festivities, such as Christmas and New Year's Eve take on a "communal" characteristic in this complex. For example, all the households got together to celebrate Christmas in 1991. They cooperated in the preparation of food, and they also had a piñata and a "posada." The event was planned primarily by the women of the apartment complex. They decided upon their own contributions and responsibilities. Mrs. Morales said there was much praying, singing, and that people were very enthusiastic, especially the women. She said that the men got together to buy bottles of wine. Most of the festivities in the apartment complex are organized in a similar way. However, Mrs. Morales is often disappointed because her husband works many hours and is frequently absent from these events.

Mr. Morales was absent for Leticia's First Communion and Sol's birthday. The fifteen-year-old daughter of Mrs. Morales' neighbor was Leticia's godmother. Another girl in the complex was also part of this religious ceremony and five families got together to celebrate the event. Several tables with tablecloths were set up in the garages. They were decorated and the girls sang many songs. For Sol's birthday, Mrs. Morales and several neighbors went to Chuck-e-Cheese for pizza. Reciprocally, Sol participated in the neighbor's "quinceañera" festivity. Mrs. Morales said that she spent about $300 for the girls' shoes and dresses.

The economic situation of the household can also be seen in its members' recreational activities. On Sundays when Mr. Morales is at home, the whole family goes out to eat or to amusement parks and other places. In 1991 the family spent about $1,650 in these activities. They went to Disneyland, Santa Maria, Las Vegas, and four times to see Mexican singers in Los Angeles. When Mr. Morales is not around, the family goes to the park or rents videos for the children.

Similarly to the Renterias, the Morales also watch television, and the young girls play dolls with other girls. Felipe likes to play with toy cars, and he often "repairs" them. However, and in contrast to the Renterias, reading and drawing are more salient activities for this family. Mrs. Morales often reads stories and religious literature to the children, and Leticia also enjoys reading by herself. Although, Sol likes to draw, she prefers to jump and run around the complex.

Although the relationship between Mrs. Morales and her husband appears to be more harmonious than that of the Renterias, she sometimes resents the fact that her husband has to work very hard to support the family. She told me that her husband was not going to be very good for the family if he gets tired and sick from working too much. She wishes that her husband had more time to spend with the family. Mrs. Morales would like to work in the future once her children are older. She would like to contribute economically, and she is interested in studying cosmetology.

DISCUSSION AND CONCLUSIONS

The activities of individuals and the way they perceive each other are shaped and constrained by the configuration of their households. The configuration of these units in California is delimited by the social and historical development of the Mexican-origin population and its mode of incorporation into the Los Angeles economy. Within this context and to a large degree, many of the activities carried out for the maintenance and reproduction of the unit are carried out along gender lines. The allocation of labor along this domain and its impact on household structure and organization highlights the specific concerns of individuals within the unit. In addition, the relationship of each household to the larger cluster also affects relationships with other relatives.

In the Renteria household, each spouse has played a different role in the maintenance and reproduction of the unit. Mr. Renteria has worked in several jobs, all characterized by instability due to conditions of the local economy. In addition, his disability has affected his monetary and labor contribution to the household. Mrs. Renteria has worked for many years in occupations characterized by low wages. Nevertheless, her economic contribution to the household has been substantial. She has also been responsible for overseeing many of the subsistence needs of the household, including child care and household chores. Although Mrs. Renteria is greatly assisted by her sister in this domain, she thinks that her husband should help now that he is at home. The fact that he refuses to do "women's" chores in addition to his drinking and refusal to contribute more money to the household has created a conflictive environment within the unit.

As a survival strategy, Mrs. Renteria has followed a cultural pattern of creating a cluster within her own property. Many economic and social exchanges characterize the relationship between the members of each household. Due to the thickness of their relationship, she is very aware of her relatives' wants and needs. To a more limited extent, Mrs. Renteria is also in contact with her husband's relatives. However, she is less aware of their situation, and she believes they have economically taken advantage of her family.

The relationship among the Morales is more harmonious. Their activities for the maintenance and reproduction of the unit are complementary. However, Mr. Morales has had to work in two jobs in order to provide for the economic needs of the family. This aspect has had a very strong impact on other aspects of household life. For example, he is often absent from the many social and ceremonial activities carried out by Mrs. Morales. Of greater importance for the family is the fact that Mr. Morales may get sick due to his heavy workload.

Social and affective needs are more salient in the configuration of the Morales household. To a great degree, these needs are met by Mrs. Morales' intensive participation in social and ceremonial exchanges with people from other households in the apartment complex. Although Mrs. Morales has no relatives in this setting, she has recreated many of the features of a household cluster by establishing strong friendship and fictive kinship ties with several families in the apartment complex.

Many of the activities performed by the Renterias and Morales have been shaped and constrained by the impact of political, economic, social, and cultural forces (the system) impinging upon the historical development of the Mexican population of Los Angeles. They have responded dynamically and creatively to their circumstances by selecting the best possible options available to them. However, not withstanding this dynamism, their activities—derived in great part from their position within the household and the larger cluster—often result in conflict and contradiction. This systemic feature illustrates the complex nature of cultural processes as they operate in U.S. Mexican households.

NOTES

1. Susan Keefe, "Real and Ideal Extended Familism Among Mexican Americans and Anglo Americans: On the Meaning of 'Close' Family Ties," *Human Organization*, 43 (1984): 65-70. See also Angela Valenzuela and Sanford M. Dornsbusch, "Familism and Assimilation among Mexican-Origin and Anglo High School Adolescents" (Chapter 5, this volume). Elsa O. Valdez, "Chicano Families and Urban Poverty: Familial Strategies of Cultural Retention" (Chapter 6, this volume).

2. Patricia Zavella, *Women's Work & Chicano Families: Cannery Workers of the Santa Clara Valley* (Ithaca, NY: Cornell University Press, 1987), 159–160.

3. Sherry B. Ortner, "Theory in Anthropology since the Sixties," *Comparative Studies in Society and History*, 26 (1984): 126–166.

4. Ortner, "Theory in Anthropology since the Sixties," 148.

5. Anthony Giddens, *The Constitution of Society: Outline of the Theory of Structuration* (Berkeley: University of California Press, 1984), 193.

6. Pierre Bourdieu, *Outline of a Theory of Practice* (Cambridge: Cambridge University Press, 1977).

7. Immanuel Wallerstein and Joan Smith, "Households as an Institution of the World Economy," in J. Smith and I. Wallerstein (coord.), *In Creating and Transforming Households: The Constraints of the World-Economy* (Cambridge: Cambridge University Press, 1992), 7.

8. Hans-Dieter Evers, Wolfgang Clauss, and Diana Wong, "Subsistence Reproduction: A Framework for Analysis," in J. Smith, and I. Wallerstein (eds.), *Households and the World-Economy* (Beverly Hills: Sage Publications, 1984), 23–26. See also Peggy Barlett, "Introduction: Dimensions and Dilemmas of Householding," in R. Wilk (ed.), *The Household Economy: Reconsidering the Domestic Mode of Production* (Boulder: West View Press, 1989).

9. Harriet Bradley, *Men's Work, Women's Work: A Sociological History of the Sexual Division of Labour in Employment* (Minneapolis: University of Minnesota Press, 1989), 8. See also Heidi Hartmann, "The Family as the Locus of Gender, Class, and Political Struggle: The Example of Housework," *Signs: Journal of Women in Culture and Society*, 6(1981): 366–394.

10. R. Netting, R. Wilk, and E. Arnould (eds.), *Households: Comparative and Historical Studies of the Domestic Group* (Berkeley: University of California Press, 1984), x–xxii.

11. Vélez-Ibáñez, "Plural Strategies of Survival and Cultural Formation in U.S. Mexican Households in a Region of Dynamic Transformation: The U.S.- Mexico Borderlands." Paper presented to the Wenner-Gren Panel on Industrial Disorders in Society, Dragoon, AZ, 1990. See also Eric Wolf, "Afterword," *Urban Anthropology and Studies of Cultural Systems and World Economic Development*, 17, 1 (1988): 105–109.

12. Vélez-Ibáñez, "Plural Strategies of Survival and Cultural Formation in U.S. Mexican Households." Also, Javier Tapia, "Cultural Reproduction: Funds of Knowledge as Survival Strategies in the Mexican American Community." Unpublished Ph.D. dissertation, University of Arizona, Tucson, AZ, 1991.

13. Ronald Gallimore and Claude Goldenberg, "Activity Settings of Early Literacy: Home and School Factors in Children's Emergent Literacy," in E. Forman, N. Minick, and C.A. Stone (eds.), *Education and Mind: The Integration of Institutional, Social, and Developmental Process* (Oxford: Oxford University Press, in press).

14. Vélez-Ibáñez, "Plural Strategies of Survival"; Tapia, "Cultural Reproduction."

15. Vélez-Ibáñez, "Plural Strategies of Survival."

16. Individuals from related households frequently get together for social and ceremonial occasions. However, assistance in house or car repairs, or childcare may be quite limited.

17. Vélez-Ibáñez, "Plural Strategies of Survival"; Tapia, "Cultural Reproduction."

8

INDEPENDENT LIVING AMONG MEXICAN AMERICAN ELDERLY: THE NEED FOR SOCIAL SERVICES SUPPORT

DIANA J. TORREZ

The belief that the extended family in the Mexican American culture takes care of its elderly continues to exist in U.S. society. This belief, in part, is due to research studies conducted in the 1970s and 1980s which romanticized the extended family.[1] However, other research studies have concluded that the extended family, particularly among Mexican Americans, is a myth.[2] Extended family includes parents, their children, and other kin who reside in the same household and share economic resources. Although it is true that some Mexican American elderly live in extended families, most do not. Lacayo revealed that only 10 percent of minority elderly have this living arrangement.[3] Although studies such as Becerra, Markides, and Miranda report that the older Mexican Americans continue to have a strong commitment to extended family ties, the families of the elderly are unable to offer financial assistance, as a result of their low socioeconomic status.[4] However, the persistent assumption of the extended family continues to bolster a long-standing belief that minorities take care of their own. This stereotypical belief often detracts from the fact that there is an increasing need for social services among Mexican American elderly.

Mexican American elderly are often unaware of the social services to which they are entitled or how to access these services. In addition, when Mexican American elderly attempt to access social services, they often encounter barriers. As a result, Mexican American elderly underutilize social support services. Awareness of, accessibility to, and utilization of these social services is essential to Mexican American elderly's ability to live independently. The imperativeness of increasing the accessibility and enhancing the quality of social service programs that serve the Mexican American community is apparent when one realizes that the number of Hispanics older than 65 is projected to grow 500 percent by 2030.[5] Since social services programs have the potential for improving the quality of life of Mexican American elderly, this chapter examines the effect of social service utilization on Mexican American elderly's lives.

The effect of social support services on Mexican American elderly was analyzed by examining data collected through the Wesley United Center Errand and Assurance (E & A) Program in Fort Worth, Texas. The primary goal of this program is to provide the elderly (60 years and older) with services that help them maintain their independence and remain at home and a part of the community. A program which provides services such as these is of particular importance to the Mexican American elderly, whose problems become more serious and complicated with age. Since the traditional extended family support system has to a great extent been disabled, Mexican American elderly are in need of a social support system that assists them in accessing the social services to which they are entitled. I hypothesize that programs such as E & A positively impact the lives of Mexican American elderly by providing a social support system that improves their access to the social services to which they are entitled.

SOCIAL SUPPORT THEORY

The need among Mexican American elderly for formal social support systems will be examined within the framework of Ell's social support system theory.[6] She defines social networks as including all of an individual's social contacts, such as family, friends, neighbors, and formal helpers. Social support is defined as emotional support and advice, as well as the material aid and services that people obtain from their social relationships. However, Ell suggests that social networks and social support are conceptually different, and that social networks do not guarantee social support.[7] Lockery also noted that a high social density, large family, or an informal support network is not an accurate indicator of social support.[8]

It is necessary to distinguish between the formal and informal components encompassing the social support system. Cantor asserts that an informal support system can be distinguished from a formal support system as a result of its individualistic and nonbureaucratic manner.[9] More specifically, informal services are provided by the family, neighbors, and friends. In contrast, formal support services are provided by bureaucratic governmental and voluntary organizations.

Studies such as Brody, Markides, and Lubben and Becerra report that the primary source of informal support for the elderly, particularly minorities, continues to be the family.[10] Researchers report that the levels of interaction and support from children are higher for Hispanic elderly than for either whites or African Americans.[11] However, in order to accurately comprehend the social support that the Mexican American elderly receive from their children, it is necessary to further discern between the instrumental and affective components of informal social support. Instrumental social support provides the elderly with services such as transportation, money, or chores, whereas affective social support offers assistance in the form of love, companionship, and understanding.[12]

Mutran noted that the ability to provide instrumental support is in part due to the economic ability to give.[13] As noted, Mexican Americans' low socioeconomic levels have hindered their ability to provide instrumental support to their elderly. Affective support, however, is not mitigated by income levels. As a result, affective support is the type of social support that Mexican Americans are most able to provide their parents. Studies have recognized this aspect and have cautioned against the tendency to overromanticize and stereotype Mexican American family life.[14] Weeks and Cuellar, for instance, found in their San Diego study that although the Mexican American elderly who lived alone were four times more likely to have extended kin in the area, they were less likely to turn to them in times of need.[15]

Sokolovsky concluded that much of the literature that reported that ethnic families were a resource of informal social support had been overly optimistic.[16] More specifically, he stated that the overidealization of minority subcultures has resulted in policies that placed a great deal of emphasis on the family and its "informal supports as the savior of its elderly member."[17] However, as noted, the socioeconomic status of Mexican American families has hindered their ability to provide informal assistance to their elders. It is, therefore, essential to consider and develop social support programs that assist Mexican American elderly to access social support services that allow them to maintain their independence as long as possible.

DATA SOURCE AND METHODS

Tarrant County administers five E & A programs, and one of these programs is housed in Wesley United Center. This center, due to its geographical location, provides services to a large number of Mexican Americans. As a result, this E & A program was selected. The research participants were selected from an E & A list of Mexican American clients containing sixty-one clients. A caseworker from the program assisted with contacting all of the clients on this list, requesting permission for an interview and arranging the interviews. All those clients who consented to an interview were included in the study. Forty-six clients were interviewed in their homes. Fifteen Mexican American elderly were not interviewed for various reasons: Some of the elderly may have been ill or taking care of sick relatives, others had difficulty hearing, and others were bedridden and could not converse. The majority of the interviews were conducted in Spanish, since the clients were better able to express themselves in Spanish. The length of the interviews was between one and two hours.

The Mexican American elderly interviews focused on (1) the types of services currently being received from the E & A program, (2) the manner in which these services affected the quality of the respondent's life and assisted him or her in maintaining his or her independence, (3) the strategies by which the respondent believed these services could be improved, and (4) services not presently available in the E & A program that could improve the quality of life for Mexican American elderly and increase their likelihood of remaining independent and in their homes. The elderly's knowledge of existing social services and the extent to which they utilized these services was also probed. The author also delved into the health, family support, and the life experiences of the Mexican American elderly.

RESULTS

The interviews revealed that Mexican American elderly were in need of social services, particularly as their health began to deteriorate; however, access to these services was often limited. This was evidenced by the fact that the elderly primarily became aware of social services through informal, word-of-mouth sources. Consequently, the E & A program significantly impacted the lives of many of its clients by increasing their knowledge of and access to needed social services.

The interviews also revealed that the adult children of the elderly were rarely able to extend material assistance to meet their parents' needs. Due to limited economic resources and the effects of industrialization and urbanization, services often could not be provided by their children. Although many of the Mexican American elderly interviewed continued to have contact with their children, the contact was infrequent (once a week) and brief (one to two hours) or consisted primarily of phone calls or letters. It was not the intense or frequent interaction that the myth of the "Mexican American extended family" suggests. It is, however, important to realize that although the degree of interaction has decreased, the family remains a very important element in the Mexican American culture. This was evidenced by the fact that in almost all of the homes, numerous photographs of sons, daughters, and grandchildren decorated the walls, shelves, and dressers. These photographs often depicted transitions from one life stage to another. For instance, the photographs portrayed the elderly's children in childhood, adolescence, adulthood, and parenthood.

Despite the cultural significance of the family, the limited resources of their children made it difficult, if not impossible, for the Mexican American children of the elderly in this study to extend economic or social support to their parents. In the majority of cases, the children of elderly were employed in low-paying working-class jobs or blue-collar jobs. Although the occupational prestige accorded their children's jobs may have been greater than the jobs they had occupied in the past (blue-collar versus manual labor jobs), their earnings remained low and as a result, they, like their parents before them, continued to struggle economically. In addition, their work schedules combined with their family responsibilities left them little time to extend assistance to their parents.

Becerra and Shaw have noted the negative effect of contemporary economics and urbanization on the extended family social support systems.[18] The increasing urbanization of Mexican Americans, together with increased acculturation have contributed to the erosion of the extended family. Alfaro-Correa and Nanda have also asserted that the concurrent growth in the number of children and elderly among Hispanics creates conflicting demands on limited family resources.[19] The interviews revealed that in nearly every case, the children of the elderly were still caring for their own children. In addition, in the majority of cases the children of the elderly were employed outside the home. Consequently, the families struggled with time as well as economic constraints. As a result, today the families of Mexican American elderly are not able to provide the support and assistance traditionally associated with the extended family. This lack of an extended family social support system combined with Mexican American elderly low income levels, low education levels, and language barriers lends support to their need for a social support system that will assist them in accessing services.

It was evident from the interviews that the respondents were individuals who had struggled economically throughout their lives. They were proud of the fact that until recently they had not required the assistance of any public agency. Following are quotes from the interviews.

> I told you I never bothered anyone. I never needed to. I have always worked and have never been sick. Well, I will tell you one thing. For me no one does anything. I am used to doing what I want. First I was married, but my husband has died and now I do everything.

However, as a result of deteriorating health, most of the elderly interviewed had begun to need assistance with activities of daily living. Their inevitable health decline and its adverse effect on their independence was source of great frustration for many of the Mexican American elderly.

Previous research has documented Hispanic elderly's higher rates of disability relative to non-Hispanics.[20] This incidence of disability and the limited resources of the Mexican American family often result in unmet social service need for the elderly. Although their family continues to provide affective informal support in the form of phone calls, letters, and limited visits, the resource constraints previously noted hinder their ability to provide the elderly with the informal instrumental support once provided by the extended family. The elderly are, as a result, in need of social services such as transportation to physicians' appointments, assistance with home repairs, and assistance with the process of applying for services to which they are entitled such as medicare, medicaid, social security, and supplemental security income.

In many instances, however, the elderly were unaware of the services for which they were eligible, or if they were aware of them, they were uncertain of the mechanisms by which to access social services. Despite the resistance of the elderly to accepting help from programs, they were well aware of the fact that given their limited economic and social resources, they had few options. One of the most commonly utilized services of the E & A program is the transportation service. For instance, the elderly often need transportation to physicians, grocery stores, and pharmacies. Despite this, the interviews revealed that the most important service the program renders its clients is case management. This service includes information about and referral to other services for senior citizens, advocacy and reading, writing, interpreting, and translating business or personal correspondence. The program has helped many of its clients apply for social security, medicaid, medicare, and supplemental security income. In addition, the program has assisted the elderly to apply for and receive low cost or free cataract testing and surgery, hearing tests and hearing aids, and it has also assisted the elderly in completing the necessary forms to qualify for the city's program offering major and minor home repairs.

De Armas reported that the federal, state, and city government systems and the private and public agencies that provide services to the elderly are extremely complex and frustrating for the elderly.[21] As a result, the elderly are often discouraged from applying for services to which they are entitled. For minority elderly, such as Hispanics, this problem is further compounded by additional barriers encountered in their community, such as "lack of information, transportation, language difficulties, unfamiliarity with rules and lack of ethnic service providers."[22] Consequently, minority elderly underutilize services.

The fact that the services provided by the E & A program have significant impact on the lives of Mexican American elderly was supported by the elderly's responses when they were asked how their lives would be affected if the program did not exist. Since transportation and the supplemental allotment (a service that provides a monthly supplemental allotment of food for individuals who identified as "in need") were the two most frequently utilized services, these were the services to which many of the elderly made reference. They stated that without the program it would be extremely difficult to find transportation to doctors' appointments and to pharmacies to fill prescriptions. They also noted that the supplemental allotment they received often was essential in extending their food supplies through the month.

Although transportation and the supplemental allotment were obviously important services, it should be apparent from the previous discussion that the most valuable services provided by the program were the case management services of referral, advocacy, and interpretation. These are services for which Mexican American elderly have the greatest need, since their families are often unable to extend informal instrumental assistance. As a result, the case management services that assist the elderly in applying for social security, medicaid, home repairs, reduced cost cataract and hearing aids, and other such services are essential for the Mexican American elderly's ability to live independently and remain at home.

CONCLUSIONS

The traditional Mexican American extended family has undergone significant changes. Gratton noted that two primary factors contributing to this change have been industrialization and urbanization.[23] This change has resulted in the unavailability of the family support systems that Mexican American elderly anticipated in their old age. Therefore, Mexican American elderly need programs to provide them with services that the traditional extended family social support system may have previously provided. In addition, low income, low educational levels, and high rates of disability make the Mexican American elderly's needs for social services greater than that of other elderly. Despite this, studies such as Gelfand have reported that ethnic elderly often lack knowledge about available services. Further, due to lack of transportation, minority elderly may be unable to travel beyond their neighborhoods to access these services.[24] Consequently, Mexican American elderly underutilize social services. Therefore, programs such E & A that provide transportation to the elderly and play a pivotal role in increasing the Mexican American elderly's access to and utilization of health and social services are essential for the Mexican American community.

Social service accessibility is vital to Mexican American elderly, as an increasing number of elderly live alone and without the extended family support systems of the past. As Margarita Treviño noted, it is necessary to be aware that "their problems do not change from the time when they were younger, their needs only become greater in magnitude and more complicated with age."[25] Since this study revealed that social services are needed by Mexican American elderly and that these services do positively impact their lives need for services, it is necessary to be cognizant of mechanisms that will increase their access to social services.

The interviews revealed that all of the elderly in this study became aware of the E & A program through informal sources. This is consistent with past research, which has documented that Mexican Americans are more likely to be referred to services through informal referral.[26] Word-of-mouth tends to be the most common source of informal referral. It is essential that policymakers be aware of the extent of the elderly's knowledge of programs and services when developing mechanisms to increase Mexican American elderly's access to social services. Since this study and others have found that the most common source of referral is informal, one strategy for increasing awareness of social services might be to distribute social service information at churches, community organizations, physicians' offices, pharmacies, and grocery stores.

Acknowledgments: This study was conducted under the auspices of the Gerontological Society of America's 1992 Technical Assistance Program. This project was supported, in part, by Tarrant County Area Agency on Aging and Award number 90AM0470 from the Administration on Aging, U.S. Department of Health and Human Services.

NOTES

1. See Marjorie H. Cantor, "The Informal Support System of New York's Inner City Elderly: Is Ethnicity a Factor?" in Donald E. Gelfand and Alfred J. Kurtzik (eds.), *Ethnicity and Aging: Theory Research and Policy* (New York: Springer, 1979); Elizabeth Mutran, "Intergenerational Family Support among Blacks and Whites: Response to Culture or to Socioeconomic Differences," *Journal of Gerontology*, 40 (1985): 382–389; and Carolyn J. Rosenthal, "Family Supports in Later Life: Does Ethnicity Make a Difference?" *Gerontologist*, 26 (1986): 19–24.

2. For example, F. Solis, "Cultural Factors in

Programming of Services for Spanish-Speaking Elderly," in A. Hernández and J. Mendoza (eds.), *National Conference on the Spanish-Speaking Elderly* (Kansas City, KS: National Chicano Social Planning Council, 1975); Noel F. Laurel, "An Intergenerational Comparison of Attitudes toward the Support of Aged Parents: A Study of Mexican Americans in Two South Texas Communities." Ph.D. dissertation, University of Southern California, Los Angeles, CA, 1976; and David Maldonado, "The Chicano Aged," *Social Work*, 20 (1975): 213–216.

3. Carmela G. Lacayo, *A National Study to Assess the Service Needs of Hispanic Elderly—Final Report* (Los Angeles, CA: Asociacion Nacional Pro Personas Mayores, 1980); also, C.G. Lacayo, "Current Trends in Living Arrangements and Social Environment Among Ethnic Minority Elderly," in E.P. Stanford and Fernando M. Torres-Gil (eds.), *Diversity: New Approaches to Ethnic Minority Aging* (New York: Baywood Publishing, 1992).

4. Rosina M. Becerra, "The Mexican American Aging in a Changing Culture," in R.L. McNeely and John L. Colen (eds.), *Aging in Minority Groups* (Beverly Hills, CA: Sage, 1983); Kyriakos S. Markides and N. Krause, "Old Mexican Americans: Family Relationships and Well-Being," *Generations*, 10(4) (1986): 31–34; and M. Miranda, "Latin American Culture and American Society: Contrasts," in A. Hernández and J. Mendoza (eds.), *National Conference on the Spanish-Speaking Elderly*.

5. S.P. Wallace and C. Lew-Ting, "Getting by at Home—Community-Based Long Term Care of Latino Elders," *Cross-Cultural Medicine: A Decade Later. [Special Issue]. Western Journal of Medicine*, 157 (1991): 337–344.

6. K. Ell, "Social Networks, Social Support and Health Status: A Review," *Social Science Review*, 58 (1984): 133–149.

7. Ell, "Social Networks."

8. Shirley A. Lockery, "Caregiving among Racial and Ethnic Minority Elders," in E.P. Stanford and Fernando M. Torres-Gil (eds.), *Diversity: New Approaches to Ethnic Minority Aging* (New York: Baywood Publishing, 1992).

9. Cantor, "The Informal Support System."

10. Elaine M. Brody, "Parent Care as a Normative Family Stress," *Gerontologist*, 25 (1985): 19–29; Markides and Krause, "Old Mexican Americans," 31–34; and, James E. Lubben and Rosina M. Becerra, "Social Support among Black, Mexican and Chinese Elderly," in Donald E. Gelfand and Charles M. Barressi (eds.), *Ethnic Dimensions of Aging* (New York: Springer, 1987).

11. Cantor, "The Informal Support System"; Ramón Valle and Charles Martínez, "Natural Networks of Elderly Latinos of Mexican Heritage: Implications for Mental Health," in Manuel Miranda and Rene A. Ruiz (eds.), *Chicano Aging and Mental Health* (Rockville, MD: National Institute of Mental Health, 1980); and M. Sotomayor, "A Study of Chicano Grandparents in an Urban Barrio," Ph.D. dissertation, University of Denver, 1973.

12. Lockery, "Caregiving."

13. Mutran, "Intergenerational Family Support," 382–389.

14. Maldonado, "The Chicano Aged," 3; and José Cuellar, "El Senior Citizens Club: The Old Mexican American in the Voluntary Association," in Barbara Myerhoff and Andrei Simic (eds.), *Life's Career—Aging* (Beverly Hills, CA: Sage, 1980).

15. John R. Weeks and José Cuellar, "The Role of Family Members in the Helping Networks of Older People," *Gerontologist*, 21 (1981): 388–394.

16. J. Sokolovsky, "Ethnicity, Culture and Aging: Do Differences Really Make A Difference?" *Journal of Applied Gerontology*, 4 (1985): 6–17.

17. Sokolovsky, "Ethnicity, Culture and Aging," p. 6.

18. Rosina M. Becerra and David Shaw, The *Hispanic Elderly: A Research Reference Guide* (Lanham, MD: University Press of America, 1984).

19. A.I. Alfaro-Correa and J.P. Nanda, *Utilization of Health and Social Services among Elderly Hispanics*. Testimony submitted to the joint hearing of the House Select Committee on Aging and the Congressional Hispanic Caucus, 1991.

20. S.P. Wallace and C. Lew-Ting, *Cross-Cultural Medicine: A Decade Later. [Special Issue]. Western Journal of Medicine*, 337–344; C. Hanis, R.E.

Ferrell, S.A. Barton, L. Aguilar, A. Garza-Ibarra, B.R. Tulloch, C.A. García, and W.J. Schull, "Diabetes Among Mexican Americans in Starr County, Texas," *American Journal of Epidemiology*, 118 (1983): 659–672; M.P. Stern, S.P. Gaskill, H.P. Hazuda, L.I. Gardner, and S.M. Haffner, "Does Obesity Explain Excess Prevalence of Diabetes among Mexican Americans? Results of the San Antonio Heart Study," *Diabetologia* 24 (1983): 272–277; and Benjamin S. Bradshaw and Edwin Fonner Jr., "The Mortality of Spanish-Surnamed Persons in Texas: 1969–1971" in Frank D. Bean and W. Parker Frisbie (eds.), *The Demography of Racial and Ethnic Groups* (New York: Academic Press, 1978).

21. E.P. De Armas, "The 'Super System' and the Spanish-Speaking Elderly," in D.J. Curren, J.J. Rivera, and R.B. Sánchez (eds.), *Proceeding of the Puerto Rican Conference of Human Services* (Washington, DC: National Coalition of Spanish-Speaking Mental Health Organizations, 1975).

22. D. Guttman, *Perspective on Equitable Share in Public Benefits by Minority Elderly* (Washington, DC: The Catholic University of America, Administration on Aging, 1980).

23. B. Gratton, "Familism among the Black and Mexican-American Elderly: Myth or Reality," *Journal of Aging Studies* 1 (1) (1987): 19–32.

24. Doonal E. Gelfand, *Aging: The Ethnic Factor* (Boston: Little Brown and Co., 1982).

25. Margarita C. Treviño, "A Comparative Analysis of Need, Access, and Utilization of Health and Human Services," in Steve R. Applewhite (ed.), *Hispanic Elderly in Transition: Theory, Research, Policy and Practice* (New York: Greenwood Press, 1988), 39.

26. Frances M. Carp, "Communicating with Elderly Mexican Americans," *The Gerontologist*, 10 (1970): 126–134.

PART III

CHALLENGING SOCIAL INSTITUTIONS

9

LIBERATION THEOLOGY AND SOCIAL CHANGE: CHICANAS AND CHICANOS IN THE CATHOLIC CHURCH

GILBERT R. CADENA   LARA MEDINA

Solidaridad es torrente que da vida
es mil Pueblos unidos al andar.
Solidaridad es camino de esperanza
es proyecto de nueva sociedad[1]

A history of conflict and resistance characterizes the relationship between Chicanas and Chicanos and the Roman Catholic Church.[2] As part of the largest ethnic group in the Catholic Church, Latinos and Chicanos make up the majority of Catholics in the Southwest United States. Today, however, Latinos are leaving the church; they are joining evangelical denominations or creating autonomous religious communities outside of the church. Those remaining are struggling to carve space for their identity and ideology within the church.

This chapter provides an introduction to some of the social changes taking place within the Catholic Church. Our interest lies in how Catholicism is becoming a catalyst for social change among many Chicanos. The social forces influencing this relationship include: Latin American liberation theology, the number of Latino theologians, and rapid demographic changes. A gradual institutional transformation is occurring that is characterized by social and religious conflict over the means of religious production. In other words, Chicano religious leaders are articulating a religious world view challenging the status quo and power of the Euro-American Catholic Church. To examine how this is being done, we discuss the changing demographics of Catholics, theories of religion and social change, liberation theology, and focus on a base community as an example of organizing within the socioreligious sphere.

DEMOGRAPHIC OVERVIEW OF CHICANAS AND CHICANOS IN THE CATHOLIC CHURCH

Today, about three-quarters of Chicanos identify as Catholic. Studies show that first generation Mexicans have higher rates of Catholic affiliation when compared to second and subsequent generation Chicanos.[3] For example, in the National Latino Political Survey, 73 percent of Chicanos and 82 percent of Mexican-born identify as Catholic. Protestants account for 16 percent of Chicanos and 8 percent of Mexicans.[4] Most studies suggest Chicanos and Latinos are very religious people.[5] Both Chicanos and Mexicans receive significant guidance (62 percent) from religion, with only 6 percent of both groups stating they receive no guidance from religion.[6]

Within the Catholic Church, Chicanos and Latinos comprised about 28 percent of the Catholic Church in 1980 and about 35 percent in 1990. Soon after the turn of the next century, Latinos will be about one-half of the Catholic laity. More than a dozen (arch)dioceses are over 51 percent Latino and over twenty-seven (arch)dioceses are between 25 and 50 percent.[7] According to the Secretariat of Hispanic Affairs in Washington DC, the following (arch)dioceses total over 50 percent Latino: Amarillo, Brownsville, Brooklyn, El Paso, Los Angeles, Las Cruces, Lubbock, Miami, Santa Fe, San Angelo, San Antonio, Tucson, and Yakima. Los Angeles represents the largest archdiocese in the United States, where Latinos total approximately 65 percent of the Catholic laity.

While the majority of Chicanos identified as Catholic since the mid 1800s, the hierarchy and religious leadership never reflected this relationship. The number of Chicana/Chicano priests, bishops, and sisters never exceeded over 5 percent of the religious leadership. For example, about 3 percent of Catholic priests are Latino or about 1,900 out of 54,000 U.S. priests.[8] Of these only about 200 are Chicano.[9] Of 104,000 sisters, less than 1,000 are Latina. Of the nearly 400 Catholic bishops, about 5 percent or twenty, are Latino. Of these twenty, eight are Chicano. From 1848 to 1970, the hierarchy appointed no Latino bishops, until Fr. Patricio Flores became auxiliary bishop in the San Antonio archdiocese.

If we look at the pipeline of future Chicano priests and sisters and the pool of potential bishops, the numbers are not promising. While half of the dioceses claim to offer special programs in "Hispanic" ministry, Latinos make up only one percent of diocesan seminarians. Throughout the United States, in 1987 to 1988, only 290 Latinos attended Catholic seminaries and theological centers. In contrast, 958 Latinas/os attended Protestant seminaries and theological centers.[10]

The church today faces a significant loss of its clergy. From 1965 to 2005, the church will lose 40 percent of ordained ministers, and the average age for ministers will be 55 years old.[11] At the same time, the Catholic church will increase about one percent a year, due primarily to Latina fertility rates and immigration.

Euro-American Catholics will decrease in numbers, due to low fertility rates and an aging population. When comparing other ethnic Catholics, religious leadership remains concentrated among Irish Catholics. Irish-Americans, for example, make up about 17 percent of the church, but total 49 percent of the bishops, 39 percent of the diocesan, and 34 percent of religious priests. German and Scandinavian-Americans are about 20 percent of the church, and total 25 percent of the bishops, diocesan, and religious priests.[12]

Studies show that Catholics have achieved social and economic parity with Euro-American Protestants.[13] However, when income is controlled for ethnicity, differences vary among ethnic groups. For example, data from the General Social Survey (1980-1984) show Italian, Irish, and Polish Catholic families earned between $27,858 to $30,321 in annual income.[14] These three Catholic ethnic groups earned more than Presbyterians, Episcopalians, Lutherans, Methodists, and Baptists. Only Jewish Americans earned more than Catholics. However, out of eleven selected groups, Latino Catholics earned the least with $16,426, or 57 percent of Italian Catholics.

Other studies show a general level of dissatisfaction and alienation from official church activities. For example, mass attendance in most surveys show a bimodal relationship in attendance. Among Chicanos, 41 percent attend mass at least once a month, and 47 percent never attend religious services. Mexican-born individuals have slightly higher attendance rates, with 51 percent attending at least once a month and 41 percent never attending mass.[15] Gonzáles and La Velle's national study found the vast majority (88 percent) of Latino Catholics not actively involved in parish activities and most (60 percent) not encouraged to be involved.[16] Marin and Gamba found in San Francisco only 12 percent very active in church activities and over half (53 percent) dissatisfied with the priest in their current parish.[17]

Cadena's research on Chicano priests found a majority (58 percent) not satisfied with the way the Catholic Church responded to social problems in the their community. Eighty-four percent of Chicano clergy feel Chicanos do not have an adequate voice in the decision-making process of the U.S. Catholic Church, and over 82 percent believe Chicanos are discriminated against by the church.[18] Throughout six generations, Gonzáles and La Velle found 82 percent of Latino Catholics feel the Catholic Church should make greater efforts to include Latino culture and tradition in Church activities.[19]

The U.S. Catholic Church has attempted to minister and respond to Latino laity through the creation of diocesan Offices of Hispanic Affairs. Fifty-two percent of dioceses have such an office. Yet, closer examination reveals a less than serious effort by the church. For example, in a study conducted by the Secretariat for Hispanic Affairs, most of these offices are located within another department, such as Catholic Charities. Almost 50 percent of the dioceses have *no* budget for Latino pastoral ministry. The number of priests, sisters, and pastoral workers working in Hispanic Affairs is less than one percent of its diocesan personnel.[20]

The data reflect a church stratified by ethnicity, class, and gender. An unequal distribution of power, and the ethnic hegemony of the bishops and priests account for the near monopoly of the decision-making process in the church.

From seminaries to chancery offices, religious orders, and religious organizations, with few exceptions, Latinos remain segmented at each level. Yet, in spite of this stratification, many are creating avenues for social change by adhering to liberation theology. These liberationists, or advocates of liberation theology, participate in the process of transforming religious discourse by addressing inequalities affecting Latinas/os inside and outside of the church.

RELIGION AS A SOURCE OF SOCIAL CHANGE

To understand how religion can be a source of social change, the writings of Italian social theorist Antonio Gramsci, Venezuelan sociologist Otto Maduro, and Cuban-American theologian Ada Maria Isasi-Díaz are important to consider. For each of them, religion can serve as a catalyst in bringing about social change, as religious leaders join the side of subordinate groups and participate in socioreligious movements.

From Antonio Gramsci, the concept of hegemony helps to explain the power and control of the Catholic Church. Hegemony refers to control over a group of people, not by forced domination, but by consent through political and ideological leadership.[21] The laity internalizes the ideology of the hierarchy and believes their world view is "natural" and legitimate. Church hegemony is reinforced in society with churches supporting the status quo of the state. The Church maintains its hegemony by controlling its religious leadership and through institutional discrimination. On the other hand, counter-hegemony attempts to challenge the dominant world view and to contribute to ideological and structural change by a subordinate group. Liberation theology provides an example of counter-hegemony by Latinos struggling against ethnic, gender, and class inequalities.

For Maduro, the "relative autonomy of religion" describes the dynamic relationship between religious institutions to society at large.[22] All religious institutions are partially influenced by the dominant social forces of society; however, institutions remain partially independent of those forces. Sometimes this autonomous relationship seeks to create a more traditional world view. For example, in 1967 Pope Paul VI reaffirmed the church's ban on contraception, despite the recommendation of a commission he appointed to study the reality of modern Catholic lives. At other times the autonomous relationship challenges the status quo and advocates a new religious or social system, such as Latin American liberation theology that demands a "preferential option for the poor" and a "political faith" to be lived by Christians.

Ada Maria Isasi-Díaz emphasizes the role of the community as "the real theologians."[23] As actors and producers of religious thought, community members analyze the causes of oppression and link their religious understandings to social action. The "theological technicians," or those trained in the academy assist in this process. As enablers, they must be members of the community and remain accountable to the liberation of the community. This vision of leadership creates a radical shift in the use of power and the relationship of leaders to a community.

Religious authority lies among the community, where social analysis and religious ideas are generated and clarified.

[handwritten: Spanish Crown Catholic → Colonies]

✳ *LIBERATION THEOLOGY*

The emerging U.S. Latino theology represents an example of religious cultural resistance where theologians, clerics, and laity use their social experiences as the starting point for theological discourse. For Latino liberationists, traditional Euro-American theology has failed to understand the culture and religiosity of U.S. Latinos. It remains inadequate in addressing issues of class, and racial/ethnic, gender, and religious inequalities. Liberation theology offers an alternative for those estranged or alienated from the Roman Catholic Church.

Latin American liberation theology has significantly influenced the foundations of U.S. Latino theology. For Latin American theologians and advocates, the primary task of liberation theology is to free the oppressed from their inhumane living conditions. Generally, liberation theology seeks to (1) interpret the Christian faith from the perspective of the poor, (2) critique societal structures that cause poverty, and (3) critique the activity of the Church and of Christians through the lens of the poor.[24] The motivating factors are compassion with the poor and "energetic" protest against the causes of collective oppression and the denial of basic human rights that are contrary to the plan of creation. Liberation theology calls for an authentic commitment to the struggle of the oppressed.[25] According to Gustavo Gutierrez, the first theologian to systematically write about liberation theology, liberation has three dimensions:

[handwritten: Three Dimensions of Liberation]

1. Liberation means freedom from oppressive economic, social, and political conditions.
2. Liberation means human beings take control over their own historical destiny.
3. Liberation includes emancipation from social sin and the acceptance of a life following Jesus's commitment to the poor.[26]

There are two basic acts of this theology. The first act takes liberating action; the second reflects on the action in light of faith. Liberating action goes beyond charity or reform measures. The strategy of liberating action means the poor, subordinate groups, and those in solidarity with them, come together to understand the causes of their oppression and to organize themselves into groups or movements that challenge the unequal structures of society. The second act, faith reflecting on action, requires participants to question the role of Christianity in the strategies for liberation. In this act, faith seeks guidance through the word of God as found in the scriptures. The scriptures are read from the perspective of the poor and require a "theological-political rereading" of the Bible.[27]

The doing of liberation theology can be further divided into three basic stages: (1) the socioanalytical stage, (2) the hermeneutical stage, and (3) the praxis stage. The socioanalytical stage requires an analysis of the actual conditions of poverty using the tools of Marxism to understand class struggle, economic factors, and the power of ideologies. The hermeneutical stage requires a reflection on what the word of God has to say about the situation of oppression. Liberationists refer to the scriptures by seeking the practical meaning of its contents for the purpose of application to contemporary social situations. The practical stage requires arrival at a specific course of action to be taken to rectify the oppressive situation. Action is essential to liberation theology as it sees the only true form of faith to be "political love."[28] In essence, this theology moves from the analysis of the social reality to seeking inspiration for action from the Bible to arriving at concrete strategies for action.

Contributions of U.S. Latina/o Theologians

Liberation theology began to have influence in the United States in the late 1960s and early 1970s. This coincided with the rise of the militant Chicano movement. However, as Chicano priests and Chicana sisters were being influenced by liberation theology, most Chicano activists and organizations severed ties to the Catholic Church. As an exception, Cesar Chavez used the power of Catholic symbolism and the strength of the farmworker's religious identity as a tool to fight the power of agribusiness.

It is important to understand the differences between Latin American liberation theology and U.S. Latino theology. First, the social context is different. Latin American liberation theology emerged from a context of extreme conditions of poverty and political turmoil in countries such as Brazil, Peru, Chile, Mexico, Nicaragua, and El Salvador. The liberating strategies required a focus on class oppression, the role of foreign multinational corporations, U.S. foreign policy, and Latin American oligarchies and military dictatorships. In the United States, the first writings by Chicano theologians in the late 1970s and early 1980s emphasized cultural survival within a historical legacy of racism.[29] As Chicanas and Latinas began to write in the late 1980s and early 1990s, their experiences in confronting patriarchy and sexism as well as racism and classism influenced their theological contributions.

Liberation theology in both Latin America and the United States is concerned with social justice and the means to achieve it. However, in the United States the social and material conditions are not as extreme as in Latin America. U.S. Latino political movements tend to be reformist in nature, rather than revolutionary. Similarly, U.S. Latina/o liberationists give attention to group empowerment and social transformation rather than revolutionary change.

Virgilio Elizondo, a Chicano priest and the first theologian to write about Chicano socioreligious issues, suggests the source of creativity of the Chicano people lies in their *mestizaje*. As *mestizos*, Chicanos live on the outskirts of U.S. society. It is precisely the experience of being marginalized that calls Chicanas/os to challenge modern-day structures of oppression, including the Church.[30] Elizondo sees this as their prophetic call and mission:

In fidelity to his [her] way, Mexican-American Christians are challenging the oppressive powers of today, both within the Latin American world and in the U.S.A. They do not want to inflict violence on others, but they know they have the mission to make known in no uncertain terms the injustice and violence that the establishments are inflicting . . .[31]

Elizondo's work highlights the role of *mestizas/os* in creating a new reality, one that brings together the best of diverse cultures that make up the Chicano: the Indian, the Spaniard, the African, and the Asian. The *mestiza/o* is one who bridges the gap between cultures and ethnic groups straddling two different cultures: the Mexican culture and the Euro-American culture. Theologically speaking, he claims that Chicanos play a vital part in upholding the gospel, which brings about a reality of justice.

The contributions of Latina theologians have made a great impact on the course of U.S. Latino theology. In 1988, Ada Maria Isasi-Díaz and Yolanda Tarango, a Chicana sister, wrote *Hispanic Women: Prophetic Voice in the Church*. The lives of Latinas and their religious understandings provide the foundation of this book. As feminists these women seek to challenge patriarchal religious structures that exclude the experiences of women. Their contributions highlight the role of the church in justifying patriarchy:

The church sanctions—justifies—the patriarchy in society by being itself a patriarchal structure. If the church is holy and patriarchal, is not patriarchy holy? If the church were to denounce patriarchy, it would be an important moment in the process of the liberation of women. For this reason, as Roman Catholics we must continue to call the Catholic Church to repent of the sexism inherent in its structures and in some of its tenets.[32]

Their work articulates the religious motivations of Latinas and the praxis they engage in as they struggle towards liberation. This is a struggle not only to survive physically, economically, and culturally, but the struggle to be active agents in the making of their history. Religious understandings play an important role in Latina liberation as they provide the source of one's action in history. It is the sense of the divine in the lives of Latinas that gives them the strength for the struggle—"a struggle that is not a part of life but life itself."[33]

As in liberation theology, praxis is critical to this theology. Action and reflection occur simultaneously during praxis. Accordingly, the emphasis is on "doing theology," which is to act in the world out of a commitment to the liberation of Latinas and oppressed communities. What represents justice for Latinas cannot be defined in conflict with what is justice for other communities of struggle. Community takes a primary role in this theology for several reasons. First, with experience as the starting point, it must include personal as well as communal experience. One without the other leads to individualism or abstraction. Second, liberation is linked to the full participation of humans in community, and third, community is an essential element of Latino culture, as it gives identity to Latinos in a hostile society.[34]

The contributions made by Isasi-Díaz and Tarango represent the voices and experiences of women not traditionally included in theological discussions. Their work takes religious authority away from the exclusive realm of male academics and places it in the hands of Latinas whose faith and lived experiences inform their actions. The experiences of Latinas as the starting point radically challenge religious and academic structures to include these experiences in the norm of religious discourse.

Since the writing of this book, Isasi-Díaz uses the term "Mujerista theology" to refer to Latina theology. The name was chosen because *mujer* is most often used in the music of Latino cultures to refer to Latinas, whether it be protest songs or love songs. A *mujerista* is one who makes a preferential option for women and who struggles to liberate herself and other women. She works for justice and understands her call to bring forth a new people with strong women and strong men.[35] *Mujerista* theology gives voice to their religious understandings always using "a liberative lens, which requires placing oneself radically at the core of our own struggling *pueblo.*"[36]

Mujerista theology concerns itself with the issue of power and calls for a reinventing of power. For *mujeristas*, power "is the ability to enable all persons to become the most they themselves can be" and always in relationship to the community.[37] This kind of power seeks to create "political, economic, and social conditions needed for the self-realization of all persons."[38] Power must be a shared power rather than power over others. Shared power lies in direct contrast to the kind of power that exists within the majority of societies' structures influenced by patriarchy. As patriarchy is the institutionalization of male dominance over women, such structures require having a hierarchy of individuals with power over those on the bottom levels of the institution. *Mujeristas* condemn such abuse of power and call for the issue of power to be at the heart of theological discourse.

Other important U.S. Latina/o theologians making further contributions to this discourse include: María Pilar Aquino, Jeanette Rodriguez-Holguin, Marina Herrera, Roberto Goizueta, Orlando Espín, Gloria Loya, Allan Figueroa Deck, Arturo Banuelos, C. Gilbert Romero and Sixto García. It is beyond the scope of this article to summarize their work; however, each are making valuable strides in the development of Latina/o theology.[39]

CALPULLI: A MODEL FOR SOCIAL CHANGE

Pastoral practitioners and community activists Rosa Marta Zarate, a Chicana religious sister, and Patricio Guillen, a Chicano priest, deserve recognition as religious leaders having an impact on U.S. Latina/o theology. Zarate and Guillen represent the community "doing theology" with their involvement in the formation of base communities in San Bernardino County in Southern California. Base communities are small groups of people formed around theological reflection and community organizing. Involved in critical social analysis they link action to religious faith. These groups are modeled after the *comunidades eclesiales de base* of Latin American liberation theology, which formed as a result of the absence of clergy in the rural areas of Latin American countries. Religious leaders may take a role in the formation of these communities, but the emphasis rests on the laity taking leadership in the work of these small church communities. Reflection, action, and worship are central aspects of these groups.

Since the early 1970s, Sister Zarate and Father Guillen organized base communities in San Diego, San Bernardino, Imperial Valley, and Riverside, California. Today, they and a team of lay people successfully apply the tenets of liberation theology by creating a system of profit and nonprofit cooperatives employing residents from the local community. Their goal is to create economically self-sufficient organizations that operate based on the principles of shared profit, shared responsibility, and shared power. The inspiration for their efforts comes not only from liberation theology but also from knowledge about the economic systems of their Mesoamerican ancestors. The cooperative system, or *calpulli*, of native communities provides the framework for much of the educational, economic, and cultural work that Zarate and Guillen facilitate. Their organizational plan includes establishing centers of learning and work owned and operated by the community. The philosophy behind *calpulli* stresses that social economic change is possible with the collective efforts of a community rather than individual workers.

Since 1987, the nonprofit centers focus on vocational training, English as a second language, youth employment training, continuing education, and immigrant services. The profit centers include a travel agency, tax and legal counseling, a bookstore, a gardening and landscaping service, clothing manufacturing, and food service. Decision making in the cooperatives uses a consensus model and all workers own a share of the cooperative.

A strong characteristic of *calpulli* is the emphasis placed on the indigenous cultural history of *mestizos*. Calpulli takes seriously indigenous knowledge and values existing prior to the European invasion in the Americas. Sr. Zarate, Fr. Guillen, and the members of Calpulli seek to recover this knowledge and pass it on to the broader community. From 1991 to 1992, they intensified their learning and commitment to indigenous knowledge in a number of ways. For example, they coordinated a series of workshops for the community on the Mesoamerican system of *calpulli*. Dr. Clodomiro Siller, a Mexican anthropologist, led the workshops and initiated a study of the codices, the ancient sacred and historical books of Mesoamerica. In addition, they studied the *Relational Letters of Hernan Cortes*, the works of Bartolomé de las Casas, and other historical documents. From their studies, a team wrote an open letter to the Pope regarding the Roman Catholic Church's proposed 1992 Quincentennial Celebration. A four-page document was sent to the Apostolic Pro Nuncio, the Papal representative to the United States, and published in several magazines and newsletters. The letter called for the institutional church to ask forgiveness of the Indigenous peoples of America for the sins, past and present, committed against them. We further recommend that acts of reparation be included as integral to the commemoration of the encounter of cultures. These acts of reparation should be reflected in acts of solidarity with the struggles of the Indigenous of America in their efforts to redress the injustices committed against them.[40]

Calpulli also participated in the Peace and Dignity Journey, a spiritual run beginning simultaneously in Alaska and in Argentina. The runners met in Mexico City on October 12, 1992 to commemorate 500 years of resistance by the indigenous people of the continent. Calpulli helped coordinate a team of runners to run a 180-mile link from San Bernardino to Blyth, California, and participated in the October 12 event. In the organizing of this event, contact was made with sixteen local indigenous groups living in southern California.

Calpulli seeks to create solidarity networks with other organizations seeking self-autonomy and self-determination for the purpose of empowering the poor and working for social change. They have relationships with *campesino* groups, Native American communities, community-based organizations, social scientists, and student groups. Overall, Calpulli seeks to educate, develop, and accompany the community as it seeks to create alternative social systems that provide sustenance and dignity for all involved.

In addition to community organizing, Sr. Zarate is an accomplished composer and singer of music that reflects the religious and political motivations of Latinos struggling for justice. Her music is informed not only by Christian gospel values of justice, but also by Mesoamerican religious understandings. For example, a recent song speaks of the indigenous female deity, Cihuacoatl or Tonantzin, who remains a source of strength for many Chicanas and Chicanos:

> Tonantzin, mi nina.
> Llorona de tantos siglos
> las rosas en el cerro florecen ya
> la lucha del pueblo sera
> canto de victoria. . . .
>
> Madre Tonantzin el Indio
> sigue de pié, resistiendo;
> y en su pisada andariega
> nadie ha podido vencerlo.
> La milpa sigue creciendo,
> alimentando esperanza.
> Y el Indio escribe su historia,
> al Indio nadie lo entierra.[41]

Zarate's artistic work is an example of Latina theology being informed by the aspirations of *el pueblo*.

DISCUSSION AND CONCLUSION

This chapter shows that the Catholic Church is not a monolithic institution always promoting cultural conservatism. For liberationists, the struggle for cultural resistance and social change is carried out in their attempts to create an alternative world view and challenge the religious structures of domination through praxis. This conscious transformation is an inseparable part of political and economic change. The emergence of liberation theology, the new critical mass of Latina/o theologians, and Latino demographic shifts, all contribute to a movement for social change within the Church.

The relationship between Catholic hegemony and Latino counter-hegemony is important in understanding religious domination and ethnic group subordination. The church is an example of a hegemonic institution through its control and maintenance of a system of ethnic, gender, and class inequality. In order for liberation theology to impact the lives of the masses of Latino Catholics, religious leaders must be active participants in social and political struggles, providing the organic link to grassroot communities. The methodology of praxis, theological reflection, and social action grounds their work to the lives and social context of Chicanas/os and Latinas/os today.

While most Catholic theologians work primarily within the institutional framework of the Roman Catholic Church, it is important to recognize the non-Christian sources of religious expressions vital to the self-determination of Chicanas and Chicanos. Critical readings of indigenous sources such as the *Popol Vuh* and the numerous codices that portray the values of indigenous communities must be included in theological reflections. Calpulli successfully does this in their ministry. Many Chicanos, as *mestizo* peoples, often find their motivations and behavior come more from the ethics of indigenous ancestors than they do from the Christian influence. For example, the values of community, respect for elders, and religious observances represent indigenous "ethics" existing long before the Christian presence in the Americas. In addition, important values such as the relationship to the land, the valued role of homosexuals, or the role of female priestesses can be learned from native knowledge.

The ways in which Chicano Catholics create avenues for change within the institutional church reflect the ongoing importance of religion in their lives, regardless of the historical alienation felt within the Catholic Church. Base communities, such as Calpulli, create an environment of renewed religious commitment addressing the local, regional, and international concerns of its members. Although similar base communities are not the dominant model of church in the United States, Calpulli does provide an alternative model that has the capacity to strengthen the religious affiliation of many Latinos disaffected from the institutional Catholic Church. This relationship is based on collective action, rather than abstract faith.

This relative autonomy of religion contributes to an emerging U.S. Latino theology, which allows particular groups in the church to advocate a progressive religious and political agenda. As Latinas and Latinos transform the church, the impact the church has in society will reflect the social and religious interests of the future majority of U.S. Catholics.

NOTES

1. "Solidarity is the power that gives life, it is a thousand communities walking united. Solidarity is the road of hope, the project of a new society." Rosa Martha Zárate Macías. Lyrics from "Solidaridad," *Concierto a Mi Pueblo* casette tape, (San Bernardino, CA, 1990.) Translated by authors.

2. This paper uses the term "Chicano" to refer to the Mexican-origin population living in the United States. "Latino" is used when data cited reflects the Mexican-origin, Puerto Rican-origin, Cuban-origin and other Latin American-origin populations, or connotes a pan-ethnic solidarity of collective action.

3. Roberto O. Gonzáles and Michael La Velle, *The Hispanic Catholic in the United States* (New York: Northeast Catholic Pastoral Center for Hispanics, 1985), 25; Rodolfo O. de la Garza, Louis DeSipio, F. Chris García, John García, and Angelo Falcon (eds.) *Latino Voices: Mexican, Puerto Rican, and Cuban Perspectives* (Boulder, CO: Westview Press, 1992), 37.

4. de la Garza et al., *Latino Voices*, 37–39.

5. Ruth T. Doyle and Olga Scarpetta, *Hispanics in New York: Religious, Cultural and Social Experiences*, 2nd edition, (New York: Office of Pastoral Research and Planning, 1982), 29–37; Gonzáles and La Velle, *The Hispanic Catholic in the United States*, 23–26; Gerardo Marin and Raymond J. Gamba, "Expectations and Experiences of Hispanic Catholics and Converts to Protestant Churches," Technical Report No.2 (San Francisco, CA: University of San Francisco, February 1990), 6–7.

6. de la Garza et al., *Latino Voices: Mexican, Puerto Rican, and Cuban Perspectives*, 38.

7. NCCB/USCC Secretariat for Hispanic Affairs, "National Survey on Hispanic Ministry" (Washington DC: NCCB/USCC Secretariat for Hispanic Affairs, 1990), 3.

8. Manual J. Rodriguez, *Directory of Hispanic Priests in the United States of America* (New York: Spanish Heritage, 1986), 125–126.

9. Gilbert R. Cadena, "Chicanos and the Catholic Church: Liberation Theology as a Form of Empowerment," Unpublished Ph.D. dissertation, University of California, Riverside, 1987, 45.

10. William Baumgaertner (ed.), *Fact Book on Theological Education 1987–88* (Vandalia, OH: Association of Theological Schools, 1988), 93, 110.

11. Richard Schoenherr and Lawrence A. Young, *Full Pews, Empty Altars* (Madison, WI: University of Wisconsin, 1993), 25.

12. Andrew Greeley, *The Catholic Priest in the United States: Sociological Investigations* (Washington, DC: United States Catholic Office, 1972), 28–30.

13. Andrew Greeley, *Religious Change in America* (Cambridge: Harvard University Press, 1989), 79.

14. Annual family earnings is based on the head of households under age 40.

15. de la Garza et al., *Latino Voices: Mexican, Puerto Rican, and Cuban Perspectives*, 39; Gonzáles and La Velle also found this dichotomy of mass attendance among U.S. Latinos.

16. Gonzáles and La Velle, *The Hispanic Catholic in the United States*, 126–130.

17. Marin and Gamba, "Expectations and Experiences of Hispanic Catholics and Converts to Protestant Churches," 6, 17.

18. Gilbert R. Cadena, "Chicano Clergy and the Emergence of Liberation Theology," *Hispanic Journal of Behavioral Sciences*, 11 (1989), 115.

19. Gonzáles and La Velle, *The Hispanic Catholic in the United States*, 162–164.

20. NCCB/USCC Secretariat for Hispanic Affairs, "National Survey on Hispanic Ministry," 6–7.

21. Antonio Gramsci, *Selections from Prison Notebooks* (New York: International, 1971), 181–182.

22. Otto Maduro, *Religion and Social Conflict* (Maryknoll, NY: Orbis Books, 1982), 87–88.

23. Ada María Isasi-Díaz and Yolanda Tarango,

Hispanic Women, Prophetic Voice in the Church (San Francisco: Harper and Row, 1988), 104–109.

24. Phillip Berryman, *Liberation Theology* (New York: Pantheon, 1987), 6.

25. Leonardo Boff and Clodovis Boff, *Introducing Liberation Theology* (Maryknoll, NY: Orbis Books, 1987) 2–3.

26. Gustavo Gutierrez, *A Theology of Liberation* (Maryknoll, NY: Orbis Books, 1973), 36–37.

27. Boff and Boff, *Introducing Liberation Theology*, 33–34.

28. Boff and Boff, *Introducing Liberation Theology*, 39.

29. See Virgilio Elizondo, *Galilean Journey: The Mexican American Promise* (Maryknoll, NY: Orbis Books, 1983); Andres G. Guerrero, *A Chicano Theology* (Maryknoll, NY: Orbis Books, 1987).

30. Elizondo, *Galilean Journey: The Mexican American Promise*, 104.

31. Elizondo, *Galilean Journey: The Mexican American Promise*, 104.

32. Isasi-Díaz and Tarango, *Hispanic Women, Prophetic Voice in the Church*, x.

33. Isasi-Díaz and Tarango, *Hispanic Women, Prophetic Voice in the Church*, 103.

34. Isasi-Díaz and Tarango, *Hispanic Women, Prophetic Voice in the Church*, pp. 6–7.

35. Ada Maria Isasi-Díaz, "Mujerista: A Name of Our Own," in Marc H. Ellis and Otto Maduro (eds.), *Future of Liberation Theology: Essays in Honor of Gustavo Gutierrez* (Maryknoll, NY: Orbis Books, 1989), 411.

36. Isasi-Díaz, "Mujerista: A Name of Our Own," 411.

37. Isasi-Díaz, "Mujerista: A Name of Our Own," 416.

38. Isasi-Díaz, "Mujerista: A Name of Our Own," 416.

39. See Allan Figueroa Deck (ed.), *Frontiers of Hispanic Theology in the United States* (Maryknoll, NY: Orbis Books, 1992); Robert S. Goizueta (ed.), *We Are People! Initiatives in Hispanic American Theology* (Minneapolis: Fortress Press, 1992); Justo L. Gonzáles (ed.), *Voces: Voices from the Hispanic Church* (Nashville: Abingdon Press, 1992); María Pilar Aquino, *Our Cry for Life: Feminist Theology from Latin America* (Maryknoll, NY: Orbis Books, 1993): and Jeanette Rodriguez, *Our Lady of Guadalupe: Faith and Empowerment among Mexican American Women* (Austin: University of Texas Press, 1994).

40. Centro de Reflexion e Investigación Pastoral Teologica. "An Occasion for Reflection: The 500 Years." Letter to Apostolic Pro Nuncio to the United States (August 1, 1991), 4.

41. "Tonantzin, my godmother. Crying woman of many centuries, the roses on the hillside still blossom, the struggle of the people will be the song of victory . . . Indian Mother Tonantzin, continues by foot, resisting; and in your roving footsteps, no one has been able to conquer you. The corn continues to grow, nourishing hope. And the Indian writes her history, the Indian will never be buried!" Lyrics by Rosa Martha Zárate Macías. "Tonantzin, Madre Tierra." *Abya Yala* cassette tape (San Bernardino, CA, 1992). Translated by authors.

10

OF *CORRIDOS* AND CONVICTS: *GRINGO* (IN)JUSTICE IN EARLY BORDER BALLADS AND CONTEMPORARY *PINTO* POETRY

RAÚL HOMERO VILLA

> *. . . a great many men and women who up till*
> *then would never have thought of producing a*
> *literary work, now that they find themselves*
> *in exceptional circumstances—in prison, with*
> *the Maquis, or on the eve of their execution—*
> *feel the need to speak to their nation, to*
> *compose the sentence which expresses the*
> *heart of the people, and to become the*
> *mouthpiece of a new reality in action.[1]*
> —Frantz Fanon, *The Wretched of the Earth*

Two recent Hollywood films that deal wholly, or in large part, with Chicanos in and around the prison system, have brought to mass cultural view an experience long since known to the Chicano population, but not often recognized, much less understood, by the general U.S. public. Edward James Olmos' *American Me* (1991) and Taylor Hackford's *Bound by Honor* (1993) have, in different ways, cast light on the complex subculture of the *pinto*, or Chicano prisoner. Neither film is squeamish in its representation of the violence inherent to this subculture. *American Me* is particularly relentless in this respect, as part of Olmos' stated intention to "scare straight" young Chicanos away from *la vida loca* (the crazy life). But violence is not the only aspect of the *pinto* experience represented in the films. In both productions, there are important *pinto* characters whose sense of their condition as prisoners includes a sociopolitical consciousness. This consciousness acknowledges that Chicanos, along with African Americans, constitute a disproportionately large percentage of the U.S. prison population. Such knowledge, however, does not point to an innate Chicano propensity for crime, but, rather, identifies the effects of the Chicano community's generally subordinate social and economic status within a structure of racially organized power in this country.

The point to be made, therefore, is that justice is *not* blind, as the official rhetoric of the U.S. judicial and penal systems claim. The experience of *gringo* (in)justice has been a constant fact of Chicano history, and it has just as constantly been a theme of Chicano expressive culture. Specifically, in this chapter, I will plot a continuum between popular balladry in early Chicano culture and the contestative expressions of recent Chicano and Chicana prison poetry. I argue that the earlier ballads functioned, retrospectively, as a cultural taproot for the contemporary writers, providing models of social criticism, thematic strategies, and narrative or generic conventions that are adapted and transformed by socially critical *pinto* poets.

INTERCULTURAL CONFLICT: THE HISTORICAL CONTEXT OF BORDER BALLADRY AND CRITICAL PINTO POETRY

As Américo Paredes has ably demonstrated, the historical relations of *mexicano* and Anglo-American communities in what is now the U.S. Southwest have led *mexicanos* to produce a wealth of folklore whose dominant theme is "intercultural conflict."[2] In expressions as diverse as cross-cultural/out-group naming (and name-calling), jokes, and popular song, *mexicanos* fashioned popular cultural forms that creatively mediated their experiences and opinions of contact and conflict with the growing population and culture of *los gringos*.

The premier expressive practice to take up the theme of intercultural conflict was undoubtedly the *corrido*, or ballad tradition. The reasons for its primacy as a popular symbolic practice have been well documented.[3] *Corridos* were used to tell stories about any events of consequence or curiosity for the *mexicano* community, ranging from natural disasters to train robberies to military battles. However, during the period of the *corrido's* ascendancy (approximately 1836–1930) its narrative repertoire focused increasingly toward "one theme, the border conflict; [and] one concept of the hero, the man[4] fighting for his right with his pistol in his hand."[5] Self-defense, however, is only part of the reason compelling the hero of border conflict. He is almost always motivated to fight for the rights of fellow Mexicans as well as his own. Examples include Gregorio Cortez, who killed two Texas sheriffs after one of them shot his brother; Jacinto Treviño, who avenges his brother's death by killing several Americans; Rito García, who shoots several Anglo officers for unlawfully searching his home and harassing its residents; and Aniceto Pizaña, whose band of *sediciosos* (seditionists) set out to overthrow Anglo-American rule in South Texas.[6] The *corrido* and its border Mexican audience, then, identified the individual hero's plight as representative of the repression increasingly experienced (in proportion to the increase of the Anglo-American population in the U.S. Southwest) by the collective Mexican-descent population. In this way the *corrido*, in its epic heroic genre, provided the first sustained popular narrativization of the Chicano experience of *gringo* (in)justice within the imposed borders of the U.S. Southwest.

In its glorification of the hero's armed response to the *rinches'* (Texas Rangers) violation of his own or his community's civil and human rights, the *corrido* narrativized popular Mexican wisdom regarding the Anglo-American legal establishment. In "Rito García," for example, the hero wisely reasons,

Conociendo bien las leyes	(Knowing well how the law works
del país americano,	in the American nation,
me pasé a buscar abrigo	I went in search of refuge
a mi suelo mexicano	on my own Mexican soil.)

And when he is later tried in a Texas court:

Allí no alcancé clemencia,	(There I found no mercy,
ni me quisieron oír,	they didn't even listen to me,
pues voy a la penitencía	now I'll go to prison
eternamente a sufrir.	and suffer all my life.
. . .	. . .
. . . voy a la penitencía	I'm going to prison
por defender mi derecho.[7]	for defending my rights.)

The heroic narrative tradition has produced the most potent and lasting *corridos* of social conflict and resistance. At a more fundamental level, the existence of the present United States-Mexico border, already a major condition of possibility for the heroic *corrido* genre, would itself become a fundamental theme and narrative element in the creative mediations of intercultural conflict.

In a purely practical sense, the formation of a new geopolitical boundary line between the United States and Mexico in 1848 required, from the Anglo-American perspective, that it be regulated, administered, and policed. The border line itself, marking the defeat of Mexico in the Mexican-American War, became for *mexicanos* on both sides another violation under the rubric of intercultural conflict. Consider, as Américo Paredes describes it, that when the Rio Grande "became a dividing line instead of a focus for normal activity, it broke apart an area that had once been a unified homeland. People ended up with friends and relatives living in what had legally become a foreign land, hedged in by all kinds of immigration and customs restrictions."[8] The disruption of kinship and community networks, of the normal forms of social intercourse and commerce was understood by many border Mexicans as a related violation to the violent physical assaults by the *rinches*. As such, "illegal activities" that undermined the United States' regulation of border transit and exchange were often represented in *mexicano* folklore as forms of incipient rebellion whereby the "smuggler, the illegal alien looking for work, and the border-conflict hero became identified in the popular mind. They came in conflict with the same American laws and often with the same individual officers of the law, who were all looked upon as *rinches* . . ."[9] Such perceptions expressed a clear logic of resistance. The folkloric idealization of the smuggler and "illegal alien" rhetorically subverted official government definitions of criminality. Furthermore, by equating officers of the law with *rinches*, United States enforcement agencies were semantically identified with the oppressiveness of the *rinches*.

In the *corrido* poetics of intercultural conflict, there is an intuitive articulation of dissent from Anglo-American discourses and categories of justice and legality. These social poetics also contained thematic elements and discursive strategies that would be taken up by critically conscious *pinto* poets. In the dominant heroic narrative, for example, although the fate of the hero was often violent death at the hands of a large posse of *rinches*, imprisonment was sometimes the result, as in the case of Rito García, cited above, and Gregorio Cortez, the most famous *corrido* hero.

Although Cortez is drawn into violent retribution and flight because of the unjust shooting of his brother by a Texas sheriff, he is not shot in the field of action, but rather tried in a court of law. "Rito García," which precedes "Gregorio Cortez" by sixteen years, alludes to the actual trial experience. García, quite aware of the *rinches'* "field justice," and "knowing well how the law works in the United States" flees to Mexico. But when he is betrayed and sent back to the American authorities, his intuition about the U.S. legal system is borne out: "I found no clemency there; they would not even listen to me."[10]

The hero's sense of inevitable guilt within the United States' legal system resurfaces constantly in later *pinto* poetry as a politicized popular insight, fueled by the escalated Chicano-police conflict of the urban barrios. Raúl Salinas expresses this sensibility powerfully in his classic poem "Un Trip Through the Mind Jail":

> Ratón: 20 years for a matchbox of weed. Is that cold?
> No lawyer   no jury   no trial   i'm guilty
> Aren't we all guilty?[11]

The interrogative "Is that cold?" asks a rhetorical question: "Is this what you call justice?" And, of course, disproportionate punishment, with scarce recourse to fair judicial process, is what passes for "justice" in the experience of many Chicanos.[12] Furthermore, the commonness of this experience in the modern barrio allows Ratón's "cold" experience to represent another instance of the individual-collective nexus which made the *corrido* such a potent symbolic expression of its audience's cultural, group perspective: If "i'm guilty / Aren't we all guilty?"

The poetic expressions of an individual-collective nexus often mirrored the actual involvement of the Chicano community in key legal conflicts that were then creatively rendered in oral and literary texts. In the case of the greatest *corrido* hero, Gregorio Cortez, the lyrical narrative ends precisely where the historical narrative of his community's activism begins: when he is brought to trial. His legal battles over the next three years were no less dramatic than the tales of his pursuit and capture. Although only one man was on trial, the larger Chicano community became a collective protagonist, with their efforts leading not only to support for Cortez's defense, but to the formation of a number of tentative civic organizations that lasted beyond the trial and appeal process. According to Américo Paredes, "Gregorio Cortez and the *corrido* about him are a milestone in the Mexican-American's emerging group consciousness. . . . The readiness with which Mexicans in the United States came together in his defense showed that the necessary conditions existed for united effort."[13]

In 1942, the mass trial of Chicano "gang" youths for the murder of José Díaz, popularly known as "The Case of Sleepy Lagoon," revealed similar conditions for united effort. The Sleepy Lagoon Defense Committee, a broad based coalition of Chicanos and sympathetic non-Chicanos, carried on its battle in the face of legal proceedings that have been amply documented as a farce of justice and due process.[14] This case deserves particular mention here not simply because of the sensational nature of the events or its notable place in the Chicano historical and popular imagination. Of equal or greater significance is the very way in which the charges were made. Not one, or even a few, but twenty-two members of the 38th Street Club were accused of criminal conspiracy. By the logic of this collective accusation, every defendant, even if he had nothing to do with the killing of Díaz, could be charged with his death. Guilt by cultural association was never so clearly and officially revealed.[15] Alfredo Mirandé, in his book *Gringo Justice*, appropriately titled a chapter on this case, "Sleepy Lagoon: The Chicano Community on Trial."[16] In the trial of Gregorio Cortez, the Chicano community understood and reacted to the collective resonances of an individual Chicano's battle with the Anglo-American legal system. Conversely, the Sleepy Lagoon case exposed the ideological notion that Mexicans were culturally prone to criminal violence. This view, which traced Chicanos' supposed blood lust back to the sacrificial practices of Aztec society, was openly expressed in a report presented by Capt. E. Duran Myers, Chief of the Los Angeles County Sheriff's Office Foreign Relations Bureau, to the Grand Jury investigating "Mexican juvenile delinquency" at the time of the trial.[17] The Chicano community *was* on trial, as the mass indictments and inflammatory Mexican-baiting yellow journalism made painfully evident to Chicanos in Los Angeles and elsewhere. The oppressive truism critiqued by Raúl Salinas ("i'm guilty/Aren't we all guilty?") was presaged by such historical evidence as this.

FROM LA PENITENCIA TO LA PINTA: TRADITIONAL VISIONS AND CRITICAL REVISIONS OF THE PRISON EXPERIENCE

Thus far we have considered certain themes and socially critical insights, produced within and against the history of intercultural border conflict, which were given their first sustained narrativization in the heroic tradition of the *corrido*, and carried on in some recent Chicano prisoner poetry. This comparative analysis suggests a partial history of the folkloric roots of contemporary Chicano literature. However, in order to specify the particular genealogy of *pinto* poetics, we must identify *corrido* accounts of the prison experience itself as they contribute to the larger master narrative of intercultural conflict. Though the examples are far fewer than the dominant heroic narratives, the prisoner *corrido* is a specific precursor to critical *pinto* poetry. In rare instances as well, the heroic *corrido* may allude to the prison experience. "Rito García," for example, includes two brief references to the hero's impending penitentiary fate (though it does not substantially reflect on his actual imprisonment). To its credit, the text does reveal one anticipated detail of imprisonment, which at first reading or listening might seem merely a generic figure of speech:

Me voy a la penitencia,	(I'm going to prison,
porque así lo quiso la suerte,	as luck would have it,
voy a arrastrar la cadena	I'll be dragging a chain
hasta que venga la muerte.[18]	until the day I die.)

Considering the *rinche* field justice usually meted out to the border conflict hero, García's prison sentence substitutes a death-in-stasis for a death-in-flight. This notion of imprisonment as a form of death-in-life figures prominently in much of the critical *pinto* tradition. Lorrie Martínez provides a compelling example of this institutional violation of the *pinto*.

> There's nothing left to say.
> I will die a slow death,
>
> they have tortured my mind
> physically my body is
> bruised and my heart is cold.
>
> In the smoke I could
> smell the dead bodies. . . .[19]

Raúl Salinas, relatedly, composed a eulogy for a fellow *pinto*:

> . . . he died. . .
>   2 years later—
> in the putrefying bowels
>   of a dismal prison—
> death's impact
>   SLAPS!
> the face of consciousness
>   and jars the torpid brain
>   AWAKE![20]

Américo Paredes has described how the "prisoner's song usually shows us the protagonist in his cell, yearning for his sweetheart or mother, counting the prison bars or listening for the footsteps of the executioner—all the while consoled by an angel or little bird."[21] He also notes the prisoner's characteristic repentance or regret for his criminal activity. These elements comprise a narrative genre of the sorrows of the prisoner. This genre is typically void of the explicit social critique so present in the border-hero narratives, tending mostly toward a confessional melodrama. Significant exceptions exist, however, in which a prisoner *corrido* manifests a clear critique of the U.S. judicial system. "Manuel Garza de León" is such an exception, since as Paredes argues it

> is not so much about the "sorrows of the prisoner" as it is about the intercultural conditions that have put the protagonist behind the bars. A man goes to prison under laws he had no part in making, according to concepts of justice he does not understand. He feels that he is in prison . . . because he is a Mexican. . . . It was not a judge who sentenced Manuel to thirty years; it was an "American." And the prison guards who harass him with their dogs are called *rinches* too.[22]

The *corrido* of "Manuel Garza de León," which dates from around 1915, is a precursory model for reading socially critical *pinto* writing. Unlike the typical prisoner ballad, this one expresses a critical insight, in the best tradition of the heroic *corrido*, that lays bare the over-determined racial ideologies in the dominant discourses and practices of justice and punishment. In light of this popular critique, which would be quite apparent to the ballad's native audience, even the melodramatic details which describe the suffering of the prisoner and his loved ones serve a critical cause by highlighting the subjective, emotional effects of this injustice.

While there are countless examples of the uncritical use of sentimentality by contemporary *pinto* poets, many follow the example of "Manuel Garza de León" by using the melodramatic *corrido* conventions in the service of a social critique. Sometimes this takes the form of directly evoking a precursory *corrido* text. Such is the case with Ricardo Sánchez, who in "EXISTIR ES . . . an experiment in writing in and around a few songs from the *barrio*"[23] uses, among other songs, "El Contrabando de El Paso" as a counterpoint in narrating his quest for a Chicano identity. Sánchez freely associates with images from this *corrido* of a prisoner's laments, using them as impressionistic punctuation to his own existential odyssey. For example, when "oblivion loomed on the horizon as my only destination," he evokes the *corrido* protagonist's own question of destination: *"le pregunto a mister hill/que si vamos pa' luisiana . . ."*, while the train in the *corrido* recalls how "the train of my thoughts still rannnnnn on and on. . . ."[24] Similarly, the *corrido* protagonists' sentencing to Leavenworth evokes how Sánchez "was encloistered in a prison of inculcated hates" and in an actual prison.

More common than the suturing of a traditional *corrido* text into the *pinto* text is the reworking of the prisoner ballad's generic elements in the narrative and thematic poetics of the *pinto* text. Two related, generic elements have been consistently transformed in this way. One is the force and meaning of grief, both in the prisoner's lament and (generally) the mother's sorrow; the other is the tone of moralism or moral censure. In the traditional melodramatic narrative, the prisoner's lament is often focused on a twin regret. First, of the painful fate which has befallen him; and second, of the pain he has caused his loved ones, especially his mother. The latter motif is evident in "El Contrabando de El Paso," when the convict narrator typically seeks his *"madre idolatrada/ [para] pedirle la bendición"* ("beloved mother/ [to] ask for her blessing"), or concludes with an offering of his affection (and of his song, as well), as if in reparation for his filial shortcomings: *"Ahi te dejo, mamacita,/un suspiro y un abrazo. . . ."* ("Mother of mine,/I leave you a sigh and an embrace. . . ").[25] Raúl Salinas, in the dedication that opens his book, *Un Trip Through the Mind Jail y Otras Excursiones*,[26] invokes a similar appeal in offering the poems to his mother:

> Amá, whether you read
> this or not;
> Here's hoping
> it makes up
> for
> the graduation picture
> (cap/gown & diploma)
> that never graced
> your class-confusing
> cuarto de sala.

And yet, even as he employs a conventional motif, he transforms it by using it to illustrate a political critique of U.S. foreign policy. For example, later in the dedication, he asks his mother to accept his poem as compensation:

> Also, for the
> lack of first-after-
> basic training
> photos proving
> involvement in
> immoral wars.[27]

Luis Talamántez, in "Reflections of a Convict"[28] engages a sustained meditation on the cultural-critical wisdom born of the sufferings of his "aged abuela." The principal lesson of her wisdom, not surprisingly, is the knowledge of intercultural conflict. From her own experience she came to know:

> The ways of the pale foreigners
> In our land and way of life
>   always the bringer of our troubles
>   . . . the inquisitors
> Beckoning to us with their crook'd finger
> their rednecks and panzas swollen with poisons
>   . . . of greed and consumption—their eyes hard like hearts . . .
> calling us to come to them
>
> To be abused, used and screwed.[29]

This socially critical knowledge is further illustrated by the intimate violation of her own family's wholeness by the military and judicial institutions of the U.S. government.

> It was not enough that they had taken
> Grandma's sons away to war—
> but that they've taken her grandsons
> to jail. . . .
>
> . . .
>
> No one would think to convince grandma that the gringo
> did not take her son away . . . long ago
> Just to leave him far away . . . on Iwo Jima
>
> . . .
>
> Now no one can tell her that the gringo
> does not have her nieto prisoner
> > hurting him silently as our people
>
> have learned to be hurt and defeated,
> > keeping him
> > > so that she may never see him again either.[30]

Here Talamántez shows that the *abuela's* grief is not simply an emotional response to overwhelming circumstances, a powerless response to a fate beyond her control. Her lament reveals an experiential political consciousness in which a pointed ideological critique of "gringo" institutional practices is expressed in an ·emotive register.

This critical articulation of grief is a revision of the generic lament that is its precursor, for in the traditional narration of the mother's (and the prisoner's) grief, *fortuna* (fate), *destino* (destiny), *suerte* (luck), and *la mano de Dios* (the hand, or will, of God) figure prominently as explanations for being imprisoned. We may recall here Rito García's statement that *"asi lo quiso la suerte."* Implicit in the traditional narrative, then, is a resignation or sense of acceptance which precludes any questioning of the possible racial and political over-determinations of the prisoner's "fate." Quite the contrary in Talamántez's poem, where the *abuela* knows only too clearly that her grief does not respond to heavenly whims but to concrete institutional practices (prison, the draft) acting against her family and her community.

The revision of popular, or "typical" perceptions as critical consciousness is central to the strategic intention of socially conscious *pinto* writing. Raúl Salinas, for one, shows the traditional unreflective resignation of the mother in "Un Trip . . . ".

> Indian mothers, too unaware
> of courtroom tragi-comedies
> folded arms across their bosoms
> saying, "Sea por Dios" [It's God's will].[31]

only to subvert such religious mystifications elsewhere:

> And so, dear friend & brother,
>   The System
>   (not God!)
>   created you . . .
>   that system
>   took
>   you
>   away.[32]

As Salinas sets up a tension between an uncritical popular perception (the will of God) and his own critical perception of "The System," so too do other *pintos* inscribe this tension in the relations between characters in their poems, textualizing the consciousness-raising that their poems hope to spark in the reader.

In "A Visit With Mama"[33] Pancho Aguila confronts, consoles, and tries to convert the "misery/my mother cries about . . . ," by redirecting her grief through a critical social analysis:

> . . . I tell her
> the misery is in the world—
> I am not the beast—
> the beast lives on the outside
> devouring the country

By inverting the moral and critical hierarchies embedded in his mother's misery, the poet offers a transformative vision of a reconstructed social landscape:

> I tell her, cheer up,
> the sweet wine
> clears against the sun.
> All my visions
> are a marble of song
> sculpting the temple
> in offering to a new world.

Similarly, in "Mt. Tamalpais,"[34] the protagonist must reconcile the memory of his *tío's* view of prison with his own socially critical perspective born of "nearly nine years of prison/ in the waters of life."

> over-looking San Quentin
> where my Tío Tonio once told me,
> "Bad men live there."
> Now, listening to the comrade teacher,
> "Many revolutionaries come from prison." (Ibid)

Such inversions of a dominant moral hierarchy voiced in the common sense of Tío Tonio ("Bad men live there.") is a major critical thrust of the contestative *pinto* tradition. This tradition employs a radical, oppositional method of reinterpreting many pronouncements of dominant American social discourse to uncover their ideological biases. In their poetics, these *pintos* are, as José D. Saldívar has noted of other Chicano poetry, "offering concrete theories of social resistance."[35] This oppositional poetics is powerfully employed by Raúl Salinas in "El Tecato."[36] Salinas evokes the dominant moral rhetoric that is applied to the *tecato* (junkie) and then with biting irony juxtaposes it to his unflagging paternal responsibility:

> that scourge . . . that social leper
> beamed with pride
>   because he knew he could
> (in spite of sickness)
>   well provide [for his children].[37]

Salinas then gives a more accurate and humane assessment of the *tecato* as

> a sick, addicted father/brother/son,
> who recognized his children's need
>   for food and nourishment
> while no one recognized his need
>   for drugs of treatment[38]

And yet, to subvert the moralistic judgments applied to the *tecato* is not enough, for the actual life history of Elías Perales, on which the poem is based, shows us how the social power of moralistic rhetoric can transcend semantics in the exercise of deadly material force:

> So the predators [narcotics officers] gunned him down
>   in the manner of that social madness
> that runs rampant across the land,
>   dressing itself in the finery & raiments of
>   JUSTIFIABLE HOMICIDE!!![39]

These indeed are the empire's new clothes, its discursive "finery & raiments," nakedly revealed by Salinas' penetrating critical vision.

Clearly, Salinas dismantles the duplicitous facade of dominant legal and moral rhetorics, exposing to view some tragic effects of their institutional enforcements.

Such discrepancies between U.S. dominant discourses and the real life experiences of oppressed people exemplifies the sort of compelling duplicities that similarly inspired *corridistas* to make cultural heroes of so-called "criminals" and "bandits." In the poetics of these *corridistos* and *pintos*, laying bare what the dominant discourses really say is the first step towards what Fanon described as "a new reality in action.[40]

NOTES

1. Frantz Fanon, *The Wretched of the Earth* (New York, Grove Press, 1963), 223.

2. Américo Paredes, *A Texas-Mexican Cancionero: Folksongs of the Lower Border* (Urbana: University of Illinois Press, 1976); *"With His Pistol in His Hand": A Border Ballad and Its Hero* (Austin: University of Texas Press, 1982 [originally published in 1958]).

3. José E. Limón, "The Rise, Fall and 'Revival' of the Mexican-American Ballad: A Review Essay," *Studies in Latin American Popular Culture*, 2 (1983): 202–207; Américo Paredes, *"With His Pistol in His Hand": A Border Ballad and Its Hero*; John Holmes McDowell, "The *Corrido* of Greater Mexico as Discourse, Music, and Event," in Richard Bauman and Roger D. Abrahams (eds.), *"And Other Neighborly Names": Social Processes and Cultural Image in Texas Folklore* (Austin: University of Texas Press, 1981), 44–75.

4. The hero of border conflict was invariably male, showing a clear patriarchal, or male-dominant, perspective in the genre. This perspective assumed that it was predominantly, if not exclusively, a man's role to act publicly, and often violently, to defend himself as well as "his" family, "his" property, and "his" land. Befitting such a gendered bias, women in the corridos were typically invisible, made dependent on a man, or, in the worst cases, figured as treacherous. For an analysis of the representation of women in the *corrido* tradition see María Herrera-Sobek, *The Mexican Corrido: A Feminist Analysis* (Bloomington: Indiana University Press, 1990).

5. Américo Paredes, *"With His Pistol in His Hand": A Border Ballad and Its Hero*, 149.

6. Pizaña unsuccessfully attempted to establish a Spanish-speaking republic in South Texas in 1915 using guerilla insurgency and appeals to other racial minority groups throughout the Southwest as his principal actions. His appeal to coalition and armed rebellion was laid out in a document called "El plan de San Diego," named after the town of San Diego, Texas from which he launched his campaign.

7. Transcribed in Paredes, *A Texas-Mexican Cancionero*, 58). The translations throughout this essay are my own.

8. Paredes, *A Texas-Mexican* Cancionero, 43.

9. Américo Paredes, "The Problem of Identity in a Changing Culture: Popular Expressions of Culture Conflict along the Lower Rio Grande Border," in Stanley R. Ross (ed.), *Views Across the Border: The United States and Mexico* (Albuquerque: University of New Mexico Press, 1978), 75.

10. Transcribed in Paredes, *A Texas-Mexican* Cancionero, 59.

11. Raúl R. Salinas, *Un Trip Through the Mind Jail Y Otras Excursiones* (San Francisco: Editorial Pocho-Che, 1980), 58–59.

12. Armando Morales, *Ando Sangrando (I Am Bleeding): A Study of Mexican American-Police Conflict* (La Puente, CA: Perspectiva Publications, 1972).

13. Paredes, *A Texas-Mexican* Cancionero, 31.

14. Carey McWilliams, *North From Mexico: The Spanish-Speaking People of the United States* (New York: Greenwood Press, 1948), 228–233; Alfredo Mirandé, *Gringo Justice* (Notre Dame, IN: Notre Dame University Press, 1987), 156–172; Rodolfo Acuña, *Occupied America: A History of Chicanos*, 3rd edition (New York: Harper & Row, 1988), 255–256.

15. The charges of criminal conspiracy were never upheld, although seventeen of the defendants were found guilty of a variety of crimes ranging from assault to first-degree murder. The battle for justice by the Sleepy Lagoon Defense Committee, however, brought about a unanimous decision on appeal reversing all the lower court rulings, but only after the defendants had spent nearly two years in jail, unable to procure the necessary bail during the long appeal process. In Rodolfo Acuña, *Occupied America: A History of Chicanos*, 255–256.

16. Alfredo Mirandé, *Gringo Justice*.

17. McWilliams, *North From Mexico*, 233–235.

18. Transcribed in Paredes, *A Texas-Mexican* Cancionero, 58. My emphasis.
19. Lorri Martínez, "Slow Death," *Where Eagles Fall* (Brunswick, ME: Blackberry Press, 1982), n.p.
20. Raúl R. Salinas, "In Memoriam: Riche," *Un Trip Through the Mind Jail*, 49–50.
21. Paredes, *A Texas-Mexican* Cancionero, 44.
22. Paredes, *A Texas-Mexican* Cancionero, 44–45.
23. Ricado Sánchez, *Canto y Grito Mi Liberación* (Garden City, NY: Anchor Books, 1973), 144–153.
24. Sánchez, *Canto y Grito Mi Liberación*, 152.
25. Paredes, *A Texas-Mexican* Cancionero, 104.
26. Salinas, *Un Trip Through the Mind Jail.*
27. Salinas, "Dedicatoria," *Un Trip Through the Mind Jail*, 16.
28. Luis Talamantez, "Reflections of a Convict," *Bilingual Review*, 4.1-2 (1977): 123–125. Reprinted with permission of copyright holder, Bilingual Press/Editorial Bilingüe, Arizona State University, Tempe, AZ.
29. Talamantez, "Reflections of a Convict," 123.
30. Talamantez, "Reflections of a Convict," 124–125.
31. Salinas, *Un Trip Through the Mind Jail*, 60.
32. Salinas, *Un Trip Through the Mind Jail,*. 49–50.
33. Pancho Aguila, *11 Poems*, Chapbook published as part of *Mango*, 1.3-4: n.p.
34. Aguila, *11 Poems*, n.p.
35. José David Saldívar, "Towards a Chicano Poetics: The Making of the Chicano Subject, 1969–1982," *Confluencia: Revista Hispánica de Cultura y Literatura*, 1.2 (1986): 10–17, 10.
36. Salinas, *Un Trip Through the Mind Jail*, 52.
37. Salinas, *Un Trip Through the Mind Jail*, 52.
38. Salinas, *Un Trip Through the Mind Jail*, 52.
39. Salinas, *Un Trip Through the Mind Jail*, 52.
40. Fanon, *The Wretched of the Earth*, 223.

11

CHICANO CULTURAL RESISTANCE WITH MASS MEDIA

DIANA I. RÍOS

The mass media are mainstream Anglo American, pervasive and influential in our society. Socialized in part by a widely encompassing Eurocentric media, Chicanos have encountered the potential danger of losing distinct cultural values and ethnic group identification. In spite of a long history of engagement with mainstream print media, radio, television, and a tremendous variety of popular culture mainstream products, Mexican American[1] audiences have withstood and progressed through the onslaught of all too often antagonistic media. I have no intention of becoming an apologist for the Hollywood culture machine or for the status quo manufacture of news.

However, there are important elements among Chicano audience members that have mediated the impact of culturally hostile mainstream media, and these mediating factors need to be investigated and explained. A "magic bullet" theory of direct media impact cannot explain the linkage that average adults have with mass media, nor can it elucidate the process by which Chicanos discriminantly negotiate forms of communication for sustenance and advancement in the United States. To say the least, the long-time defunct magic bullet theory, which posits that messages from media sources become inserted into the unsuspecting minds of the public, does not account for individual difference characteristics among the masses nor for individual needs and intentions for mass media.

In media studies, a more common approach to the study of media and audiences has been to acknowledge that audiences are not unwary dupes. Building from this premise, researchers have been shedding more light on the linkages between audience identities, cultural allegiances, and discernible media use practices. Within the new era of audience investigation, I posit that Chicanos use media for two culturally significant functions or purposes that are unique, along with more general intentions. Within the two functions of cultural and structural assimilation and cultural maintenance are processes in which Chicanos are involved. The process of "purposive" media use for Chicanos entails resistance and conditional acceptance of mainstream culture elements, which make media content useful and meaningful. This process is dominant culture resistance coupled with selective acculturation. The processes of resistance and conditional acceptance of mainstream media are what I identify as forms of struggle within a Euro-American dominated cultural system. In addition, given the availability of ethnic-oriented media, Chicanos can selectively use Chicano-Latino[2] media content for maintaining cultural values and fortifying a sense of Mexican American group belonging. The companion process with ethnic-oriented media is not equivalently demanding of resistance because these media allow many more opportunities for Chicano cultural maintenance.

This investigation is based on a qualitative interview sample of thirty-eight Mexican-heritage adults in Austin, Texas. It was designed to address the following key questions about Mexican-American cultural functions for mainstream and Chicano-oriented mass media:

1. In what ways are Chicanos using mainstream and Chicano television, radio, and newspapers for purposes of acculturation and structural assimilation?
2. In what ways are Chicanos using mainstream and Chicano television, radio, and newspapers for purposes of cultural maintenance and ethnic group reinforcement?

Media use for cultural maintenance describes a process of upkeeping Chicano cultural values and ethnic group identification, and is therefore resistant to dominant mainstream culture and more accepting of Chicano culture. Media use for acculturation (cultural level assimilation) describes the use of media to support cultural change toward dominant Anglo values and norms. Chicanos can use media for selective acculturation in order to learn cultural interaction and survival skills necessary in an Anglo-American world.

A closely related process to media use for acculturation is media use for structural level assimilation (or integration). Chicanos want access and participatory opportunities in social, educational, political, and economic realms of U.S. society that are Anglo controlled and dominated. Mass media can be used selectively to help obtain these goals by providing information and cultural knowledge.

Overall, the relationship that Chicanos have with media is complex and cannot be simply understood as a direct impact process from media to passive consumer. The functions of the mass media for Chicanos are multiple and non-mutually exclusive. Cultural resistance to dominant culture is among the most relevant exercises for Chicanos within the dual function framework, because this practice allows Chicanos to protect positive ethnic group identity from the Eurocentric agenda of mass media. Chicano-Latino media and popular media forms typically are used as an imperfect cultural refuge for Mexican-heritage audiences.

FUNCTIONS OF COMMUNICATION: MEDIA USES AND GRATIFICATIONS

"Media uses and gratifications" describes a functionalistic relationship that audiences have with communication sources and source content. Audience members are said to be goal-oriented, and thus seek out and use interpersonal and mass communication that will satisfy (gratify) particular needs or goals. The development of the mass media uses and gratifications approach occurred in conjunction with a research movement away from an all-powerful media effects position in mass communication research. Attributing the mass media with almost boundless potential to manipulate and influence the public had previously eclipsed concerns with individual differences.[3] Uses and gratifications is not yet a single grand theory, nor has it been through a development phase that squarely addresses media use and gratifications based on non-Anglo-American media or audiences. Fortunately, the flexible quality of the uses and gratifications model allows for the integration of theory that can better explain media use and gratifications among ethnic minority population groups.

Theoretical incorporations are important when addressing ethnic media users such as Mexican Americans during this current era of uses and gratifications related research because of the necessary introduction of theories of culture and ethnicity. The uses and gratifications approach has been used in conjunction with other theories in studies such as those on white ethnics in Cleveland[4] and Mexican Americans in the Southwest.[5] While the Southwest landmark research project was mostly descriptive, the other study incorporates theories of acculturation, assimilation, and ethnic persistence. Some attempts have been made within the realm of uses and gratifications to explain differential ethnic audience needs.[6] However, the lack of consistent cultural and ethnic considerations in uses and gratifications investigations has left much more to be explained for ethnic minority audiences.

AUDIENCE-CENTERED FUNCTIONS

One of the most important concepts in the uses and gratifications approach is the "active" or "purposive" audience. This conceptualization of audience contrasts with old beliefs of an all-powerful media, as well as with the assumption that media use is always a pastime or a reflection of chance. Aside from the instances where individuals may "just leave it [the TV] on" or are "too tired to change the channel," the uses and gratification model focuses on what are assumed to be the majority of selections, which can be motivated by psychological or sociological need. Audiences are conceptualized as exhibiting differential needs that "spring from their location in and interaction with their social environment."[7] Furthermore, audiences are assumed to be self-directed and even capable of circumscribing potential media-directed effects.[8] Though the concept of audience selectivity has gained more favor over the decades, the power that uses and gratifications attributes to audiences continues to be in debate.

Other issues that merit discussion are the valuable implications that uses and gratifications and similar approaches within audience-response literature[9] offer for improved audience research on historically disenfranchised populations. As detailed in the Chicano audience research by Ríos,[10] improved conceptualization of active, and thus more enfranchised, ethnic audiences can be possible within the arena of uses and gratifications. In the study at hand, where a Chicano uses and gratifications research framework is used, audiences become empowered, because they are allowed a more respectable position as purposive and not mindlessly consumptive beings. I posit that these theoretically enfranchised "active" audiences can be described as having at least two cultural-specific functions for media that are achieved through a complex relationship with media. This position contrasts with that which describes Chicanos as simply becoming acculturated by Euro-American mass media or otherwise being victimized by media messages.[11]

DATA SOURCE AND METHODS

Population Context and Respondents

Population data give the reader a clearer understanding of the social context from which respondents in this study come, and may also allow the reader to form some tacit comparisons to other Mexican Americans living in other parts of the United States. In Travis County, where Austin is located, 106,435 individuals identified themselves as Mexican origin. In the Austin capital, 93,323 individuals identified themselves as Mexican origin, where all Latinos (106,868) numbered 23 percent of the city's population[12]. Mexican-heritage people in Austin surely have a cultural presence in the city, but do not command the same sociopolitical power as do Chicanos in cities with higher Chicano concentrations.

The interview sample presented here was composed of thirty-eight Mexican-heritage adults (nineteen women and nineteen men) between the ages of twenty-two and fifty-five years old who lived in Austin, Texas or in bordering cities. Respondents' ages were mostly distributed in the thirties and forties. Proportionally, most respondents were born in the United States, while others were Mexican immigrants. In order to ensure diversity, interviews were conducted with members of the working and professional classes.

Procedure

The entire two-phase multimethodological study, on which this essay is partially based, was carried out from June 1992 to January 1993 in Austin, Texas.[13] The initial qualitative period of research spanned the period from June 1992 to September 1992, during which time I was in the field on a full-time basis and on occasions on a part-time basis.

There are important issues concerning data-gathering methods in uses and gratifications studies that are addressed in this investigation. First of all, uses and gratifications research is not usually conducted using qualitative methods. So, a standard "mainstream" interview schedule that asked non-cultural-specific questions about media would certainly have proven inadequate.[14] In light of the need for more latitude in question types asked to respondents and the need for me to gain more contextual community information, qualitative field methods were planned. The main and secondary procedures I used for qualitative data collection were face-to-face interviews and participant observation, respectively. Respondents were typically interviewed in their homes and were promised anonymity and confidentiality. The respondents were volunteers gained through "snowball" sampling, a sampling technique where respondents are gained through interpersonal networks.[15]

The interview guide I used in the field was composed of bilingual Spanish and English open-ended questions, and some closed-ended questions, by which to solicit direct information and a range of opinions. Questions were constructed from the following criteria, though this text focuses primarily on media-related responses: demographics; language usage; language abilities; language attitudes; cultural attitudes, cultural pride, and ethnic identification; sociostructural assimilation; media exposure; learning from media; and finally, media offering anything good to Mexican-heritage people. The following are some examples from the many questions that were asked during interviews:

1. Do you listen to the radio? What are some of your favorite stations? Why?
2. In your opinion, do you think *Arriba/La Prensa/ The Austin American-Statesman* has anything positive or good to offer people of Mexican background or heritage? Why? Why not?
3. In your opinion, can people of Mexican heritage learn anything from Univisión/the other English language channels? Why? Why not?

These questions presented above should not be confused with quantitative survey questions that are rigid and closed-ended by design. I exercised flexibility with questions when speaking with individuals, which made my agenda of questions, from specific criteria, not always possible or reasonable to use among all respondents. Furthermore, the open-ended nature of the questions gave respondents the opportunity to talk about issues that they personally thought were important. Sometimes, respondents reconstructed a question posed to them, and then proceeded to give their point of view.

FINDINGS FROM THE FIELD

Media Availability and Resistance

Chicano Austinites expressed awareness of the limited media offerings for the Mexican American community and saw this as connected with the potentially harmful effects of the media. To address the first issue, Mexican heritage people in greater Austin had a particular media menu from which to choose. Austin is served by the major television networks and is wired for cable television. Univisión was available with good reception by subscribing to cable, or could be viewed with reception interference without subscription. Only two Spanish-language radio stations catered to Austin listeners, while late at night in non-stormy weather Chicanos were blessed with radio signals from San Antonio stations (San Antonio is located about two hours away by speedy car). There was one large city paper, the *Austin American-Statesman* and a variety of alternative community papers. Two small, well-circulated papers, *Arriba* and *La Prensa*, focused on the Chicano communities in Austin and surrounding cities. For the size of the Chicano-Latino population in this capital city of Austin, I and others wondered why more ethnic-oriented media were not offered.

To address the second issue, when asked directly in the field, respondents tended to consider mass media not only limited in its helpfulness to Chicanos but also saw media in general as potentially clashing with Chicano values. These opinions indicated a tacit belief in a magic bullet phenomenon, and were much more commonly voiced opinions in formal and informal conversations than the academic opinion of mitigated impact. With the bulk of media offerings coming from the Anglo American perspective, individuals in the field would have considered the uses and gratifications model to be at least counterintuitive and probably outright wrong, even though they themselves demonstrated discriminant media use. I needed to rely on indirect responses in natural settings in order to discern ways in which Chicanos were making mainstream and Chicano media serve their needs. I argue that in spite of the relative paucity of Chicano content in Austin's mass media offerings, Mexican Americans exercise the ability to subvert media and use content that suits cultural goals. Cultural struggle with mainstream media through critical awareness and cultural reinterpretation must be a prerequisite for Chicanos to find Anglo American-constructed and controlled media entertaining or informative to any degree. Chicanos had well-founded concerns about media availability and content, but tended not to give others enough credit for processes of resistance and selective use for acculturation, structural assimilation, or cultural maintenance.

Media Functions for Linguistic Acculturation and Maintenance

Being bilingual was seen as a positive Chicano characteristic by almost all respondents with whom I spoke. Spanish was a facet of ethnic group identity which respondents did not want to lose, in spite of the pressure to communicate only in English in a dominant English-speaking environment. English was considered the language of the land and was perceived as one important step toward access to better education, careers, and living conditions. Cultivating or maintaining two languages was considered important in order to be competent in both Chicano and Anglo domains. The media, however, were not overwhelmingly considered to be the best avenues for learning or improving English (media function for linguistic acculturation) or strengthening Spanish language skills (media function for linguistic maintenance). From the perspective of parents in reference to their children, "learning" cultural or linguistic elements from the mass media in general tended to be perceived as something that parents wished their children would not do, because the parents were afraid that children would "learn bad things." Overall, limited patterns did surface in regard to immigrants' use of English-language media for learning or improving English.

Though U.S.-born English-dominant-speaking respondents were not certain about how helpful English language mass media had been for them personally for language improvement, U.S.-born Chicanos and immigrants considered it possibly useful for Mexican immigrants. One professional U.S.-born woman commented on English language radio, and observed that it would be difficult for a person with little or no knowledge of the language to use radio effectively: "You wouldn't understand anything and you wouldn't learn anything." Some immigrants who were Spanish-language-dominant did feel that television was helpful because they could see how words were pronounced in English. A working-class immigrant who spoke mostly Spanish at home and at work with the other *Mexicanos* described why English language television was useful to him: " . . . with the movements of the lips pronouncing the words, it can help an individual a lot." A problem immigrants encountered with English language television, however, was that character dialogue went by too quickly for them to understand everything or try to ask someone for explanations. Some immigrants who spoke mostly Spanish voiced that English language newspapers could be more helpful than broadcast media like television because the respondents could spend more time trying to understand stories. An immigrant man said that he could look in the dictionary or ask his bilingual high school-aged children for assistance with print media.

The function of Spanish language mass media to improve or maintain Spanish was not a commonly voiced practice among the respondents, most of whom were dominant English speakers. Some respondents indicated that this function was reasonable, but others did not see it as such. A U.S.-born working-class man commented about Mexican-heritage people learning Spanish from TV: "I guess they can learn more Spanish that they use on TV that we don't use around here in Texas. [But] I think that's minimum." U.S.-born, dominant-English-speaking respondents appeared to feel that Spanish language improvement or learning was an issue best dealt with informally in interpersonal communication situations in the household, with Spanish-speaking relatives, and in formal education contexts.

Television Use for Surveillance, Maintenance, and Assimilation

The functional use of media for surveillance ("knowing what's going on" or obtaining knowledge of your environment) and more specific purposes involved the use of English- and Spanish-language television, English- and Spanish-language radio, the mainstream press, and Mexican American newspapers (printed in English and Spanish). The idea of surveillance for respondents sometimes meant nothing more than finding out what was going on in the sports world or what the weather was going to be like. However, surveillance could also take on ethnic group significance in the use of mainstream or Chicano media. When taking on Chicano cultural significance, surveillance is transformed into a form of cultural maintenance, which is at once dominant culture resistance. By the same token, when surveillance becomes a way in which to move up in society, it can become a form of structural level assimilation. I must clarify that in the field, with few exceptions, Chicanos who were "making it" or trying to improve their situations did not lack ethnic pride or believe that their personal status improvements meant that Chicanos as a whole were being heartily accepted into Anglo-American spheres. "Moving up" was perceived as a process of participation in Anglo-dominated society without the replacement of Chicano cultural characteristics with those that were Anglo-American.

Mainstream network, cable television news, and Spanish language news from Univisión were mentioned often as ways in which individuals could keep up with events near and far away. Watching Univisión was one way in which individuals could strengthen their sense of belonging to a Chicano-Latino U.S. community. In general, having information and keeping up with information appeared to be important for most respondents in order for them to be knowledgeable about the community, U.S. and Latin American events. Few people expressed apathy about media functionality for finding out about things around them. Typically Chicanos actively sought to be informed and armed themselves with information for work and everyday conversation with others. A working class man said: "The TV is what I can't live without, because I can look at it, watch a movie, the news. I can get what I want to know out of the TV." A professional man who traveled a good deal as part of his job talked about how important news information was to him: "To keep up with the world, CNN, because it's up to date, it's what's happening right there and then. I like to keep up . . . " A Mexican immigrant service worker said: "I watch the news every day. In the morning in Spanish and at six o'clock in English for the weather and for what's happening in Austin." A professional woman who was a Mexican immigrant and an active community worker expressed how she could not let anyone interfere with her watching the news. She vigilantly sought out the news anchored by Dan Rather and would have sought out additional news programs on cable, if she had had the service: "Every evening with Dan Rather, nobody can interrupt my news program . . . Maybe I could get something out of Univisión, the news, but I don't get cable, so I'm deprived."

Television Use for Entertainment, Maintenance, and Assimilation

Television use for entertainment garnered a mixed bag of responses in relation to cultural functionalities and cultural processes involved during viewing. Variety in intentions is not unusual since television is a multifunctional medium by nature.

I found it difficult to assess entertainment use as clearly a resistant or maintenance practice, or part of a practice of acculturation, since programming content varies with channel along with variations in opinions. Respondents would often indicate nonspecific general relaxation purposes for television. With Spanish-language media, it was somewhat easier to conclude that cultural maintenance, and thus dominant culture resistance, was being practiced, since non-English languages are considered threatening and dangerous to the English language of the United States. Furthermore, cultural content of Spanish-language media is additionally threatening to a mainstream that wants to protect Anglo-American culture power. What made my interpretation of respondents' television entertainment use especially slippery was when respondents criticized Spanish-language entertainment, not because of ethnic-group-related cultural reasons, but because of shows they thought were silly, stupid, or offensive to Chicanas and other women. They easily vocalized the same criticisms about certain English-language shows. So, individuals indicated resistance to elements, whether in Chicano-oriented or dominant media, that they did not think were acceptable. An unexpected pattern of Chicano family maintenance revealed itself among respondents whose selective and critical use of media went beyond themselves as individuals because of their roles as parents raising the next generation of Chicanos. Some examples of varied opinions about television entertainment are presented below.

Commenting on U.S. soap operas and Spanish language *telenovelas*, there were a variety of negative and positive statements. One U.S.-born working-class woman criticized the whole genre because she felt such programming did not promote positive behaviors for Mexican-heritage people to follow. She demonstrated her resistance to soaps and *telenovelas* by turning off the television, changing the channel, or engaging in community volunteer work: "I don't like to watch soap operas, they fight too much. I don't need that total gossip and all that fighting . . . sex with this man and that one. I want to lead a better life than that . . . all that yelling and yelling and yelling . . . ." She goes on to describe how soap operas are distractions when groups are trying to accomplish community projects: "When I go make *tamales* some have to leave because of their *novela*. [The television characters] don't have any shame! They should keep it all inside *them* instead of telling everybody. I used to be in charge of the *tamaladas.*"

Another U.S.-born working-class woman held other sentiments, especially for Spanish language entertainment programs: "I love *novelas*! *Muchachitas*, *La Risa del Diablo*, and another one. I like them better in Spanish." An immigrant woman commented that she favored Spanish language Univisión entertainment programming that included *novelas*. She had achieved some college education in Mexico and obtained a job as an office worker in Austin. From speaking with her about her immigration experience and adjustment to the United States, it seemed that watching these shows was a way she could be in contact with the popular culture and community she missed in Mexico. Univisión became a communication channel that could indirectly help her maintain her identity as a *Mexicana* living in the United States. This woman exercised cultural maintenance through Univisión, and was also passing on a viewing practice to her U.S-born daughter: "In Spanish, *Corte Tropical, Desde Hollywood, Fama y Fortuna, Charitin, Paul Rodriquez, Muchachitas'* (a *telenovela*) . . . We have to divide the TV, me and my daughter. I like the movies, the old ones from Mexico, *novelas*, but not in English."

English-language television use spanned watching scandalous daytime soap operas to family-oriented programs. One working-class woman used mass media for entertainment a good deal, especially television. One predominantly English-speaking Chicana's, and others', limited use of Spanish-language television was not a result of their lack of cultural identification, but limited by their Spanish language ability and the limited offerings of the one Spanish-language channel received in the city.

Some respondents expressed that they preferred programs that promoted good family values, and shows that they felt they could use to understand others in real life. Even if shows were in English, and not featuring Mexican-heritage people, Chicanos felt that something could be gained for the maintenance and well-being of their families. One working-class woman talked about a show she liked: "Some of the shows on TV are realistic to what happens to some girls or guys we might know." A working-class man liked to watch Bill Cosby's situation comedy program: "Cosby . . . Good day-to-day programs that help families outside TV-land deal with certain situations . . . how to deal with kids." A professional man explained his reasons for disliking and liking types of programming. He described favoring public broadcasting: "PBS, 'Nature' series, concerts . . . I flip through the channels. I don't like programs that don't show good family morals, especially showing children being oppositional with parents . . . like 'Roseanne,' 'Married with Children' . . . they're funny but bad examples for children."

Two professional Chicanas voiced strongly how they wanted their children to have more respect for women. This was part of the Chicano family cultural maintenance work and bad-cultural-influence resistance work in which they were active. These women, from separate households, had histories of working for Chicana/o social causes as well as being primary care providers. They recalled media images on television and at the cinema that were derogatory and sexist. They preferred that they themselves and their children avoid unacceptable elements in media whether Chicano or mainstream, but they also ferreted out elements in media that they thought were acceptable and useful. For example, one woman finds a positive role model in one television character and is highly critical of some variety show hosts, and describes what she sees as good and bad programming:

> I like Murphy Brown because she's her own woman, educated and intelligent . . . I hate that fat guy on Univisión who has a slew of goddesses, an army, an <u>army</u> of goddesses, of women practically half naked. That's exploiting women. He interviews his guests in a bed! *Sábado Gigante* is another mess. It's a big, big, long advertisement where all these Mexicanos and Cubans are made fools on national TV.

Radio Use for Entertainment and Maintenance

Access to and quality of Spanish-language radio in Austin proved to limit what could have been more frequent radio use among the respondents. There were only two Spanish-language radio stations available to Mexican Americans and Latinos in the community. This Spanish-language radio access limitation circumvented stronger cultural intentions for Chicanos wanting to take advantage of this medium. Access to out-of-town stations was inconsistent. Radio frequencies from stations from in San Antonio, a prominent Latino city south of Austin, could sometimes be picked up, depending on your location in Austin, the technological sophistication of your receiver, the time of day and weather conditions. A professional woman described why she did not like the Spanish-language radio stations, which were quite limited in comparison with the offerings of other U.S. cities: "Spanish radio in Austin sucks . . . They can't even speak Spanish correctly. It's way better in Chicago, San Antonio, and in south Texas. You can't even get the stations here all the time. The wind has to be blowing in the right direction." She tended to use audiotapes of her favorite Chicana/o and Latina/o artists and attended Chicana/o and Latina/o *pachangas* or live band dance parties for cultural maintenance instead of relying on the radio for satisfaction.

From previous experience, another professional woman had found that Spanish-language radio could be culturally affirming. She would have preferred to use Spanish-language radio while living in Austin, given better accessibility and content. In regard to content, she felt that the radio stations should have presented stronger relevant Chicano content:

> I don't listen to the radio in Spanish because I don't relate to it here in Austin. It's way better in San Antonio. They cater to the needs of the Chicanos. They have talk radio in Spanish and Tejano, Chicano music . . . they cater to the different segments of Chicanos and we don't have that here.

The woman went on to make some pointed observations about what Austin radio in English could and could not offer her culturally. She had a favorite rock-and-roll oldies radio station in English, which brought teenage memories of her Chicano *barrio* in San Antonio, but was highly aware of the cultural limitations of English language radio:

> The radio in English keeps me informed, instantaneously, as to local, national and international events. But something for me culturally, not as a *Chicana*, in that it's backward . . . It would have to give equal access. . . . The D.J.'s would have to be sensitive when they talk about the so-called "American." When they announce famous peoples' birthdays, they're all English surnames! They don't say, today's Flora Beltrán's birthday or Benito Juárez' birthday. The rest of the Tejanos here are nonexistent.

Newspaper Use for Maintenance and Assimilation

Except for those who did not use newspapers, a number of respondents used the *Austin American-Statesman* for general news but relied on newspapers, such as *La Prensa* and *Arriba* to keep abreast of issues in the Chicano community. These two Chicano newspapers played important Chicano cultural maintenance and empowerment roles in the city. It was through the use of these two Chicano community papers that readers felt they were actively fighting off political, economic, and social oppression in the city. It was through these papers that they could get information to move up and see how other Chicanos were making progress. Newspaper readers expected and counted on civic information, such as the success or defeat of proposals that would have direct impact on the community. Respondents were also understandably interested in the successes or setbacks of community action coalitions. For example, during the summer of 1992, much of Austin was concerned over clean water swimming in the quaint Barton Springs, in addition to related water issues. Mexican Americans held more interest in the possibility of finally having an Eastside Mexican American Cultural Center, and putting a stop to multinational oil companies' Chicano and Black neighborhood contamination abuse.

The Mexican American papers appeared to be useful to Chicanos as an instrument promoting group solidarity around Mexican American neighborhood issues and group ethnic identification. Non-mainstream ethnic papers appeared to be most functional for respondents in their keeping up with information about current Mexican American topics. One homemaker-professional woman expressed:

> . . . *La Prensa* comes and fills in the gaps by covering what the *Austin American-Statesman* doesn't cover, that the Neighborhood section doesn't cover. Like the tank farm issue with Exxon. The *Statesman* didn't follow through. They let it die out. Same thing with the Mexican American Cultural Center. They just quit reporting on it and *La Prensa* just kept on covering the issues dealing with the Chicanos . . . somebody has to!

One working-class woman expressed how a Chicano paper provided social linkages in the community: "*La Prensa* keeps you informed about exactly what's happening in your Mexican community." A working-class man stated how the mainstream paper did not provide him with much Chicano community information: " . . . the *Statesman* will not tell you the whole story. I don't think you can learn anything from it. Like about the tanks here in Austin. They do a little writing about it, but they don't come to see what's actually going on."

Besides the interest on the fuel terminals, or tank farms, located in the part of the city that is inhabited mostly by people of color, another topic of Chicano interest included Chicano student progress in education, upcoming cultural events, and positive stories on Mexican Americans and Latinos. An immigrant woman who often gave volunteer time in the public schools checked in the paper to see stories of progress in the schools of high Mexican-heritage student enrollment.

Another woman, who enjoyed attending and participating in community events, often checked the ethnic papers like *La Prensa* and *Arriba* for new events. One blue-collar worker stated that *La Prensa* "tells something positive about the Mexicano, that he's doing something good, progressing . . . ". One professional described *Arriba* as a "feel-good paper with good things to say about the community, entrepreneurs, and small businesses." Another professional man unequivocally stated that the ethnic papers were community voices: "That's my people talking, and I say that with a certain degree of pride."

The only major city daily, the *Austin American-Statesman*, was mentioned as being useful for surveillance and other practical purposes. Because of the huge community coverage differences between the *Statesman* and the Chicano papers, I discerned that Chicanos did not bother to seek cultural affirmation in the city paper. Still, several respondents said they read it every day of the week. If respondents could not afford to subscribe to the paper at home, they could often read it at work or get it passed along to them from someone they knew. One respondent stated the fact that the *Austin American-Statesman* had a monopoly on its readership: "It's the only newspaper in town." This paper tended to be useful for more general surveillance and information than for specific Chicano-oriented information. According to respondents, ethnic-oriented papers served specific cultural and ethnic identification functions that the mainstream press could not emulate. In spite of the cultural gap, individuals had favorite parts or sections of the main paper, such as: City and State, Lifestyle, Homes, Business, Classified Ads, Sports, Food, editorials, weekend coupon inserts, and the front page. In general, the mainstream newspaper served the function of letting people know "what's going on around you, in the city or in the world . . . " and filled general utilitarian needs, but did not function as ethnically specifically as Mexican American newspapers.

The use of the mainstream newspaper, according to some respondents, served to satisfy some informational needs for business and employment. Some respondents expressed that they could use the newspaper to get a job and get a better job. Two working-class respondents stated that they had checked the classifieds daily for a job and had eventually found something. Some respondents expressed that using the mainstream city paper, in conjunction with other papers, helped them maintain and improve their professional positions. Among a number of professionals, small trade papers or specialty magazines served professional needs, such as in the areas of real estate and information management systems. They needed to know what was going on in their professions and they sought out and applied specific information in their work.

A fortyish professional expressed that he thought that Latinos should make better use of information that was available in newspapers. This information, he said could be very useful in helping to improve individual opportunity and economic status. He stressed that Latinos did not know how to take advantage of key information from newspapers and other media. Overall, the use of media for specialized surveillance within work and employment in order to improve access in the socioeconomic levels can be described as structural assimilationist or integrationist. It should be restated that structural access for Chicanos did not mean that their identification with their group ceased. Respondents perceived that increased opportunity and participation in the economic structure was something which was needed in order for Chicanos to gain equitable power and reap equitable benefits.

CONCLUDING REMARKS

This field research in the Austin Mexican American community allowed for in-depth research on contemporary cultural topics and issues. I found that ethnic consciousness and pride was strong among almost all respondents. There were few respondents who exhibited distance from their ethnic group. Those who had established within them a critical perspective had it sharpened from first-hand experiences. These respondents could acknowledge their heritage strongly and could be critical of societal factors that were barriers for Mexican Americans. Barriers as interpreted for this study would be poor mainstream news coverage of the community, not enough cultural specific news or relevant news for Chicanas and Chicanos, problems with consistent broadcast access to Mexican American radio stations, popular media content in mainstream, and ethnic media that did not promote ideal values and behaviors as they are expected in the Mexican American community. Much popular television content could not be said to be as culturally specific or affirming as was needed for Mexican American individuals and their families. Overall, it was apparent that Chicanos have been highly adept at resistance and selective acceptance of media content. Chicanos therefore use what is available and make the best of the news and the entertainment they get from media.

Patterns that were not expected were the references to one's family and to specific family members. Though I interviewed individuals alone and asked mostly individually based questions, respondents also wanted me to know about themselves as heads of households, as adults often making media use decisions for themselves as well as others. Family-based analysis was beyond the scope of the project, but it was sometimes difficult to unravel statements respondents made in the field as individually based media use responses or family unit responses. For Mexican American families, this was often perceived as one and the same.

Field work revealed evidence of Chicano-group-based functional and active media use patterns in the community. Also, field work revealed that Chicano active media use has its own limitations. To be able to gain more exposure or more effectively use mass media, respondents needed more available media. In short, qualitative field work allowed for my study of a community site with which I was not completely familiar, the identification, confirmation, or elimination of variables and question types for future research, and much needed documentation on active media use patterns among Mexican Americans. In the immediate future, replications in other U.S. cities are necessary in order to identify regional Chicano purposive media use as well as national patterns. With further field data, a more precise "Chicano Uses and Gratifications" model can be established. A replication of this work is being conducted by this researcher in Albuquerque, New Mexico.

NOTES

1. The terms Chicano and Mexican American will be used interchangeably in reference to people of Mexican heritage living in the United States.

2. Ethnic-oriented media for U.S. Latinos tends to be more Mexican in orientation in the Southwest as a reflection of Mexican-heritage concentrations, the imports of Mexican programming and cultural products, and the construction of local broadcast and print media from Mexican-American perspectives. Though U.S.-Latino media may also be constructed by and used by Latinos of non-Mexican heritage, I will use the shorter description, Chicano media, in this chapter for brevity.

3. K. Rosengren, L. Wenner, and P. Palmgreen, *Media Gratifications Research* (Beverly Hills, CA: Sage, 1985).

4. Leo W. Jeffres, "Media Use for Personal Identification: Linking Uses and Gratifications to Culturally Significant Goals," *Mass Communication Research*, 10 (1983).

5. Judee K. Burgoon, Michael Burgoon, Bradley S. Greenberg, and Felipe Korzenny, "Mass Media Use, Preferences, and Attitudes among Adults," in *Mexican Americans and the Mass Media* (Norwood, NJ: Ablex, 1986)

6. See C. Stroman and L. Becker, "Racial Differences in Gratifications," *Journalism Quarterly*, 55 (1978): 767–771; Bradley S. Greenberg and J. R. Dominick, "Racial and Social Class Differences in Teen-agers' Use of Television," *Journal of Broadcasting*, 13, 4, (1969): 331–343; E. B Lee and L. A. Browne, "Television Uses and Gratifications among Black Children, Teenagers, and Adults," *Journal of Broadcasting*, 25 (1981): 203–208.

7. Rosengren et al., *Media Gratifications Research*.

8. E. Katz, H. Hadassah, and M. Gurevitch, "On the Use of the Mass Media for Important Things," *American Sociological Review*, 38 (1974): 164–181.

9. Janice Radway, *Reading the Romance: Women, Patriarchy and Popular Literature* (Chapel Hill, NC: University of North Carolina, 1984).

10. Diana I. Ríos, "Mexican American Audiences: A Qualitative and Quantitative Study of Ethnic Subgroup Uses for Mass Media," Unpublished doctoral dissertation, University of Texas at Austin, 1993.

11. See critique in Diana I. Ríos, "Processes of Ethnic Change and Persistence: Mexican Americans, Ethnicity and Acculturation," Paper presented at the annual meeting of the Speech Communication Association, Atlanta, Georgia, 1991.

12. U.S. Bureau of the Census, *Census of Population and Housing Summary Tape File 1A*, Washington, DC: Author, 1991).

13. The entire research project was designed with an initial qualitative data-gathering phase that provided much needed foundational data for the much larger quantitative survey to follow.

14. In one study, Lee and Brown questioned their usage of a standard uses and gratifications survey instrument for their Black sample population when it appeared that response choices were limiting. This pointed to the need for not only culturally appropriate variables in ethnic group questionnaires, but also to the need for qualitative data-gathering procedures that would allow for open-ended questions.

15. The ethnographic techniques and field work design follows that which was carried out by Williams in the following Texas-based research: Norma Jean Williams, "Changing Patterns in the Mexican American Family," Unpublished doctoral dissertation, University of Texas at Austin, 1984; Norma Williams, *The Mexican American Family: Tradition and Change*, (New York: General Hall, 1990).

12

GANGING UP ON THE GANG

RAÚL TOVARES

News stories about Chicano[1] gangs promote an unflattering picture of this subculture and often present it as either a direct or subtle threat to the community. Some evidence, however, suggests that newspaper reports greatly exaggerate the activities of Chicano youth gangs by presenting information that depicts this group as pathologically violent, addicted to illegal drugs, and beyond the control of official authorities.[2]

In contrast to these media images of Chicano gangs, several researchers have reported that most of these gang members are not prone to violence,[3] that attitudes toward drug use among members of gangs is as common as among adolescents in general,[4] and that gang members do not demonstrate a high degree of nonconformity to social rules and regulations.[5] This discrepancy between news items about Mexican American gangs and the findings of several researchers demands a closer look at news stories about Chicano gangs.

In the past, some researchers have concerned themselves with how fairly Mexican Americans were treated in newspapers.[6] The counting of headlines and column inches, key words or phrases, number of stories, and other quantitative measures, while providing some valuable information, can also serve to obscure methodological problems and ignore important questions about the production of news. For example, how does the salience of a story compare with its repetitiveness? Does one headline on the front page count as much as three stories run on consecutive days, but which appear on the back pages? More importantly, the concept of objectivity in the process of news production is often left unchallenged in quantitative measures of news stories. Tuchman, Downing, and Fishman[7] provide evidence that seriously questions any claims of objectivity on the part of the news media. Far from being objective, news seems to be intimately tied to the political, economic, and social systems in which it is created. Stories about Chicano gangs are no exception.

The Chicano gang story is more a product of the needs of media institutions and government agencies than a reflection of the everyday experiences of Chicano teens and young adults. The need for media and government institutions to protect and promote their interests best explains the manner in which the Chicano gang is presented in the news. The corporate structure of media institutions compliments the needs of the bureaucratic structure of government agencies, so that the reproduction of the prevailing ideology is reproduced in news in general and the Chicano gang story in particular. This is the primary reason that the Chicano gang is so often presented in the news media within two frames of reference. These two frames of reference can be described as either a call for more police action—retribution—or a call for more social services—rehabilitation—or some combination of both.

In the literature review that follows, I will first examine some of the findings of researchers who have studied Mexican American gangs. Then I will focus on works that report on how events in general are constructed for presentation as news. Within this context of general news production I will then look at how gang stories in particular are presented in two Texas newspapers.

LITERATURE REVIEW

While many of the scholars who have studied Chicano gangs have noted the tendency of the press to associate these groups with criminal behavior, few have focused their attention exclusively on this particular issue. Moore[8] for example, writing about currents of gang hysteria that periodically run through many cities in the United States, claims that "These outbreaks of fear usually begin with reports from law enforcement people, and are greatly helped along by newspapers and other media" (p. 1).

Similarly, Vigil points out that:

> most *cholos* and *pachucos* . . . are nonparticipants in deviant, antisocial patterns. Because of police and media influences, the public has nevertheless tended to perceive such styles as reflective of criminal behavior.[9]

Other researchers have delved deeper into the issue of the media and Chicano gangs in an effort to understand how the media operate in the creation of stereotypes. Turner and Surace[10] provide us with a study of how one newspaper, *The Los Angeles Times*, utilized the expression "zoot-suit" during the late 1930s and early 1940s to create a negative image that associated young Mexican Americans with illegal activities. The term "zoot-suit" referred to the style of dress worn by many in the 1930s and 1940s, including some Mexican American young men. However, it should be noted that while "zoot-suit" was a term attributed to those who wore this style of dress, Mexican American youths preferred the term "drapes" to describe their fashion preference. McLemore and Romo provide a description of this style:

They wore tight cuffed trousers that bloused at the knee and were belted high on the body. Their costumes also included wide-brimmed hats, long-tailed coats, high boots, ducktail haircuts, and ankle-length watch chains. Anglos called these costumes "zoot-suits" and tended to identify those who wore them as "hoodlums."[11]

Turner and Surace reason that because of the association of Los Angeles history with Mexican history, the term "Mexican" could at best elicit ambiguous feelings about members of this ethnic group. Substituting the term "Mexican" with "zoot-suit" created a different set of associations:

The symbol, *Zoot-suiter*, evoked none of the imagery of the romantic past. It evoked only the picture of a breed of persons outside the normative order, devoid of morals themselves and consequently not entitled to fair play and due process.[12]

The identification and labeling of Mexican American youths as beyond mainstream society, according to Turner and Surace, helped legitimize the search for and attack on Mexican American teenagers and young adults in Los Angeles in the summer of 1943, between June 3–10.

One criticism of Turner and Surace's[13] work is that their position tacitly supports what others have labeled as a "hypodermic needle" approach to the study of mass media. Such an approach posits the media's ability to "inject" ideas and feelings into the mind of the consumer of news stories, films, or radio. In the case presented by Turner and Surace, it was through the manipulation of the terms "Mexican" and "zoot-suit" that *The Los Angeles Times* was able to contribute to the unleashing of the wrath of the community on young Mexican Americans. While Turner and Surace acknowledge that the question of whether daily papers reflect community sentiment or actively mold it has not been answered, they fail to discuss just how much influence they believe the media have in shaping public sentiment and influencing behavior. Perhaps even more importantly, they fail to discuss how other institutions, such as the police, government agencies, and corporations also contribute to the creation of images of both themselves and other groups.

More recently Marjorie Zatz[14] authored an article on Mexican American gangs. Her analysis of the gang phenomenon in Phoenix, Arizona led her to conclude that "it was the social imagery of Chicano youth gangs, rather than their actual behavior, that lay at the root of the gang problem in Phoenix." Zatz points out, based on quantitative data gathered from Juvenile Court referrals, that gangs and gang-related crimes were a reality. However, contrary to the reaction to gang-related crime, the police did not organize special units to deal with regular street crime, corporate crime, and other types of illegal activity. She notes in her study of court referrals in Tucson, Arizona, that those Chicanos believed to be members of gangs were mostly guilty of having been involved in "minor squabbles." She reports that only one referral out of 518 "gang boys" was for a non-fighting violent crime.

Zatz[15] believes that it is the image of Chicano youth as "different" that facilitated the police and media's promotion of a "moral panic." Identifying Chicano youths as responsible for community disorder justified increasing the number of social control agents in the *barrio*: "As a consequence, legal control over the resistive behavior of this economically and politically subordinate group, and the threat that it posed to the state, was legitimized."[16]

What is not clear in Zatz's[17] study is the role ethnicity played in the creation of the moral panic about Chicano gangs in Phoenix and Tucson. She notes that white, middle-class youths may be seen as deviant without being threatening. On the other hand, Chicano youths who are dark-skinned, speak Spanish, and congregate in urban areas are seen as "different" and threatening.[18] However, moral panics related to gangs have been created in societies much more homogeneous than many of the communities in the United States that are experiencing gang problems.[19] In such cases, social class differences, rather than ethnic differences, may serve as a basis for, or contribute to, the creation of a moral panic.

Moore and Vigil,[20] after ten years of studying neighborhood gangs in Southern California, found it "difficult . . . to support the view that gangs are simply crimogenic."[21] They point out that gang activities are usually centered on normal adolescent concerns, such as peer respect and acceptance, security and protection, and age and sex role identification.[22] With respect to drug use, a topic commonly associated with gang behavior, Moore and Vigil write, "gang members do not consider such activity deviant. In holding this opinion they are far from unique among American adolescents."[23]

The studies just cited clearly indicate that the gang phenomenon is certainly more rich and complex than the gang stories appearing in newspapers lead readers to believe. This tendency in the media toward one-dimensional portrayals about gangs should come as no surprise. Minority groups have a long history of being presented in news stories in a less-than-accurate manner.[24]

Newspaper stories and television news segments about Latinos tend to focus on the most unusual, sensational, and negative incidents.[25] The result is that often this group, like Blacks and recently arrived immigrants, is portrayed in what has come to be referred to as a "problem people" news frame. Such a frame can include crime, welfare, school failure, and unemployment as backdrops for profiles of minority group members.[26]

This context, or frame, within which information about Latinos, including Mexican Americans, is presented is in large part the result of the process by which reporters get their information. Inherent in this process of news gathering is a bias toward those organizations and persons who know and understand the needs of newsworkers and media institutions.

News has been described by Tuchman[27] as both a frame, which constructs social reality, and ideology,[28] which blocks inquiry. As a frame, news defines our world and allows us to interpret events in that world within a given social structure. As ideology, however, news "blocks inquiry by preventing an analytic understanding through which social actors can work to understand their own fate."[29]

A key element in Tuchman's[30] view of news as a frame is the definition of news as a social institution. Three primary aspects define news as a social institution. First, news is produced in an institutional setting for consumers. Second, news is associated with other legitimized institutions. Third, news is searched for, collected, and produced by professionals working within an organization. "Thus it [news] is inevitably a product of newsworkers drawing upon institutional processes and conforming to institutional practices."[31]

One of the most obvious, yet often overlooked, features of news production is that it takes place within an institution designed to maximize profits. Tuchman[32] explains how the network of reporters, wire services and "beats," what she refers to as the news net, serves to accentuate some news items and overlook others. Paying a reporter to cover City Hall means that events and information generated there will be more likely to get into the newspaper: "Obviously, reporters cannot write about occurrences hidden from view by their social location, that is, either their geographic location or social class."[33]

Besides creating a definition of news, the news net also makes the collection of news cost effective. The efficiency of the news net as an information-gathering system and the conscious effort of institutions such as City Hall, the courts, and the police department to generate information that can easily be packaged as news gives them a clear advantage in the control over the information about gangs that the public will read in the papers or see on local television news.

While the news frame limits the audience's access to that knowledge that is collected via the news net in a cost-effective manner, packaged in a timely fashion, and delivered to a mass audience, the construction of that frame is, to a large extent, determined through the recognition of certain sources of information as legitimate institutions. These legitimate institutions, primarily government agencies, large corporations, prominent individuals, and some social service organizations that are managed and/or funded by elites, promote the prevailing ideology. The organization of news beats and bureaus around these central sources of information ties the newsworker to the ideology of the state and corporate structure.

> Through naive empiricism . . . information is transformed into objective facts—facts as normal, natural, taken-for-granted descriptions and constitution of a state of affairs. And through the sources identified with facts, newsworkers create and control controversy; they contain dissent.[34]

Far from being objective, then, news stories tend to promote the interests and perspectives of state and corporate entities and other legitimate organizations. It is through this process that the view of Chicano gangs incorporated into the news frame is more likely to be that held by political, economic, and social elites.

Evidence that a process similar to the one described above may be going on in the production of news about gangs in Texas can be found in a report issued by the Research and Policy Management Division of the Texas Attorney General's Office:

> There is little support for sensational images of gangs as heavily armed and highly organized narcotics distribution networks. Gangs of this description exist, however, in some of the larger cities.[35]

It cannot be denied that in many cities in Texas a small number of Chicano youth do engage in criminal acts and disorderly conduct. Exaggerating the problem and placing it in a "problem people" news frame, however, can only serve to create a biased view of gangs that may lead to fear and panic in communities. To what extent newspapers in Houston and Austin exaggerate the activities of Chicano gangs is a topic we turn to next.

METHODOLOGY

This analysis of how the Chicano gang is presented in newspapers will focus on two Texas dailies, *The Houston Chronicle* and *Austin American-Statesman*. The reason for selecting these two papers is a practical one: Both are indexed and available via computer services. *The Houston Chronicle* is available through Lexis/Nexis and the *Austin American-Statesman* is available through NewsBank CD News. The year 1992 was chosen because it is the first complete year when stories appearing in *The Houston Chronicle* are accessible through Lexis/Nexis. *The Houston Chronicle* became available on Lexis/Nexis in June of 1991. The *Austin American-Statesman* is available from January 1991.[36]

For the purposes of this study, a Chicano gang story is defined by the following criteria: (1) It must be written by a member of the newspaper staff; (2) it must report on an event or incident in the community served by the paper; (3) the gang featured, discussed or referred to in the story must consist of persons under the age of 21; (4) the words "gang" or "gangs" and "Mexican American," "Chicano," or "Hispanic," must be included in the story.

The computer searches resulted in a total of sixty-nine stories located in *The Houston Chronicle* and forty-three stories located in the *Austin American-Statesman*. Not surprisingly, a number of gang stories identified by the computer searches did not fit the definition of Chicano gang stories given above. Many were "wire" stories and therefore not "local." The Los Angeles riots, the arrests of the persons accused of beating truck driver Reginald Denny, and an Albanian *gang* attacking a *Hispanic* in New York, are some examples of wire stories that were registered as "hits" in the computer search but fell outside the parameters set by the definition of Chicano gang stories. Out of a total of sixty-nine stories found in *The Houston Chronicle*, three of which were repeats, twenty-two were wire stories. In the *Austin American-Statesman* search, of forty-three "gang" related stories, three were repeats (stories printed in different editions of a paper were counted as one), ten were wire service stories. This left a total of forty-four local stories in *The Houston Chronicle* and thirty local stories in the *Austin American-Statesman*.

Many of these local stories, however, also failed to qualify as gang stories. Although the words "gangs" and "Mexican American," "Chicano," or "Hispanic" appeared in these local stories, only eleven of *The Houston Chronicle* stories were determined by this researcher to qualify as locally produced Chicano gang stories meeting all the criteria outlined above. Ten *Austin American-Statesman* local stories qualified.

FINDINGS

Two findings in this analysis stand out as most important. The first is that *The Houston Chronicle* appears more disposed than the *Austin American-Statesman* to print the names of gangs and identify them by the ethnicity of their members, in this case, "Hispanic." This type of association is important because it could serve to marginalize minority group members who become identified with gangs. The second important finding, closely related to the first, is that, in keeping with the "problem people" news frame, the gang is overwhelmingly presented as a negative phenomenon that must be stopped by either retributive policies that call for increased police action or rehabilitative measures that call for increased social services.

In the eleven local gang stories identified in *The Houston Chronicle*, four included the names of gangs: January 26, 1992: Little Dogs; April 28, 1992: OBT (Old Baytown); September 20, 1992: Pelly Rats, Eastside Locos, UNLV, Lynch Mob; November 4, 1992: MexMafia. On the other hand, the *Austin American-Statesman*, the ten gang stories defined as local gang stories never mentioned local gangs by name.

The Houston Chronicle local gang stories mentioned "Hispanic gangs" three times: April 28, 1992, " . . . members of a predominantly Hispanic gang known as OBT . . . " May 16, 1992, "Deputies were alerted about a gang fight between Asian and Hispanic gang members . . . " October 18, 1992 "Progress is also being made with the predominantly Hispanic gangs . . . " In addition to these examples, *The Houston Chronicle* search results also included stories in which the ethnicity of a gang is indicated, but the words "Hispanic" and "gang" are separated by a few words. For instance, on September 20, 1992 " . . . violence had increased between the other two gangs, which are predominantly Hispanic." On May 15, 1992, "among male juvenile gang members, 46 percent are Hispanic; 34 percent are black; 16 percent are white; and 4 percent are Asian." In a story that appeared November 14, 1992, the Hispanic gang can be easily deduced after *The Houston Chronicle* informed readers that the young man arrested for murder claimed to be a member of the MexMafia. Again, in sharp contrast to *The Houston Chronicle* local gang stories, the *Austin American-Statesman* stories never refer to "Hispanic gangs."

The second major finding relates to how the gang stories are contextualized within the "problem people" news frame. Whether they are calling for more police action (retribution) or an increase in social services (rehabilitation), all of the stories remain well within the "problem people" news frame. In the stories labeled "retributive," the message is that more police action is needed to solve the gang problem. In those categorized as "rehabilitative," the members of gangs or those perceived to be "at risk" of joining gangs, are presented as needing direction in the form of mentors, role models, or social programs to help them develop into responsible members of the community. While both papers, *The Houston Chronicle* and the *Austin American-Statesman*, published local gang stories in 1992 that can fall into both categories, it was found that *The Houston Chronicle* carried more stories that can be classified as "retributive," while the *Austin American-Statesman* carried more stories with a "rehabilitative" theme.

As expected, given the present tenor of the gang discourse in the news media, there is an almost total lack of stories, except for one in the *Austin American-Statesman*, that present the gang as a positive experience in the life of Chicano youths. In the October 6, 1992 issue of the *Austin American-Statesman*, in an article titled "Wanted: Must Have Education," two researchers, Harriet Romo of South Texas State University and Tony Falbo of the University of Texas at Austin, report that gangs can provide emotional/psychological support for Hispanic students. Other than this one article, part of a series on education in central Texas, the gang stories in both *The Houston Chronicle* and *Austin American-Statesman* present the gang as a negative influence that must be overcome, either through increased law enforcement strategies, increased social services or a combination of both.

DISCUSSION

The identification of gang members with their ethnicity is one of the most interesting findings of this study. *The Austin American-Statesman* never mentions the name of a gang or prints the names of gang members. According to the City News Editor for the *Austin American-Statesman*, Ricardo Gandara, the paper has "guidelines"—not a policy—that discourage the printing of names of gangs or gang members.[37] The argument for the implementation of these guidelines is that publishing the names of gangs and gang members only serves to legitimize and bestow a certain status on the gangs and gang members. In addition to not mentioning the names of gangs or gang members, not once in the ten *Austin American-Statesman* articles is a gang associated with the ethnicity of its members, that is, referred to as a "Hispanic gang." When the terms "Mexican American," "Chicano," or "Hispanic," appear in one of these ten stories it is because an organization, such as the Mexican American Comptroller Employees Association (MACEA) is sponsoring a mentor program,[38] raising funds for an activity, or conducting some other effort designed to help kids stay away from gangs. *The Houston Chronicle*, on the other hand, frequently published the names of gangs and gang members (see findings above). Gangs or gang members were identified specifically as Hispanic in five of the eleven stories that appeared in *The Houston Chronicle*.

According to the logic of Turner and Surace's study[39] the use of the term "gang," like the term "zoot-suiter" in the 1930s and 1940s, may contribute to the defining of young Chicano teens as a group of individuals outside of the mainstream. Such a definition could lead to actions against Chicano teens that circumvent usual legal channels. For example, calls for curfews for teens, military-style boot camps for first-time offenders, and other "get tough" programs aimed at curbing gang activity could end up unfairly targeting Chicano and other minority teens. Such a process may be helped along by more subtle associations.

The Houston Chronicle gang stories, like the *Austin American-Statesman* gang stories, mention the words "Mexican American," Chicano" or "Hispanic" in relation to other aspects of the gang story not directly related to the gang. For example, a story (October 7, 1992; p. A18) headlined "Northbrook high school student arrested in boy's slaying" mentions the word "Chicano" only because members of the Houston Police Chicano Squad questioned the suspect. In a similar manner, a story that appeared on November 14, 1992 (*The Houston Chronicle*, p. A1) "Seeking solace," the term Mexican American is used because the subject of the story attended a school operated by the Association for the Advancement of Mexican Americans.

This association of the word "gang" with "Hispanic," "Mexican American," or "Chicano," is then packaged within the problem people news frame. Such stories create a context in which gangs are discussed simultaneously with crime and the need to increase state intervention either in the form of police surveillance or social services. The positive aspects of gang behavior are rarely presented.

On March 19, 1992, the *Austin American-Statesman* headline on page B1 was "East Austinites speak their minds to officials. Rising crime, gang violence anger residents." On April 4, 1992, the headline in the *Austin American-Statesman*, page B1, was "Posters picture the down side of gang life." Black-and-white anti-gang posters that associate joining a gang with fingerprints, jail clothes, handcuffs, and a prison corridor were the focus of the story. Because of the allusions to gangs as a growing problem and the association of the gang with arrest and imprisonment, both of these stories fit the "retributive" category. The rest of the eight stories in the *Austin American-Statesman* are classified as "rehabilitative," because they inform the reader about activities that focus on individuals or organizations working to solve the gang problem using means other than the threat of arrest and confinement. For example, on April 9, 1992, the *Austin American-Statesman* ran a story titled "Field's first day a 'beautiful hit." The focus is on the dedication of the new Roy Velasquez complex, which contains three baseball fields, two batting cages, and a concession stand. Organized sports are presented as a way to keep kids away from gangs. In the same vein, on May 28, 1992, the title of an article on page B1 in the *Austin American-Statesman* is "Latin American league honors volunteers who encourage youth." The focus here is on members of the community who make time to help teenagers stay away from gangs. On June 14, 1992, the title of an article on page B1 reads "Mentors help students renew focus on school. Program gets at-risk youth back on educational track." The focus of this story is how the Mexican American Comptroller Employees Association (MACEA) assists young people in developing skills that will help them finish school and secure employment.

The Houston Chronicle reported on May 15, 1992, page A33, in a story headlined "Warning on gangs: strength growing," that the Harris County Sheriff claimed 210 gangs, with a combined membership of 1,385, were operating in unincorporated areas around Houston. It is noted in the same story that the Houston Assistant Police Chief stated that the city of Houston is experiencing the same problems described by the sheriff. The sheriff also said that gang activities would not be tolerated and that gang members would be arrested. Such a story falls into the "retributive" category.

The next day, May 16, 1992, sheriff's deputies in Sugarland, Texas, a community just outside Houston, acting on a rumor, according to *The Houston Chronicle*, prevented a gang fight between Asian and Hispanic gangs by sending the gang members home. This action by law enforcement officials, based on a rumor, and in the absence of information about sheriffs talking to the Asian or Hispanic youths about the problems between the two groups, make this story "retributive."

On September 20, 1992, the headline in section C, page 1, in *The Houston Chronicle* was "Baytown going to war against gangs. Police adopting 'zero tolerance' stance." This is clearly a "retributive" gang story.

Reading the above examples of stories on gangs, one would expect an increase in reports of serious crimes to accompany the stories presented by both papers. However, the Texas Department of Public Safety reported that in 1992 the Houston Police Department recorded 465 murders, 143 *less* than in 1991. Robbery, burglary, larceny theft, and motor vehicle theft were all down in 1992.[40] The only categories in which slight increases were recorded were rape and aggravated assault. *The Houston Chronicle* reported on January 23, 1993 that crime in Houston was less in 1992 than in 1991. On that day the headline on section A, page 1 was "Houston leads state in crime reduction."

In Austin there were forty-nine murders reported in 1991. In 1992 there were thirty-seven. Robbery was down, as were aggravated assault, burglary, and motor vehicle theft. On January 3, 1993, on page A1, the *Austin American-Statesman* noted, "The number of homicides in Austin dropped by 30 percent in 1992 . . . It was the lowest number of homicides since 1989 . . . "

The local gang stories selected from both papers, *The Houston Chronicle* and *Austin American-Statesman*, while they demonstrate a definite contrast in approaches to the reporting on gangs, both remain well within the parameters of the delinquency debates that have persisted in this country since the late 1800s.[41] "Rehabilitation or retribution?" continues to be the central question that frames the debates on gangs that appear in these two newspapers.

CONCLUSION

The narrow parameters within which the Chicano gang is presented to the public in newspaper stories in Texas do not allow for meaningful discussion about the issues that contribute to the lifestyle adopted by some Chicano teens. Needed now is an amplification of this work to include more newspapers and other media to see if other gang stories can continue to be classified as either "retributive" and "rehabilitative."

It is unlikely that the gang phenomenon will disappear soon, regardless of the resources a community invests in dealing with it, or the strategies adopted, whether of the "retributive" or "rehabilitative" type. Finding solutions to the "Chicano gang problem" will require that we understand how politicians, community leaders, reporters, elites, and, of course, the teenagers themselves, contribute to the construction of the gang phenomenon. But these contributions must, first of all, synthesize theory and research. Our ideas about Chicano youth gangs must be tested against the reality experienced by the teens who are said to be members of gangs.

Questions of political power, social status, and economics must also be addressed. It is impossible to study the presentation of gangs in the media without addressing the role of political processes, community elites, and corporate interests in the drawing up of the social agenda. The merging of theory and research with respect to the gang phenomenon will hopefully move us closer to a clearer understanding of the role of the mass media in the construction of the Chicano gang.

Acknowledgments: I would like to thank the Graduate Opportunity Program and the Center for Mexican American Studies at the University of Texas at Austin for a Summer Research Fellowship that allowed me to complete this research.

NOTES

1. The terms "Chicano" and "Mexican American" will be used interchangeably throughout this chapter.
2. Ralph Turner and Samuel J. Surace, "Zoot-suiters and Mexicans: Symbols in Crowd Behavior," *The American Journal of Sociology*, 62 (1956): 14-20; Carey McWilliams, *North From Mexico* (Philadelphia: J.B. Lippincott, 1949), 227–258; Joan W. Moore, *Going Down to the Barrio* (Philadelphia: Temple University Press, 1991); Marjorie S. Zatz, "Chicano Youth Gangs and Crime: The Creation of a Moral Panic,." *Contemporary Crises*, 11 (1987): 129–159.
3. James Diego Vigil, *Barrio Gangs* (Austin: University of Texas Press, 1988).
4. Joan Moore and James Diego Vigil, "Chicano Gangs: Group Norms and Individual Factors Related to Adult Criminality," *Aztlán*, 18 (1989): 27–44.
5. Vigil, *Barrio Gangs*, 40.
6. Bradley Greenberg, C. Heeter, J. Burgoon, M. Burgoon, and F. Korzenny, "A Content Analysis of Newspaper Coverage of Mexican Americans," in Bradley Greenberg, M. Burgoon, J. Burgoon, and F. Korzenny (eds.), *Mexican Americans and the Mass Media* (Norwood, NJ: Ablex Publishing, 1983), 202–223; Judy VanSlyke Turk, Jim Richstad, Robert L. Bryson, Jr., and Sammye M. Johnson, "Hispanic Americans in the News in Two Southwestern Cities," *Journalism Quarterly*, 66 (1989): 107–113.
7. See Gaye Tuchman, *Making News: A Study in the Construction of Reality* (New York: The Free Press, 1978); John D. Downing, *The Media Machines* (London: Pluto Press, 1980); Mark Fishman, *Manufac-*

turing the News (Austin: University of Texas Press, 1980). Also Herbert J. Gans, *Deciding What's News* (New York: Vintage Books, 1980).
8. Moore, *Going Down to the Barrio*.
9. Vigil, *Barrio Gangs*, 40.
10. Turner and Surace, "Zoot-Suiters."
11. Dale S. McLemore and Ricardo Romo, "The Origins and Development of the Mexican American People," in Rodolfo O. de la Garza, F.B. Bean, C.M. Bonjean, R. Romo, and R. Alvarez (eds.), *The Mexican American Experience* (Austin: The University of Texas Press, 1985), 18–19.
12. Turner and Surace, "Zoot-Suiters."
13. Turner and Surace, "Zoot-Suiters."
14. Zatz, "Chicano Youth Gangs," 129–159.
15. Zatz, "Chicano Youth Gangs."
16. Zatz, "Chicano Youth Gangs."
17. Zatz, "Chicano Youth Gangs."
18. Zatz, "Chicano Youth Gangs," 150.
19. See, for example, Geoffrey Pearson, *Hooligan: A History of Respectable Fears* (London: Macmillan Press, 1983) for a study of the rise of "hooliganism" in Great Britain.
20. Moore and Vigil, "Chicano Gangs."
21. Moore and Vigil, "Chicano Gangs," 27.
22. Moore and Vigil, "Chicano Gangs," 28.
23. Moore and Vigil, "Chicano Gangs," 31–32.
24. See Federico Subervi-Vélez and collaborators, "Media," in Nicholas Kanellos, (ed.), *The Hispanic Almanac: A Reference Work on Hispanics in the United States* (Detroit: Gale Research Inc., 1993) 621–674; and Clint C. Wilson and Félix Gutiérrez, *Minorities and Media* (Newbury Park: Sage Publications, 1985), 137–149.

25. See Félix Gutiérrez, "Latinos and the Media," in Michael C. Emery, and Ted C. Smythe (eds.), *Readings in Mass Communication* (Dubuque, IA: Wm. C. Brown, 1989), 225–242.

26. Gutiérrez, "Latinos and the Media," 228.

27. Tuchman, *Making News*, 1–12.

28. In this context, ideology refers to the set of values, beliefs, laws, and customs used to legitimize an existing social structure.

29. Tuchman, *Making News*, 180.

30. Tuchman, *Making News*, 4.

31. Tuchman, *Making News*, 4.

32. Tuchman, *Making News*.

33. Tuchman, *Making News*, 23–24.

34. Tuchman, *Making News*, 210–211.

35. Elizabeth Buhmann, *The 1992 Texas Attorney General's Gang Report*. (Austin: Office of the Attorney General, Research and Policy Management Division, 1992), ii.

36. The first step in targeting stories in *The Houston Chronicle* was to select the Nexis library. Once this was done, the unique source file, HCHRN (*The Houston Chronicle*), was select-ed. In order to locate those stories that included the words "gangs" and "Mexican American," "Chicano," or "Hispanic," and which appeared in *The Houston Chronicle* in 1992, the following command was entered and transmitted: Gangs and (Mexican American or Chicano or Hispanic) and date (>12/31/91 and <1/1/93). To locate stories in the *Austin American-Statesman*, the year is selected first, in this case, 1992. The next step is to select "Topic 1," which was assigned the word "gangs." The prompt "Topic 2" was assigned the words "And Mexican American or Hispanic or Chicano."

37. Ricardo Gandara, telephone conversation (July 2, 1993).

38. *Austin American-Statesman*, August 30, 1992; B1.

39. Turner and Surace, "Zoot-Suiters."

40. See *Crimes in Texas, 1992*, Texas Department of Public Safety, Crime Records Division.

41. Anthony M. Platt, *The Child Savers: The Invention of Delinquency*, 2nd ed., (Chicago: University of Chicago Press, 1969).

PART IV

CHICANO IDENTITY AND POLITICS

13

BILINGUAL/BICULTURAL EDUCATION AND POLITICS IN CRYSTAL CITY, TEXAS: 1969–1989[1]

ARMANDO L. TRUJILLO

The decades of the sixties and seventies characterized a period of heightened ethnic political competition between the Chicano and Anglo community in South Texas.[2] The focal arena of competition between these two ethnic communities was the control of community governing institutions. This study analyzes the case of Crystal City, where the Chicano community achieved new levels of empowerment in the 1970s through the emergence of an alternative political party, *La Raza Unida*. Through the Raza Unida Party (RUP), the Chicano community elected their own representatives and gained political control of the school district, city, and county government. This political victory coincides with the emergence of an alternative political ideology, Chicano cultural nationalism, which countered the established Anglo ideological domination since the early 1900s.[3] The schools were an important site where this alternative ideology took form in curricular changes. Under Chicano control, schooling reforms were introduced that were very different from the acculturative type of education that Chicano students had received during the era of Anglo control. Under Anglo control, the time period from the 1920s to 1970, schooling primarily served the purpose of Americanizing Mexicano students.[4]

After the Mexicano community gained control of the schools, following the spring school board elections in 1970, curricular reforms were introduced for the predominantly Mexican American student body that were regarded to be more egalitarian and pluralistic. The most prominent symbol of this pluralistic schooling reform effort was a comprehensive prekindergarten through twelfth grade bilingual/bicultural education program. Through this program, the Chicano school administration sought to reinforce the goals of equality and ethnic community.

Barrera argues that these two goals characterize Chicano political history in as much as the first goal "refers to economic, social, and political equality between Chicanos and the mainstream white, or 'Anglo' population, [and] the second involves the maintenance of a cohesive and culturally distinct communal identity."[5] The new Chicano administration sought to achieve these goals through schooling by fostering a new sense of ethnic identity and group advancement by emphasizing bilingualism, biculturalism, and biliteracy. However, by the early 1980s resistance developed against the maintenance bilingual/bicultural education program within the teaching ranks and community.

This article presents a historical ethnographic analysis of the political factors and forces affecting the restructuring of the bilingual/bicultural education program in Crystal City. In order to shed light on this case study, it is necessary to analyze the intersection of local politics with national and state bilingual education policy changes over a twenty-year period. Organizationally, I conduct this analysis under three main sections. In the first section, I argue that politics in Crystal City were part of a larger ethnoregional push to gain equity for Mexicanos in the Winter Garden region of South Texas. The second section focuses the analysis on the schooling reforms introduced in Crystal City as part of the overall RUP plan to restructure the school system in order to reinforce the goals of the regional political movement. In the final section, I discuss the restructuring of the bilingual/bicultural education program in the 1980s and its relationship to local politics and national and state bilingual education policy change, concluding that Chicano communities striving to achieve the goals of equality and community through education must deal with an inherent contradiction—struggles to achieve equality may lead to the weakening of community.

THE WINTER GARDEN REGION AND CRYSTAL CITY

The Winter Garden region of Texas comprises an area of rich agricultural land with access to water for irrigation, spread over several counties. It is climatically well suited for growing fresh vegetables in winter and early spring. Using Hansen's classification of subregions of the Southwest borderlands, it falls within the eight-county Middle Rio Grande border area and forms a particular ecological/agricultural zone within the plains portion of the region.[6] The boundaries of the Winter Garden area are difficult to delimit with precision, because they have changed depending on the crops grown and the availability of good sources of water for irrigation. Nonetheless, as an economic region, the term has historically been applied to concentrated winter-vegetable production in Maverick, Uvalde, Zavala, Dimmit, La Salle, and Frio counties.[7]

It is important to note that the historical economic development of the Winter Garden as a vegetable-producing area has also been due in large part to the abundance of cheap Mexican and Mexican American labor.[8] This subregion follows the same historical economic development as described by Barrera for the Southwest.[9] The fact that Mexicans and Mexican Americans have provided the labor force to support the economic prosperity of South Texas and the Winter Garden region demonstrates the structural hierarchical relations of the cultural division of labor.[10] These hierarchical relations established the Anglo group not only as the land-owning elite and businessmen but also as the political force in control of community institutions and sociocultural spheres. The Mexicanos became a subordinate-wage laboring class who, if they complied with the existing social order, could with the passage of time gain access to privileged opportunities such as education. As a result of these structural relations, Chicanos throughout the Southwest and the Winter Garden region have a lower standard of living and social status, and their cultural distinctiveness has been denigrated.

Texas Chicano Civil Rights Politics as Key Mover

Chicanos in the 1960s sought to change their second-class citizenship through political mobilization, community empowerment, and cultural revitalization. In Texas, the Mexican American Youth Organization (MAYO), as a student/community youth organization, played a major role in this movement. The MAYO leaders were a group of astute, largely university-educated Chicano activists, who felt that the established political parties, Republican or Democratic, were not being attentive to the needs of the Mexican American community and sought alternative ways of organizing. Well-read in political theory and involved in community organizing, this new breed of leadership sought to confront conditions of internal colonialism that were keeping the Mexican American people in a subordinate position. As such, they provided the linkage between macro-level conditions affecting the Mexican American community and their micro-level political behavior. Their goal was to raise the Chicano community's consciousness through mobilization at the micro level and at the same time draw responses from the governing authorities at the macro level. As a result, MAYO adopted a more militant confrontational style of politics in order to draw attention and possible action to the problems and needs confronting the Mexican American community. Educational reform for equity became one of its highest priorities.

Among the tactics that MAYO used in order to confront the educational problems of Chicanos in South Texas were demonstrations and school walkouts; among the more prominent demands for educational change was a call for bilingual/bicultural education.[11] Very little research has been done on the demonstrations and school walkouts supported by MAYO in Texas, however, the evidence collected thus far indicates that they were occurring at the same time that the Bilingual Education Bill was being discussed in Congress or shortly after the bill became law.[12] What is most apparent in MAYO's short history is the success it had in forging a new world view of the Chicano community and its relationship to Anglo American society.

In 1969, MAYO's political plans were to initiate a movement to redirect the social, political, and economic resources in a ten-county area of South Texas (the Winter Garden). At their semi-annual state meeting held in San Antonio, MAYO delegates decided the counties of Zavala, Dimmit, and La Salle in the Winter

Garden area would be the target in which to launch their plan.[13] The organization sponsored the Winter Garden Project and named José Angel Gutiérrez, the first president of MAYO, as its director.

The Winter Garden area was chosen because the economic and political conditions experienced there by the Mexican population are typical of South Texas. The project had four major goals: (1) gain control of the educational system in Chicano communities, (2) bring democracy to the target counties through majority rule, (3) initiate a direct confrontation over Chicano versus Anglo issues, and (4) initiate a program of rural economic development by ending Anglo economic domination and creating Chicano-controlled businesses and cooperatives.[14] Crystal City, the county seat of Zavala County, became the community base for the Project and the potential model for Chicano self-determination efforts in other South Texas communities.

Through the activities of the Winter Garden Project, a series of events took form that led to a change in the structure of ethnic relations in Crystal City and much of the Winter Garden region.[15] Ethnic power struggles developed in many communities in the region in which control of the schools came to occupy an important role.[16] Crystal City, however, was one of the most successful sites in Chicanos' obtaining control of community governing institutions. One of the reasons for this success is attributed to the formation of a parents' civil rights/political organization named *Ciudadanos Unidos* (United Citizens). This group formed the nucleus through which José Angel Gutiérrez launched one of MAYO's Winter Garden Project aims, the formation of an alternative political party, *La Raza Unida*.

Through the Raza Unida Party (RUP), the Chicano community in Zavala, Dimmit, and La Salle Counties struggled to liberate itself from the political and socioeconomic domination of the Anglo-American minority that had been in control since the turn of the century. Political mobilization efforts were rewarded in the local elections of 1970, as the RUP candidates for school board and city council won over their Anglo opposition in Crystal City; and in the nearby towns of Carrizo Springs (Dimmit county) and Cotulla (La Salle county), the results of the RUP work also produced victories in city council and school board races.[17] In Crystal City, the RUP obtained governing majorities in both the school board and city council. After this important political victory, Crystal City and *La Raza Unida* party became a major icon for the Chicano Civil Rights Movement in Texas and throughout the Southwest.

Schooling Reform under the Raza Unida Party

After gaining local political control in Crystal City, the RUP initiated a variety of reform programs designed to empower a Chicano community that had historically been denied access to positions of power. Among the reform programs initiated were a variety of housing, mental health, health care, economic, and education programs. The institution of schooling was particularly recognized for the important role it plays in the processes of cultural maintenance and change and the transmission of cultural values and meanings (ideology). Because of the strategic role schooling occupies, the RUP perceived the control and reorientation of the schools as central in reversing the processes of acculturation that Chicano students had been exposed to under Anglo-controlled schooling.[18]

By gaining control of the school system, José Angel Gutiérrez hoped to " . . . force the educational system to extend to the Mexican student."[19] The changes that were initiated in curriculum and in policy closely linked to the demands made by Chicano students in the fall of 1969 and guided by the goals and philosophical base of MAYO, the RUP, and the broader Chicano Movement. Bilingual/bicultural education, Mexican-American history courses, and the official recognition of Mexican holidays such as the *Deiz y Seis de Septiembre* and *Cinco de Mayo* were implemented as part of the school program. As such, many of the schooling reforms sought to revitalize selected ethnic cultural attachments of Mexicanos in the Southwest. Researchers have stressed that many of the reforms introduced sought to transmit this revitalized cultural knowledge through new curriculum, classroom, and community activities, cocurricular events, and a new philosophy of bilingual/bicultural education in order to create a unique "Chicano view" of the self and society.[20]

They add that many of the new educational changes introduced by the Chicano administration were the opposite of the schooling practices under the Anglo administration. The most noted change was in the language of instruction and social interaction in the schools, where Spanish, including the local dialect, was encouraged. In the new Chicano studies classes, a concerted effort was made to dispel the misconceptions and myths concerning the role of Mexicanos in the history of the United States and Texas by acknowledging their contributions. In addition, the Chicano school administration cultivated school-community links by creating opportunities for (1) local Mexicanos to pursue or augment educational careers, (2) integrating local Chicano culture and lifestyle through curricular development, (3) valuing Spanish and Mexican/Chicano expressive culture in school and community activities, and (4) improving schooling facilities through new school projects and innovations.

BILINGUAL EDUCATION AND POLITICS IN CRYSTAL CITY DURING THE 1970s

The emergence of bilingual/bicultural education in Crystal City was the result of various forces from both outside and inside the community. The call for bilingual education was a part of the broader Chicano civil rights movement, the bilingual education movement, and the ideology of ethnicity. As such, some scholars have noted that educational leaders within the movement came to regard bilingual education as having the potential to assist in the ethnic group's quest for identity, cultural status, and political power.[21] This political sentiment in combination with the sociopolitical climate of the civil rights movement and the passage of the Bilingual Education Act in 1968 helped to provide direction for the local leadership in Crystal City.

Philosophically, the new Chicano administration sought to develop and implement a program that was different from transitional bilingual programs that were being implemented at the time. School district officials sought to develop a maintenance bilingual/bicultural education program that would assist each student in becoming proficient in both Spanish and English.[22] In this manner, the district designed a program that was both unique and innovative, different from transitional programs where the native language was used initially for instruction, but whose goal was to promote rapid acculturation by getting the student to function totally in English as soon as possible. In contrast, the bilingual/bicultural education program in Crystal City had as its primary long-term goal helping the student achieve in school through the use of two languages (Spanish and English) and becoming bilingual and biliterate before graduating from high school.[23]

The rationale for maintenance bilingual/bicultural education consists of the following factors: (1) Spanish is a widespread language throughout the Southwest that should be recognized, (2) the use of Spanish for instruction, as well as the inclusion of the history and culture of the ethnic group within the classroom, will facilitate learning and reinforce the self-image of students, and (3) cultivating bilingualism is a valuable resource for the community and nation.

The implementation of a maintenance bilingual education program was not without opposition, however. Some community members were opposed to the use of Spanish language instruction in the schools, arguing that students have to be taught in English from the onset in order for them to succeed economically and socially in the United States. Chicano school leaders, however, argued that this was faulty logic, as many English-speaking Chicanos were unable to succeed economically due to structural and racial constraints that are part of an unequal system. The Chicano administration, in pushing for bilingualism and biliteracy through schooling, argued that competency in two languages was not only a crucial factor in ethnic identity, but also a key component in the development of a new Chicano view of the world. Under this world view, bilingualism and biliteracy were vital skills that would not only increase the competitive potential of Chicanos in the local and regional market, but also insure that future Chicano leaders would have the skills and philosophical outlook to occupy leadership positions in greater Aztlán.[24] However, reforms introduced by the new Chicano administration at the city, county, and school district level faced opposition both within and outside the community. The following analyzes the nature of this opposition by looking at the sociopolitical context that surrounded the introduction of the RUP-sponsored schooling reforms.

Opposition from Outside the Community

Opposition to Chicano political mobilization in the 1960s and 1970s came from various fronts. United States Congressman Henry B. Gonzáles of Texas surfaced as a staunch critic in a series of speeches in Congress where he voiced his opposition to the tactics used by MAYO.[25] The RUP also became the recipient of a barrage of attacks from Anglo politicians for its proposed economic development plans and particular brand of politics. Texas Governor Dolph Brisco led the attack by accusing José Angel Gutiérrez and other RUP leaders in Crystal City of being un-American and attempting to create a "little Cuba" in South Texas.[26] In the educational arena, higher-level educational agencies such as the Texas Education Agency, university training programs, and federally sponsored teams to prepare schools for racial integration were often unsupportive of the new Chicano liberation-oriented programs that were seen as detracting from national goals for sociocultural integration.[27]

Opposition from within the Community in the Early 1970s

Political opposition to the RUP in the community developed from its inception in 1970 until its demise ten years later. This opposition reflects both historical and political developments and dissension within the party. Historically, ethnic relations between Anglos and Mexicanos in the Winter Garden region (since the turn of the century) have reflected asymmetrical power relations. Mexicanos had few opportunities to develop and practice their leadership skills under the Anglo-controlled political economy of the region. During the 1950s and 1960s, however, a few select Mexican Americans, under Anglo sponsorship, became leaders in civic, political, religious, and educational spheres. This small group of early leaders achieved new levels of acculturation and assimilation that allowed them to pursue a diplomatic and cooperative approach in their relations with Anglos in the community and region.[28] Crystal City had its group of Anglo-sponsored Mexicano leaders, but this group and its followers were largely unsupportive of Chicano-oriented schooling reforms, and many of them withdrew their children from the public schools.

Local resistance also developed within the ranks of the RUP. The earliest reported dissension took place within the local decision-making council of *Ciudadanos Unidos* after a series of misunderstandings. This group complained about the domineering styles of some RUP leaders and the continued dependence upon "outsiders" in key leadership positions.[29] Several important Mexicano members broke away from the RUP and formed a new group that became known as the Independents. Politically this group advocated a moderate orientation between the more militant RUP Chicanos, on the one hand, and Anglo-sponsored Mexicanos with their diplomatically oriented acculturated world views, on the other. In general, this independent group regarded the new bilingual/bicultural education program as extreme and further cautioned against breaking all ties with Anglos.

Further RUP Dissension in the mid-1970s

By the mid-1970s, serious factionalization developed within the RUP from which it never recovered. A group of largely native-born Crystal City Chicanos increasingly came to disagree with José Angel Gutiérrez' leadership style. They complained that his leadership style was too dictatorial; further, he was faulted for failing to disseminate power among the up-and-coming local native Chicano leadership. In actuality, the complaint was a continuation of criticism that had surfaced in 1972. At that time, local native Chicanos complained that the majority of the administrators and principals in the school district were being filled by "outsiders" and not by natives of the community.[30] The critique was raised again by those members of the community who had participated in the different educational programs instituted by the RUP in the early 1970s aimed at training Chicanos for leadership positions.[31] In particular, local native Chicanos who had obtained their administrative credentials through the Carnegie Foundation Administrative Internship Program felt they were ready (and qualified) to step into the administrative and leadership positions within the district. This group of discontented leaders based their argument on the following: (1) A previous statement made by Gutiérrez implying that outsiders would occupy the leadership positions only until such time that local Chicanos would obtain their training and credentials; and (2) the charge made by natives that many of the outsiders had failed to fully integrate into the community. Consequently, by the mid-1970s native Crystal City Chicanos wanted access to these positions. When José Angel Gutiérrez failed to acquiesce to their demands, the disagreement contributed to the development of a schism within *Ciudadanos Unidos* and the RUP.

Other researchers have reported that the trouble began soon after Gutiérrez and eighteen other activists had returned from a trip to Cuba. Gutiérrez had been highly impressed with the high level of party organization and discipline in Cuba and proposed creating a *Comité de Nueve* (Committee of Nine) "which would make decisions on hiring and firings in the city and schools and would be the top policy maker in the party."[32] *Ciudadanos Unidos*, the nucleus to the RUP in the community, already had a functioning committee of city and county department heads and elected officials making many of the policy decisions. Nonetheless, Gutiérrez proposed to streamline this hierarchy and make the policy-making process more expedient. The emerging local Chicano leadership, already displeased with Gutiérrez' leadership style, were able to select their own people to the *Comité de Nueve*, thus effectively neutralizing his power on issues dealing with hiring and firings.[33] By 1976, the division between Gutiérrez supporters and those politically aligned to the Barrio Club (a local nucleus of native Chicano leaders) became so serious that *Ciudadanos Unidos* split into two factions.

Locally these factions became known as Raza Unida I or the "Gutiérristas" (signifying José Angel Gutiérrez' leadership) and Raza Unida II. The latter were led by a number of local school professionals and members of the Barrio Club. While the RUP as an organization continued to serve as the overall political party of the two factions competing for control of community governing institutions, each faction organized its respective *Ciudadanos Unidos* administrative and coordinating bodies. Consequently, each sponsored its own candidates for public office as they sought control of the school board and city council. Gaining control of the school board became one of the major battle grounds where the opposing factions engaged in political in-fighting. Thus, the 1975–1976 school year was pivotal with respect to changes in the composition of the school board and school administration.

The composition of the school board turned out to be a key political arena for controlling resources and direction of the educational programs, especially with respect to hiring and firing of school personnel. Even before the official split in the RUP, the internal opposing forces threatening the unity of the party became evident soon after the spring 1975 school board elections. The superintendent of schools, who had come in as an assistant superintendent in the fall of 1970 under the RUP, left his post in August 1975 after filing charges of nepotism against several members of the school board who sided with the anti-Gutiérrista forces. The superintendent was considered an outsider and a loyal Gutiérrez supporter. The school board filled his post with a local Chicano who had recently obtained his superintendent's credentials and was a member of the Barrio Club. Thus, the departure of the "outsider" superintendent and the filling of the position with an "insider" signaled the growing strength of the local leadership challenging Gutiérrez' powerhold.

School board elections are held annually for either two or three positions. In the spring 1976 school board elections, the Raza Unida II faction candidates swept into office, officially marking their stronghold and control of the schools. Consequently, starting with the school board elections in April 1976 and subsequently up until 1980, election campaigning for school board positions generated widespread community interest as both factions mobilized and canvassed for votes. Depending on which of the factions got control of the school board, the positions of superintendent, directors, supervisors, and some teachers often changed accordingly. Thus, between 1975 and 1980 there were a total of five different superintendents in charge of the public schools.

Despite all the changes at the district administrative level, the schooling reforms introduced by the RUP in the early 1970s continued to be the central focus of the new direction education took in the 1970s, no matter which of the two factions was in control. One of the reasons the school district's educational policies remained stable is a policy document, "The 22 Bilingual Recommendation[s]," approved by the school board in 1973.[34] When I talked to educational leaders in the school district and asked them if there were any noticeable changes in the support for the bilingual education program when the Raza Unida II faction gained control in 1976, their responses indicated there were none. For example, one of the elementary school principals, a native of Crystal City, responded that when Raza Unida II gained control: "The ideology or philosophy of bilingual education for the kids was still maintained because the belief of both factions, regardless if . . . [they] were not agreeing in political ideologies, *como quiera* [however] in the education [of Chicano students] there was no disagreement."[35] The assistant superintendent of curriculum in 1989, a native of the community who had successfully completed the Carnegie Foundation Administration Internship Program, gave a similar response: "As far as the educational program, you know, it continued the same . . . the bilingual program continued the same as far as I know. . . . So, as far as the bilingual program is [concerned], you know, . . . [it] had the same goals and objectives . . .; [they] still were the same."[36]

The above responses indicate that the split in the RUP was not so much over substantive ideological issues regarding the local movement and its role in education, but rather revolved around competition for the few high-status, better-paying jobs within the district. As noted above, native Chicanos within the community who had obtained their administrative certification through the programs brought in by the RUP wanted access to administrative positions held by outsiders. Ideologically, native Chicanos espoused as strong a cultural nationalist perspective as the outsiders who had come in to man the administrative positions initially. As a result, the local political battles were often over issues of who was more "Chicano" and supportive of programs intended to benefit the Raza.[37] Thus, when the Raza Unida II faction gained control of the schools in the mid-1970s the philosophical/ideological base of the bilingual program did not change. However, as will be seen in a later section, the political dynamics of continued intra-ethnic community in-fighting eventually had its toll on the direction the maintenance bilingual/bicultural education program was to take in the decade of the 1980s.

The years between 1975–1980 produced much discontent within the Chicano community as the two political factions skirmished for control of the local governing institutions. In general, the Raza Unida II faction was seen as having its political stronghold within the school district. The Raza Unida I faction, on the other hand, generally retained control of the county government. Control of city council, however, often flip-flopped on different election years between the two factions. Continual conflict was generated over the numerous election battles fought over a five-year period to determine which faction would gain control of the various political arenas.

The year 1979 turned out to be an important watershed year for the RUP. After the 1979 state elections, the RUP lost its function as a statewide political party. In Crystal City the party remained active after the state elections; however, 1979 was the last year that RUP candidates ran in local elections. Consequently, with the disbanding of the RUP, the cultural nationalist ideology and philosophy were considerably weakened, and correspondingly, membership and unity continued to dwindle without an organized political party that could espouse a strong cultural nationalist line. As a result, many former RUP members became incorporated into the Democratic Party or remained unaffiliated with a political party. With this structured change, the philosophy of the local Chicano movement was modified and its course of action reorganized. By 1982, José Angel Gutiérrez had been ousted as county judge and replaced by an Anglo.[38] When José Angel Gutiérrez left town, members of Raza Unida I were left without a dynamic and charismatic leader, which made it easier for members of earlier factions such as the Independents and *Raza Libre* to reemerge as influential participants in local elections. While these factions were not as visibly organized as in the early 1970s, former members felt more comfortable in forming coalitions with either the more conservative or moderate elements in the community in sponsoring candidates for school board, city council, or county government elections.

This changed political milieu became most apparent at the school district level. With the demise of the RUP and the weakening of Chicano nationalist ideology, the school district battles along RUP fractional lines ended. Community politics increasingly came to reflect the more conservative national trend as new coalitions were formed and new school board members were elected. A local Mexicano and former leader of the Raza Unida II faction was hired as superintendent in July 1981. He pushed to get "politics" out of the schools. In short, with the decline of the RUP and the ouster of José Angel Gutiérrez, the citizens of Crystal City entered a new era of political involvement in the decade of the 1980s. A local publication, *Now and Then in Zavala County*, commemorating the sesquicentennial of the state and county in 1985 made reference to this changed social dynamic:

> The school system under the leadership of Superintendent _____ _____, the City under the leadership of _____ _____, and the County under the gavel of County Judge Ron Carr, are reuniting the community during the present decade with goals which can be stated as " . . . looking back to history to correct our mistakes and better what was good to begin with to together make plans for a better tomorrow for the benefit of all our community, our state and our nation."[39]

The changed political dynamics in the community, in combination with national policy trends as reflected in the reauthorizations of the BEA in 1974 and 1978[40] are factors that help to explain why Crystal City educator's commitment to the goal of a prekindergarten through high school maintenance bilingual/bicultural education program came into question. As the local community launched into the decade of the 1980s, many educators started pushing for more English instruction, de-emphasizing the goals of bilingualism, biculturalism, and biliteracy. Despite the commitment to maintenance bilingual/bicultural education on the part of some of the administrators in the school district in the early 1980s, the changing policy directives at both the national and state level played a vital role in undermining their strong stand. The following section gives a brief synopsis of the role that policy shifts in education has had in restructuring the bilingual education program at the local level.

NATIONAL AND STATE POLICY DIRECTIVES IN THE 1980s AND BILINGUAL PROGRAM RESTRUCTURING

The federal role in education from 1955 through 1980 was one of increased federal involvement for the purpose of assuring greater educational equity for ethnic minorities, women, the poor, and the handicapped.[41] This was done through a number of mechanisms, including the adoption and creation of interventions, establishing school improvement strategies and tactics, increased funding to fill the void left by the lack of state and local funds, and continued monitoring by enforcement of regulations and evaluation. In the early 1980s, however, this pattern of policy involvement by the federal government changed to one emphasizing the transfer of educational authority to the state and local levels. Under the Reagan administration (1981–1988) federal policy involvement changed from concerns on equity to concerns on excellence. In other words, the Reagan administration put in place a different set of priorities that placed emphasis on (1) excellence and standards of performance, (2) individual competition, (3) selectivity and minimum entrance standards, (4) economic and productivity concerns, (5) parental choice, (6) local initiative, (7) deregulation, and (8) the support of traditional values.[42] This different set of priorities indicates that social, welfare, and equity concerns are no longer major forces guiding national level educational policy. In their place the national rhetoric is focused on improving the nation's schools for the purpose of becoming more competitive economically. This message came across loud and clear in the report, *A Nation at Risk*, published by the National Commission on Excellence in Education in 1983. The outcome of this report was that it encouraged the design of career ladders for teachers and the upward adjustment of standards for both teachers and students. The effects have been far reaching as the focus of national educational policy has moved away from equity to excellence, and reduced the federal role in education considerably. In turn, it has increased the role of the state governments in educational policy development.

Texas was one of the states that most enthusiastically followed the policy directives initiated by the Reagan administration in the early 1980s. In 1984, newly elected Governor Mark White formed a task force, headed by business millionaire Ross Perot, and charged it with the task of formulating a plan that would bring Texas schools and the Texas economy into a competitive level.[43] One of the concerns that prompted the push for a closer integration of education and the economy was that the traditional strongholds in the Texas economy—agriculture and oil—had lost considerable ground due to strong competition from the international market. As a consequence, the Texas economy shifted away from these traditional sectors into the high-technology arena. State leaders, in turn, have placed more emphasis on education as a way of developing the human capital necessary for this growing sector. The concern with human capital development is very much evident in *A Nation at Risk*, and Texas leaders have followed the lead.

The Select Committee on Public Education, the taskforce chaired by Ross Perot, made several recommendations that were part of the national educational reform, for example, the creation of a teacher-career ladder merit system and the upward adjustment of standards. In addition, it also recommended the infamous No Pass/No Play provision for students, and further accountability testing of all teachers (the TECAT) and of students.[44] These recommendations became part of the state educational reform legislation, House Bill (HB) 72, which was passed in 1984. Some of the provisions in HB 72 (e.g., TECAT, No Pass/No Play, and teacher assessment) were very controversial after implementation; however, the state has maintained them in order to justify the increased expenditure in public education, especially increased pay for teacher salaries based on merit. One of the outcomes of the state educational reforms has been the effective deskilling of teachers, for the state controls the certification of teachers based on TECAT scores, teacher assessment (for merit pay), and mandated student testing.[45] In effect this has created a high-stakes testing environment where teachers are in jeopardy of losing their jobs based on test scores and performance evaluations. Furthermore, Texas school reforms have further entrenched the use of testing as a means of assessing student's educational progress.

The Texas Educational Assessment of Minimal Skills (TEAMS), an integral part of HB 72, is required of all school districts in Texas and mandates that students be tested at the end of first, third, fifth, seventh, ninth, and eleventh grades.[46] The results of the tests are used to determine the percentage of students scoring at, above, and below grade level. As a result of TEAMS testing, educators in Crystal City have expressed that they feel pressured to improve student's test scores. Consequently, with so much concern over the academic performance of students resting on standardized test scores, much of the push for changing the structure of the bilingual program came from the teachers and administrators themselves.[47]

Changes in the Structure of the Bilingual/Bicultural Education Program in the 1980s

As the decade of the 1970s came to an end, and a new political and educational outlook took form in the early 1980s, the Crystal City bilingual/bicultural education program began to change. The secondary bilingual/bicultural program had been defunded at the end of the 1970s and reduced in scope to include the first two years of high school only. By 1981, the program was operative only at the junior high level, where students were required to take two years of Spanish (Spanish I and II) as part of their coursework. The required courses in Spanish formed an integral component of the bilingual program and served to cultivate the student's native language. A former teacher at the junior high school from 1975–78, now an elementary school principal, recalls the junior high curriculum including the Spanish classes required of all students:

> As far as the curriculum, they had both at the junior high. They had the curriculum for the content area in English and there was a Spanish course that was required for students to take in the sixth through eighth. So because you [the students] were coming from the elementary schools, since in the elementary schools, I mean, you had both bilingual and non-bilingual English classes, so in order to keep up with the Spanish that you had learned in the elementary schools, you were required to also take Spanish in the sixth, seventh, and eighth grades. That was just to make sure that you did not forget your Spanish throughout the junior high. Pero, the rest of the . . . courses like in the content areas and in social studies were taught in English, in English.[48]

The courses in Spanish were highly regarded as an innovative aspect of the curriculum and formed the nucleus of the Spanish Language Arts component in the junior high school. Nonetheless, administrators report that by the 1984–85 school year, the school district dropped the Spanish Language Arts component and replaced it with a required English reading course. The force behind the change apparently came from the state legislature. School officials explained that the passage of House Bill 246 by the Texas legislature mandated a reading course for those students reading one year or more below grade level as determined by standardized tests such as the California Test of Basic Skills (CTBS). As an outcome of this legislation, the school board passed a policy directive making the reading course a blanket policy for all students in grades six through eight whether they were reading below grade level or not. The former director of the bilingual program for the school district recalls the action taken by the school administration:

> This meant that the Spanish language arts in the junior high was done away with. The only classes we could do away with in order to introduce the required reading classes were the Spanish language arts, and in that I feel that we have done ourselves a disservice. When the state came in with a thrust to teach reading classes we had to do away with our Spanish language arts. That's the course we [the school administrators] recommended that it be removed. We could not do away with the other required classes like science, history, or math. *Quitamos el Spanish language arts y metimos el* reading course required by the state.[49]

Two years later, the status of Spanish in the high school curriculum was further weakened when students were given the option of taking French instead of Spanish as part of their coursework in meeting their foreign language requirement.[50]

The loss of federal funding and the emergence of a new national and state educational reform agenda were two important factors leading to changes in the structure of the bilingual/bicultural education program at the local level. In the early 1980s, an in-house debate took place among the administrators and teaching staff regarding how to restructure the bilingual program, given federal and state policy changes. Some of the group sought to maintain the policy as was outlined in the *22 Bilingual Recommendation[s]*, while others sought to place emphasis on more English instruction. This latter group felt that the students were not making the transition to English soon enough and were lagging behind in their English reading. Concern over students' reading ability in English was heightened by low scores on achievement tests such as the CTBS and the TEAMS. Since these tests were in English, students in the bilingual program, who were developing reading skills in their native language first, were at a disadvantage. While the new Chicano administration had minimized the emphasis on standardized testing in the early 1970s in favor of individualized instruction, standardized testing remained an integral part of the state schooling structure and the primary means used to measure student achievement.

State educational reform policy had an adverse effect in the restructuring of the bilingual education program at the secondary and junior high school level. During the 1984–1985 school term, the bilingual program underwent further modifications. A seventeen-member committee consisting of teachers, elementary school principals, program directors, and supervisors worked on a "Proposed Modifications in the Bilingual Program of Instruction Plan." The committee had several meetings during the school year to discuss the proposed modifications in the bilingual program. Several of the members of this committee recall that meetings were often quite heated between different factions on the committee. A group of committee members, the majority, favored restructuring the bilingual program to the point that students would be required to transition into the English-only instructional track by the end of the first grade. The other group, the minority, argued that the goals of the bilingual program should still be those of the maintenance program at least up to the fifth grade.

The majority of the committee cited numerous reasons why the school district had to restructure the program into a prekindergarten through first-grade program. First, they argued that Spanish is the predominant language spoken in community and the Winter Garden region, thus more emphasis had to be placed on teaching English, especially in the schools. Second, they added that the school district was under pressure to improve TEAMS test scores under the state of Texas school reform policy. Third, they noted that both teachers and parents were concerned with low scores on standardized achievement tests and attributed this outcome to low English-language ability. Fourth, they argued that in the community context, students had few opportunities to use English, given that in the majority of informal social gatherings, as well as most business transactions, Spanish is the language of interaction. Consequently, these educators saw the schools as the primary institution where students were exposed to English; and given that they were citizens of an English-speaking country, the school had to take the responsibility and role of setting the appropriate example in teaching English. The director of the bilingual program for the district, serving on the committee at the time, expressed this sentiment:

> We are a rural community and somewhat isolated. The push for English on the part of the parents is due to this. I think it's because they feel that the only place they [the students] are going to speak English is during the time they are in school. Parents feel that the bilingualism [maintenance of Spanish] will be taken care of at the home and that the school will push the English. In a community like ours where bilingualism and biculturalism is inrooted, especially after the aftermath of the late 60s and [the RUP] . . . holidays like *Cinco de Mayo y el Diez y Sies de Septiembre . . . se festejan mas aqui que el* Fourth of July or other holidays. Ah . . . after the takeover it became OK to recognize [the Spanish language] . . . and teach in Spanish, but after a while our scores in English reading and language were low and that's when parents [and educators] started putting pressure on the school district for a change in policy.[51]

The minority on the committee, who were very much committed to a maintenance bilingual/bicultural program, did not argue against any of these concerns. They saw the acquisition of English proficiency as a vital and necessary goal, and they saw bilingual education as the appropriate instructional program to teach students English. Where they differed with the majority was in their philosophy and expanded view of what the bilingual education program provided students. An elementary school teacher and member of the committee stated:

> They are not serving the population as they should because the bilingual program was not meant to be a remedial type of education. It was to develop the concept and self-identity of the Hispanics, for them to be able to relate and not

to be assimilated into the Anglo culture but to contribute to it through their culture because America is built on many different cultures. . . . The American culture is a combination of many cultures. People have to understand that through their culture they can contribute something to America and make it greater than what it is. But don't try to abandon your culture because you cannot totally assimilate to any of the other cultures in America. They [the majority on the committee] believe that since you are in the United States you ought to be speaking English and that English is the primary language of the country. When you stop and think about it, what is the primary language of the United States? I believe that an individual in order to be a totally bilingual individual should be able to function in what I call the spheres of communication. . . .I honestly and truly believe that in order for an individual to be a good citizen of any country he must be loyal to his own language and his own culture. And when he fails to be loyal to that he has failed to be loyal to the new country that he is trying to be part of. . . . When you teach him his own language then he can easily transfer into the other language because of what he has learned in his own language. This was my argument [that] I fought tooth and nail [for] until I got to the point that I said, look I have enough problems fighting with the kids, fighting with the parents and then fighting with the administration is too much. I [will] just go ahead and do whatever they want me to do, and if they want to call it a bilingual program, I know it's a prostitution of the bilingual law, but if the state is not really worried about it, why should I be worried about it.[52]

According to this teacher and the members on the committee who agreed with his argument, bilingual education is the most appropriate pedagogy for learning English as well as the best means of integrating the culture and history of the ethnic group.[53] Nonetheless, the majority on the committee were able to have the final say. They were sufficiently convinced that bilingual education was holding back students, given the criticism emanating from the national studies and the local sentiment of some teachers, parents, and community people. Thus, with the majority sentiment pushing for more English instruction, the bilingual program was restructured and given form in the "Proposed Modifications in Bilingual Program of Instruction Plan" which, in essence, restructured the bilingual program into a transitional prekindergarten through first-grade program.[54]

According to the proposed modifications, English language use is given prominence, although Spanish native language instruction is emphasized initially. The explicit goal of the "instructional plan" is to use Spanish language instruction to facilitate the eventual transition to the English-only instructional track by the time the student starts second grade. This document specifically states that if students have not reached the transitional level in English by the time they start second grade they will, nonetheless, begin their reading and writing in the English language. In such cases, the "instructional plan" calls for the provision of further development of oral language skills in English. Spanish language instruction is used, however, whenever children do not understand a concept. This practice is referred to by teachers and administrators as the "only when needed" criterion, although, some administrators feel that this practice may " . . .still be too loose because it may mean two minutes per day for one teacher to a total reliance for others."[55]

Broader national policy changes in the early 1980s also contributed to the modifications in the bilingual program due to the greater say that parents were given under the principle of parental choice. National educational policy under the Reagan administration had made parental choice a key component of returning educational decision making to the state and local level. Texas followed the lead and changed the state bilingual program policy requiring parental consent in order to have a child enroll in the bilingual program. This change in policy led the district to establish an English-only instructional track and a bilingual program instructional track by the fall of 1985.

The structure of the bilingual program in Crystal City has remained the same since 1985, in spite of the fact that the state of Texas requires the provision of a bilingual program in grades kindergarten through fifth grade. During the spring of 1988, the Texas Education Agency made a monitoring visit to the district to observe the implementation of the bilingual education program. After the visit the agency found the district in noncompliance for failing to provide an adequate bilingual program for Limited English Proficient (LEP) students in second through fifth grade.[56]

CONCLUSION

The foregoing analysis has presented an historical ethnographic analysis of the political factors and forces affecting the restructuring of the bilingual/bicultural education program in Crystal City. In doing so, I have looked at the intersection of local politics with national and state bilingual education policy change over a twenty-year period. During this time period, the bilingual education program in the community has undergone substantial changes. In the mid-1970s, the model of education that developed under Chicano leadership was closely linked to the goals of the Chicano movement at the time. The Chicano administration in the school district sought to empower students for future leadership roles in the community and greater Aztlán through the transmission of a new sense of cultural identity and values, political socialization, and maintenance of native language. In essence, this Chicano world view promoted the goals of equality and community.

In the late 1980s, the goals of revived ethnic identity and community through bilingual/bicultural education had been abandoned. The bilingual education program had been transformed into a transitional prekindergarten through first-grade program whose primary goal is to transition limited English proficient (LEP) students into an all-English instruction classroom by the end of the first grade. The inclusion of ethnic history and culture is no longer emphasized in the school curriculum. The resultant outcome of this development has been that the goal of equality has remained a viable one within the context of transitional bilingual education. The goal of community, on the other hand, has lost considerable ground.

NOTES

1. The research reported in this chapter is based on approximately sixteen months of dissertation fieldwork in Crystal City between February 1988 and October 1989.

2. I use the terms Chicano, Mexican American, and Mexicano interchangeably. The term that many Mexican Americans use as a self-identification term in South Texas is Mexicano. The term Anglo American is used to refer to white Americans of European descent.

3. Cultural nationalism refers to the philosophical/ideological stand that emerged with certain Chicano organizations such as the Raza Unida Party. The basis for political organization was ethnic identity and links to the ethnoterritory that was lost by Mexico in the Mexican-American War of 1846–48.

4. Walter Elwood Smith, Jr. and Douglas E. Foley, *The Transition of Multiethnic Schooling in Model Town, Texas: 1930–1969* (Final Report NIE Project No. R020825 and No. 3-4003. Washington, DC: U.S. Department of Health, Education and Welfare, Office of Education, 1975).

5. Mario Barrera, *Beyond Aztlán: Ethnic Autonomy in Comparative Perspective* (New York: Praeger, 1988), 6.

6. Niles Hansen, *The Border Economy: Regional Development in the Southwest* (Austin: University of Texas Press, 1981).

7. James Weeks Tiller Jr., *The Texas Winter Garden: Commercial Cold-Season Vegetable Production* (Austin, TX: University of Texas, Bureau of Business Research, Graduate School of Business, 1971).

8. Douglas E. Foley, C. Mota, D.E. Post, and I. Lozano, *From Peones to Politicos: Ethnic Relations in a South Texas Town, 1900 to 1977* Revised edition (Austin: Center for Mexican American Studies, University of Texas Press, 1988).

9. Mario Barrera, *Race and Class in the Southwest: A Theory of Racial Inequality* (Notre Dame, IN: Notre Dame University Press, 1979).

10. For further discussion on the concept of cultural division of labor, see Michael Hechter, "Group Formation and the Cultural Division of Labor," *American Journal of Sociology*, 84(2) (1978): 293–318.

11. Ignacio M. García, *United We Win: The Rise and Fall of La Raza Unida Party* (Tucson: University of Arizona, Mexican American Studies and Research Center, 1989).

12. Discussion of the political context is found in Armando Navarro, "El Partido de La Raza Unida in Crystal City: A Peaceful Revolution" Ph.D. dissertation, University of California, Riverside, 1974; García, *United We Win: The Rise and Fall of La Raza Unida Party*. For further discussion on the passage of the Bilingual Education Act in 1969 see the dissertation by Armando Trujillo, "Community Empowerment and Bilingual/Bicultural Education: A Study of the Movimiento in a South Texas Community" Ph.D. dissertation, University of Texas at Austin, 1993.

13. García, *United We Win: The Rise and Fall of La Raza Unida Party*.

14. José Angel Gutiérrez, "Aztlán: Chicano Revolt in the Winter Garden," *La Raza Magazine* (1974): 36–49.

15. The following sources provide historical material on Crystal City and the Winter Garden region: John Staples Shockley, *Chicano Revolt in a Texas Town* (Notre Dame, IN: Notre Dame University Press, 1974); Foley et al., *From Peones to Politicos: Ethnic Relations in a South Texas Town, 1900 to 1977*.

16. Donald Eugene Post, "Ethnic Competition for Control of Schools in Two South Texas Towns" Ph.D. dissertation, University of Texas, Austin, 1975.

17. Shockley, *Chicano Revolt in a Texas Town*.

18. Smith and Foley, *The Transition of Multiethnic Schooling in Model Town, Texas: 1930–1969*. See also Henry S. Reskin (Producer and Director) and Roger Williams (Director), *The Schools of Cristal* [Film]. (Stanford, CA: Stanford Center for Research and Development in Teaching, circa 1974).

19. Gutiérrez, "Aztlán: Chicano Revolt in the Winter Garden."

20. Smith and Foley, "Mexicans' Resistance to Schooling in a South Texas Colony," *Education and Urban Society* (1978): 145–176.

21. Maria Eugenia Matute-Bianchi, "The Federal

Mandate for Bilingual Education," In Raymond V. Padilla (ed.), *Ethnoperspectives in Bilingual Education Research: Bilingual Education and Public Policy in the United States* (Eastern Michigan University, Bilingual Bicultural Education Program Ypsilanti, MI: 1979): 18–38.

22. Readers interested in pursuing further reading on the distinction between transitional and maintenance bilingual education programs should consult: Roth Kjolseth, "Bilingual Education Programs in the U.S.: For Assimilation or Pluralism?" in R. R. (ed.), *Bilingualism in the Southwest*, Second edition (Tucson: University of Arizona Press, 1982): 3–28. Tove Skutnabb-Kangas, *Bilingualism or Not: The Education of Minorities* (Clevedon, England: Multilingual Matters, 1981). For an in-depth discussion on the philosophy and structure of the bilingual/bicultural education program in Crystal City, the reader should consult *Crystal City Independent School District 22 Bilingual Recommendation[s]* (Crystal City, TX: Crystal City Independent School District, circa 1973).

23. *Crystal City ISD 22 Bilingual Recommendation[s]*, circa 1973; Jeanette Lizcano, Ambrosio Meléndrez, and Eliseo Solís, *Cristal* (Crystal City, TX: Crystal City Independent School District, circa 1974).

24. The schools, in particular, were seen as key institutions for transmitting a new Chicano world view. Through schooling, in the form of bilingual/bicultural education, the Chicano administration in the school district sought to empower students for future leadership roles in the community and greater Aztlán through the transmission of a new sense of cultural identity and values, political socialization, and maintenance of native language. José Angel Gutiérrez, the school board president of the Crystal City Independent School District from 1970–72 and founder of the RUP in Zavala County, expresses this view, and by extension the RUP's view, of education: "Obviously we are a class of illiterates. Education in this kind of society is mandatory if not a prerequisite for survival. We feel that if we are going to take over, as we are doing, we must also have the expertise to exercise that power. Education to us is also the fountain of socialization where our values get distorted and cultural imposition takes place. Not only do we want to reject that but we want to substitute that with our own values which are just as dear and important. Education, finally, is important for us because from that kind of leadership that will emerge from those schools we will have the leaders for tomorrow, to build a greater Aztlán." Quote taken from Henry S. Reskin (Producer and Director) and Roger Williams (Director), *The Schools of Cristal: An Experiment in Change* [film]. (Stanford, CA: Center for Research and Development in Teaching, circa 1974). For further information on the concept of Aztlán, see Rudolfo A. Anaya and Francisco Lomelí, *Aztlán: Essays on the Chicano Homeland* (Albuquerque, NM: El Norte Publications/Academia, 1989).

25. Henry B. González, *Congressional Record—United States House of Representatives*, 115, Parts 7, 8 (April 3, 15, 16, 22, 28). (Washington, DC, 1969).

26. Mack K. Sisk, "La Raza's Gutiérrez Blasts Brisco," *San Antonio Light* (Sept. 26, 1976); "Zavala Fund Misuse Cited," *Corpus Christi Caller* (Sept. 30, 1976).

27. See Smith and Foley, "Mexicans' Resistance to Schooling in a South Texas Colony."

28. Smith and Foley, "Mexicans' Resistance to Schooling in a South Texas Colony."

29. Smith and Foley, "Mexicans' Resistance to Schooling in a South Texas Colony;" Interviews with several Crystal City community residents during my fieldwork period, 1988–89.

30. Sally J. Andrade, *Chicano Mental Health: The Case of Cristal: An Evaluation of the Zavala County Mental Health Outreach Program.* (Austin, TX: Hogg Foundation for Mental Health, 1978).

31. One of the programs brought in by the RUP in the early seventies was the Carnegie Foundation Administration Internship Program, funded in 1973, which trained Chicano/a public school administrators with superintendents' credentials and a Master of Arts degree through San Diego State University.

32. Ignacio M. García, *United We Win: The Rise and Fall of La Raza Unida Party*, 205.

33. García, *United We Win: The Rise and Fall of La Raza Unida Party*, 206.

34. The *Crystal City Independent School District 22 Bilingual Recommendation[s]* served to give coherence and stability regarding the goals of the bilingual/bicultural education programs during the decade of the seventies.

35. Interview June 12, 1989.

36. Interview September 4, 1989.

37. For more information on the nature of these community debates between factions, see Greg Barrios (ed.), La Verdad: *History of a Chicano Newspaper* (Los Angeles: Posada Press 1981).

38. Interview with the County Commissioner, Pct. 3, Zavala County, September 1, 1989. See also minutes of the Zavala County Commissioners Court, Vol 10, January 26, 1981 for details regarding the conflict between Judge Gutiérrez and the county commissioners. The commissioners had stopped payment of the judge's salary on November 1980, because they felt he had been absent from his office and had not been performing the duties of county judge. Judge Gutiérrez requested reinstatement of his salary at the January 26, 1981, meeting; however, when the county commissioners failed to make a motion for reinstatement, the judge walked out of the meeting.

39. *Now and Then in Zavala County*, A History of Zavala County, Texas, written by the People of Zavala County (Published by Zavala County Historical Commission, 1985), 61.

40. By the mid-1970s, national bilingual education policy changed to one emphasizing educational equity through the mastery of English; it also limited both the number and type of student who could be served and the length of time they could receive native language instruction. For a comprehensive discussion on the factors and politics affecting this policy change, see Ray Padilla, "Federal Policy Shifts and the Implementation of Bilingual Education Programs," in F. T. Córdova and J. R. García (eds.), *The Chicano Struggle: Analyses of Past and Present Efforts*. (Bingham-

ton, NY: Bilingual Press/Editorial Bilingüe 1984), 90–110.

41. David L. Clark and Terry A. Astuto, The *Significance and Permanence of Changes in Federal Educational Policy, 1980–1988*. (Bloomington: Policy Studies Center of the University Council for Educational Administration, Indiana University, 1985).

42. Clark and Austo, *The Significance and Permanence of Changes in Federal Educational Policy*.

43. Linda M. McNeil, "The Politics of Texas School Reform," in William L. Boyd and Charles T. Kerchner (eds.), *The Politics of Excellence and Choice in Education* (New York: Falmer Press, 1988), 199–216.

44. McNeil, "The Politics of Texas School Reform," *The Politics of Excellence and Choice in Education*.

45. McNeil, "The Politics of Texas School Reform."

46. The end of the 1980s brought further refinement in assessment instruments. The Texas Education Agency saw the need to replace the TEAMs test with a more rigorous test, the Texas Assessment of Academic Skills (TAAS).

47. This information was obtained in an interview with the former Title VII and State Bilingual Program Director, Oct. 2, 1989.

48. Interview July 12, 1989.

49. Interview June 14, 1988.

50. This information was obtained in an interview with the Assistant Superintendent of Curriculum and Instruction, August 7, 1988.

51. Interview, June 14, 1988.

52. Interview, September 12, 1989.

53. A recent government publication that provides research evidence on the effectiveness of bilingual education programs is United States General Accounting Office, *Bilingual Education: A New Look at the Research Evidence*, GAO/PEMD-87-12BR (Gaithersburg, MD: Author, 1987).

54. The Proposed Modifications in the Bilingual Program of Instruction Plan are contained in a school Memo dated August 7, 1985. School officials I interviewed stated that the "Plan" had been submitted to the Board of Trustees for approval; however, in my review of the school board minutes I found no reference of

official approval. Nonetheless, the Plan outlines the steps to be taken in assigning students to the bilingual program or English program of instruction based on (a) parental consent and (b) the use of the *Bilingual Syntax Measure* (B.S.M.), a language assessment instrument used to test the children's oral proficiency in English. The Plan further outlines that the B.S.M. will be used in prekindergarten to assess the children's language proficiency at both midyear and end of the year. Students who score at level 4 or 5 at midyear enter a readiness program in English to get them ready to read English. Students who score a 4 or 5 at the end of the year are then transitioned into the English instructional program. Students in kindergarten follow the same pattern of testing. If they score a 4 or 5, they are then transitioned into the English instructional program. Students in the bilingual prekindergarten, kindergarten, and first grade receive English oral language development, but are also exposed to English instruction in social studies where Spanish is used when students do not comprehend. In science and math, students receive English instruction once they show evidence of a 70 percent degree of competency. The Plan also stresses that English be used in informal situations within the classroom between teacher and aide and in the playground and lunchroom. The Committee felt that the use of English in informal situations was necessary in order to provide examples of English use for the children.

55. Interview with former director of federal and state bilingual program for the school district, June 14, 1988.
56. Information on this development was obtained in an interview with the principal of the elementary school concerned, September 8, 1989.

14

SITUATIONAL IDENTITY OF SUBURBAN MEXICAN AMERICAN POLITICIANS IN A MULTIETHNIC COMMUNITY

JOSÉ ZAPATA CALDERÓN

This chapter addresses the situational character of ethnic identification of middle-class Mexican American politicians in Monterey Park, a multiethnic middle-class suburb undergoing rapid demographic changes.[1]

Specifically, Monterey Park is a microcosm of larger political and social transformations taking place in Los Angeles County, where racial minorities and new immigrants are becoming a majority, and where the dual issues of growth and increasing immigration have become important concerns of public debate.

In Monterey Park, as a result of this process, there is an imbalance being created in the power structure between the new majority of Latinos and Asians, who differ in economic and political power, and a dwindling Anglo minority who still control local political institutions.

The main material for my research has been taken from interviews with various Mexican American opinion leaders in the city council arena, including city politicians, elected public officials, and politically active businesspersons. The interviews were complemented with field notes written from my lived experience as a resident in the community, from participating in Latino organizations, and from working as a researcher in the "Changing Communities" project funded by the Ford Foundation in 1989.

Since opinion leaders do influence trends and public opinion, it is important to focus on their perceptions[2] and how they see themselves within a multiethnic community at a time when sharp demographic transformations are taking place around them. In this chapter, I begin to draw out the nature of Mexican American politics in the context of these changes by focusing on how a select group of suburban Mexican American leaders identify themselves politically in the city hall arena. An analysis of their perceptions can help in discerning what role class and ethnic factors play in the politics of "middle-class" Mexican Americans and in their relations with other ethnic groups in this multiethnic setting.

I will, first of all, give a brief overview of the demographics of Mexican Americans and Latinos in Monterey Park, and, secondly, an example from my work of the situational character that Mexican American opinion leaders exhibit in their identity and in their perceptions on the existence or nonexistence of a homogeneous Mexican American political community.

DEMOGRAPHICS

Mexican Americans in Monterey Park are part of a growing Latino majority in a region, the San Gabriel Valley, which has been targeted nationally by the Southwest Voter Registration Project as having the most potential in the southwest United States for voter registration and political empowerment campaigns.[3]

Until 1960, Monterey Park's population consisted of 85 percent Anglo, 3 percent Asian, and 12 percent Latino (see Table 14-1). In the 1970s, however, there were a number of external changes that deeply affected the city. Briefly, these included the federal government's recognition of mainland China and the exclusion of Taiwan from official diplomatic status; the emergence of the Pacific Rim as an interrelated economy; a dissatisfaction of incoming immigrant Asian families with the conditions in older and nearby Los Angeles ethnic neighborhoods; and a significant increase in the Latino population within the city. By the 1980 census, Monterey Park's population had radically changed to 40 percent Asian, 37 percent Latino, and 20 percent Anglo.

Spurred on by developers and realtors advertising and selling Monterey Park property in Hong Kong and Taiwan, the population continued its shift in 1990. In

TABLE 14–1   Ethnic Composition of Monterey Park, California 1960–1990

Ethnic Group	1960		1970		1980		1986		1990	
White	32,306	85.4%	24,476	50.5%	13,552	25.0%	9,665	15.8%	7,129	11.7%
Hispanic	4,391	11.6%	16,477	34.0%	21,079	38.8%	18,693	30.5%	19,031	31.3%
Black	11	.003%	111	.2%	661	1.2%	1,174	1.9%	330	0.5%
Asian	1,113	2.9%								
	7,441	15.0%	19,046	35.0%	31,467	51.4%	34,022	56.0%		
Total	37,822	–	49,166	–	54,338	–	61,246	–	60,738	–

Sources: Data compiled from the 1980/1990 U.S. Census and the 1986 Test Census of Los Angeles County.

1990, the Asian population became a majority with 56 percent while the Anglo population declined to 11.7 percent, and Latinos dropped to 31.3 percent.

As Latinos have been confronted with these rapid demographic changes, they have developed the commonality of having to work with other ethnic groups in the political arena to have some say in the decision-making process. At the same time, they have aligned themselves on varying sides of the political interests that dominate the city's power struggles.

PERSPECTIVES ON SITUATIONAL IDENTITY

The recent works of Felix Padilla have raised the issue of the situational character of Latino identity. His works stress that Latino ethnic consciousness is "situationally specific" according to the common conditions of inequality and the need for Latino groups to take action around similar concerns.[4] This perception goes along with the view of some academicians who define ethnic/racial identity as being in a constant process of being recreated,[5] and ethnic groups as being primarily political interest groups who organize themselves around common political interests.[6]

I argue that these interests are not only related to competition over resources, but also have a class foundation. The political positions of the Mexican American politicians interviewed for the purposes of this article take on a character of what sociologist Erik Olin Wright calls contradictory class locations.[7] These positions, often generalized under the term "middle class," are contradictory in that they sway between various class interests. As managerial professionals, they are considered part of the power structure in being able to supervise workers and in having significant say over the production process. On the other hand, they do not own the resources of production and they can be fired at any time by their employer.[8] When applied on a micro scale, all those interviewed or observed in city positions are primarily managerial professionals who have some control over the production process. For example, to name a few, a former city council member managed a store before he got into the profession of being a city manager. Today, he runs his own consultant business and employs a staff of individuals. One of the Mexican American former councilmembers is the principal of an elementary school where he supervises other employees in the school. A Mexican American developer, who has held various positions in city hall, also employs and manages others. A corporate public relations officer also has others working under him, has flexibility in his time, and has some control over how he carries out his work.

These individuals, affected by their contradictory locations in the class structure and the rapid demographic changes occurring around them, are being forced to rethink their ethnic identity in relation to newcomers and to the political power of Mexican Americans overall.

In this context, how these politicians identify themselves takes on a situational character incorporating both shared historical experiences and individual class interests.

SITUATIONAL CHARACTER OF IDENTITY

A former Mexican American city official who aligned himself more with growth interests exemplifies this situational character when he states his unclarity as to why he identifies himself as Hispanic:

> Hispanic origins. Hispanic? It's just a nice category. It doesn't mean anything to me. It is a way to classify yourself. I eat Mexican food but I don't speak the language. But, retain my culture—retained what culture? My parents consider themselves Californios. You know I belong to—am active in the California Historical Society, in the Southwest group and those kinds of things. Well, you know, I'm not too sure what else it would mean.

In identifying himself as a "Californio," this former city official referred to his class lineage as being rooted in the early 19th century California upper class of *hacendados* or landowners.

Although calling himself and his ancestors Californios, he used the term "Hispanic" repeatedly when talking about the contemporary Mexican American. At the same time, he admitted that he didn't identify to a large degree with the Mexican American culture, that his family didn't speak any Spanish, and that the broken Spanish he had once acquired was now lost because he was around "educated" people.

Another former city councilperson and businessman, now in his early sixties, related that people of his generation used to call themselves Mexican Americans but that he now primarily called himself Hispanic. Although calling himself Hispanic, he still strongly identifies with his Mexican roots:

> As a child my father left to go—he was an officer in the Mexican army and so he came here to get my mother and take her back. My mother was with her family and they didn't want her to go back. So he came and he left. And so as a result he left when my mother was pregnant with me. I never did know my father. So my father was from Mexico City. My mother was born in New Mexico. My grandfather was Eustos Zapata and he got involved in the revolutions and I guess he rode with Pancho Villa.

Another Mexican American elected leader in the community also prefers to call himself Hispanic and identifies the term with its relationship to other groups who are from Latin America:

> Hispanic is a good, easy common term. You know, it used to be Chicano or Mexican American. Now, I think there's more activity going down. There are other people who are similar to me but maybe don't have specific national origins. They don't come from Mexico but come here from Central America or Latin America.

SOCIAL CLASS AND ASSIMILATION

The responses of these Mexican Americans all manifest the common characteristic of aligning themselves with powerful developer class interests, on the one hand, and accepting their assimilation into a middle-class community, on the other. Acknowledging that they have lost use of the Spanish language, they are willing to identify themselves as Hispanic. However, they also exhibit an ambivalence in their beliefs that this term has any real meaning for their political identity.

Instead of any unifying identity, they propose the absence of an ethnic political community among Latinos in Monterey Park for various reasons, including divisions within the group, apathy, and the effects of a middle-class suburban culture.

Where Mexican Americans do identify with political activity, they agree, and are more apt to identify with the established mainstream political parties and civic groups. These leaders are no exception and take a "middle-of-the-road" attitude as to which political party they align themselves with.

The former councilperson explains his reason for being a Republican as a means of letting young people know that there were two parties in contention:

> And even being a Republican, isn't so much because I'm strong on Republicans. Sometimes in my life I thought that it was important that young people know that there are two parties. Because if we get strength politically, I don't think that we can be Mexican Americans and all Democrats. So I just thought that being a Republican—like I say once again, maybe that was a little naive that being a Republican and being Mexican American might be something some of the young people may want.

The former city official explains he is a Republican but that he usually votes either way:

> You know, I've been a registered Republican for years but I tend to vote either way. I'll probably be voting mostly Democratic this time. I guess you could say I really should have changed my registration. But I consider myself neither a Democrat or Republican.

Another Mexican American, a public relations officer for a corporation, explains that although he is a Democrat, he does not want to be counted as being firmly on one side and considers his politics to be "in the middle."

The former city official goes as far as to say that Latinos are both conservative and something other than Democrat:

> Middle-income Hispanics can be very conservative. I keep reading that they are involved as Democrats. I don't think they are Democrats. I think they are just as prone to vote against stopping all phases of development as the Anglos would.

An ethnic political identity, according to these Mexican Americans, is held back by the class divisions that exist in the community. Those who are upper income or upper middle class are thought to associate more with issues that affect the larger community than with issues that could be called "Mexican American." For example, the local city official perceives ethnic issues as being primarily the possession of lower-income Latinos:

> As far as the Hispanics go, you've got really two different income levels here. You've got the old line old-timer, real middle class, or upper-middle income. They don't see any Hispanic issues. Ok, now you've got the lower-income Hispanics who don't vote. They are the ones that are minimum income— don't have adequate housing, etc.—and they see this general income situation as being an Hispanic issue. But the ones, the Hispanics that have it, they don't see it as an Hispanic issue.

A similar perspective is expressed by the Mexican American developer who believes that Latino unity is being held back by Latinos who have assimilated into the upper echelons of the middle class:

> There are a lot of Hispanics in Monterey Park that are "White Latinos." If they (the White Latinos) had a choice to vote for an Hispanic or a Jones, they would vote for Jones. These White Latinos consider themselves middle class or upper class. They average $40,000 a year. But all of them don't turn away. Some monied Latinos will give money to elections. Some will even help Latinos who are running. But the ones I am talking about are the ones who don't want to be called "Chicano." The ones who say "I'm an American citizen." The barrier to the unity of Latinos is the "White Latino."

Since Mexican American opinion leaders in the city council political arena propose that their identity is tied to the way they align themselves on issues, they also agree that the history of Mexican American political organizing in Monterey Park has been primarily through established civic groups and not through ethnic-based organizations. The corporate relations officer expresses this view:

> I've witnessed the Rotary Clubs, Soroptimist, and things like that. You know a lot of them are strictly, you know, Hispanic or are Jewish or something like that.

So does the former city council person:

> I don't know. I can't identify a place or time in my, say in my four years in office, where I can say there's a Mexican coffee klatsch or—other than your church groups that may be just simply a Mexican American in the church in the city where they are going to meet anyhow but there's—no organization. . . .But I don't recall being involved or invited in the city to any function that had primarily Mexican American or Hispanic organization.

At the same time, he goes a bit deeper to explain that the lack of Mexican American political organizing is related to the process of assimilation:

> I still have a feeling though that Monterey Park is not only a middle-class city, it's a middle-class status for Mexican Americans and it's a status that we've not enjoyed for too many years. And I think a lot of people have the feeling that I am here, I've got it made, and I've arrived. I've achieved. And have become complacent with that. Why make waves to do anything else and go any further than what I am? I am into the melting pot and I'm just as good as anybody else or as much of an American as anybody else.

A former city councilperson agrees that the assimilation process may be responsible for his primary involvement being on "nonethnic" civic and agency advisory boards. This is also true for other Latinos, according to him, who see no viable Latino organizations bringing Mexican Americans together. The participation that is beginning to take place in the political arena, he claims, is occurring on city commissions. While he agrees that this is a good step toward getting the Mexican American people to participate, he doesn't see any organization or coalition that has the capacity to unite the Mexican American people with other ethnic groups.

DISCUSSION

Overall, all the Mexican Americans interviewed in the city council political arena are part of more established community civic groups and institutions that are multiethnic. They don't affiliate with organizations or groups that are strictly ethnically separate. They all have doubts as to whether distinct Latino/Hispanic or Mexican American politics exists. Instead, they are pretty much united that Mexican Americans and Latinos in general are moved more by issues than by ethnicity. In this context, Mexican American political leaders in Monterey Park, particularly those who have held elected offices, have the characteristics of a politically ambivalent middle class[9] and one that is very much like what is called the Mexican American generation. This generation, according to Carlos Muñoz in his book *Youth, Identity, Power*, is a generation whose political ideology leans toward assimilation while de-emphasizing Mexican roots.[10] It also follows along the lines of what other Mexican American academicians have written about the characteristics of the contemporary Chicano middle class. The historian Juan Gómez-Quiñonez proposes that, in the contemporary period, leaders in the Chicano community "nearly always come from the middle class, and are increasingly homogenous in educational background, moderation in posture and style, and cautious about overemphasizing ethnicity."[11] In a study of political socialization among Chicano youth, Martín Sánchez Jankowski characterized the middle-class Chicano as wanting to become assimilated into the political system:

> There is a feeling among members of this group that politics can be an effective means of creating an economically secure future . . . The political goals of

middle-class Chicanos are to obtain as many advantages as possible without offending those who now hold power. These attitudes emerge from having been members of an ethnic group with a history of occupying the lower rungs of the socioeconomic ladder and from understanding that they have managed to become middle-class in spite of discriminatory practices by Anglo Americans.[12]

Monterey Park Mexican American leaders in the city council arena see themselves much along these lines: part of a middle-class community and a middle-class culture with political positions that are fluid, ambivalent, and middle-of-the-road. Although they say that ethnicity has very little to do with their identity, they still try to hold on to some aspects of the Mexican American heritage and culture. By calling themselves "Hispanic," they do identify themselves ethnically. However, the use of the term "Hispanic" is perceived as a politically safe term and as more acceptable in the mainstream than the term "Chicano."

However, when the interests of these Mexican American city officials are threatened, or when ethnicity can be used as a means of mobilization against them, then ethnicity comes to the political forefront.

For example, when former mayor Barry Hatch defined American identity in terms of supporting English as the official language, all the Mexican Americans on the city council arena opposed him. Similarly, on the issue of English Only and English on signs in the city, the former Mexican American city council official took a strong stand against it:

> Well, you know, the original outcry about the signs it was really just brought about by people suddenly seeing too many signs that they couldn't read and were mainly Chinese. Whether they were Chinese or whatever they were, it was kind of a slap at you because it was suddenly there. I did take a very strong stand on the English language thing and maybe politically stronger than I should have.

The Mexican American developer also took a stand against it as long as business signs could have some section in English:

> Hatch is not satisfied. He wants "English Only" and no other language on those business signs. I support having a portion of signs being in English, but not all English. English Only is discriminatory.

The former city manager was also strongly opposed to English Only and supported bilingual education as long as it didn't lead to separatism:

> I think it was a bunch of bullshit—I didn't agree with it. I was opposed to the whole idea. I think if bilingual education can help people out of a hole you've got to give them a chance. Now, I do agree that we are in a real danger if everyone keeps insisting on cutting themselves up into ethnic and language

groups. I mean I'd rather have it cohesive. It makes it very difficult to develop a cohesive country.

The former city manager parroted a common sentiment among all those interviewed, that the Americanism of Hatch was really meant to exclude others:

Hatch is 1950s. I mean Joe McCarthy in the 1950s wrapped himself in the American flag and anyone he didn't like he branded. And I noticed that the way he talked about Americanism that he also makes it clear as he goes through.

CONCLUSIONS

The various conceptions of identity, in this context, are related to how the demographic changes are perceived and how individuals see that they are affected by them. Barry Hatch represents an extreme right-wing view in defining who is or is not a so-called "American." He advocates English Only, believes that immigrants are creating many of the ills in the society, and wants to preserve the purity of what he considers to be American. That purity is enveloped in an image of the United States as being predominately for Anglo, English-speaking people with a heritage dating back to European explorers. The Mexican Americans interviewed here, although middle-class and accepting of assimilation, responded with a situationally specific ethnic viewpoint as to their identity. This viewpoint accepts that it's all right to be proud of your heritage and to identify yourself as something other than American (Latino, Hispanic, Californio, Mexican American), to be against English only, to support bilingual education, to sympathize with new immigrants, to see the United States as a country built on diversity, and to work to promote that diversity in the development of the community. At the same time, there are ambivalent perceptions among these Mexican Americans arising out of a feeling of being displaced. With the new influx of Chinese immigrants into the city, Mexican Americans see the need to form coalitions. However, they don't agree on what type of coalitions. Some see the need for coalescing with the new immigrants while others see them as a threat.

Although proposing that ethnicity does not play much of a role in their political lives, they do perceive of ethnicity in the context of particular interests. A former Mexican American councilmember goes so far as to relate from his experience that, although Latinos may organize along multiethnic lines in Monterey Park, ethnicity can sometimes be used to serve particular political interests:

But at the time I was approached and I declared I was the only Hispanic on the ticket. And the people that encouraged me to get involved were people that knew me and felt that there was an opportunity to exploit it. I am not too sure it had that much bearing on anything. So I thought well why not. So I went into it with that in mind. . . . So, you know, being the second Hispanic to serve on the city council that kind of made me proud and I was really aware of the fact that Hispanic, Mexican American groups, do need role models.

Overall, what appears to be ambivalence of identity among these politicians is really, at its base, the situational use of identity to meet particular class goals.

On the one hand, as middle-class Mexican Americans who own property, they have a stake in the local economy and are not willing to affiliate with a political identity that may jeopardize their positions. Their loss of the Spanish language and social mobility into an integrated middle-class community motivates them to identify as "Americans like everybody else." Consequently, they argue that they do not place much importance on ethnic identity or unity. On the other hand, ethnicity comes forth as a basis for political organizing around issues that they find threatening.

Their emphasis on "issues," however, is situationally specific according to the alliances that emerge. Where Mexican Americans are distinguished along lines of power or class, in comparison to other groups, they respond ethnically.

At the same time, although they agree that the Mexican American people lack cohesiveness and political power, they are active around issues that take on a class character involving economic and political interests that go beyond any one particular ethnic group.

NOTES

1. Here, I use the terms which the participants used to identify themselves. I use the term Mexican American primarily and Chicano/Chicana secondarily in reference to a group of people of Mexican descent who permanently reside in the United States. Mexican refers to recent immigrants from Mexico. Latino refers to all people of Latin American descent in the United States. Although all subjects interviewed in Monterey Park were of Mexican origin, they identified themselves as Hispanic, Mexican American, Californio, Mexican, and Latino. While Hispanic was the most widely used term at the city hall level, Latino was most prominently used at the neighborhood level. Although the majority of Latinos in Monterey Park are of Mexican descent, the participant observations also included Latinos from Puerto Rican, Cuban, and Central American backgrounds.

2. Mario T. García, in *Mexican Americans* (New Haven: Yale University Press, 1989), proposes that the study of Mexican American leadership is a basis for understanding the dynamics of change and politics within the larger Mexican American community. Another source: John Higham, "Current Trends in the Study of Ethnicity in the United States," *Journal of American Ethnic History* (Fall, 1982: 8–9) emphasizes the importance of studying ethnic leadership as a means of grasping the nature of ethnic groups in the United States.

3. Edmond Newton, "San Gabriel Valley Becomes the New Power Base of Latino Voters," *Los Angeles Times* (21 January 1990), B1.

4. Felix M. Padilla, *Latino Ethnic Consciousness* (Notre Dame, IN: Notre Dame University Press, 1985). Also his "Latino Ethnicity in the City of Chicago," in Susan Olzak and Joanne Nagel (eds.), *Competitive Ethnic Relations* (Orlando, FL: Academic Press, 1986), 153–171.

5. George L. Hicks and Philip E. Leis, *Ethnic Encounters: Identities and Contexts* (North Scituate, MA: Duxbury Press, 1977). Also see Nina Glick Schiller, "Ethnic Groups Are Made, Not Born: The Haitian Immigrant and

American Politics," in George L. Hicks and Philip E. Leis (eds.), *Ethnic Encounters: Identities and Contexts* (North Scituate, MA: Duxbury Press, 1977) 25–36.

6. G. Carter Bentley, "Ethnicity and Practice," *Comparative Studies in Society and History*, 29, 1 (Jan. 1987) 25. Also, Joanne Nagel, "The Political Construction of Ethnicity," in Susan Olzak and Joanne Nagel (eds.), *Competitive Ethnic Relations*, 93–108.

7. Erik Olin Wright, *Classes* (New York: Verso, 1985).

8. Mario Barrera has also written about the segmented nature of the U. S. class structure and specifically about the Chicano professional-managerial class segment. He proposes that Chicanos remain a small percentage in the professional-managerial category and are still situated at the lower socioeconomic levels of that class segment. See *Race and Class in the Southwest* (Notre Dame, IN: Notre Dame University Press, 1979), 214–217.

9. Mark E. Kann in *Middle Class Radicalism in Santa Monica* (Philadelphia: Temple University Press, 1986) writes about the ambivalence of the middle-class as being rooted in their trying to "reconcile their professional ideals of autonomy, rationality, and public service with their material contribution to human dependence, social control, and even tyranny in the political economy."

10. Carlos Muñoz, Jr., *Youth, Identity, Power* (New York: Verso, 1989), 19–46.

11. Juan Gómez-Quiñonez, *Chicano Politics: Reality and Promise: 1940–1990* (Albuquerque: University of New Mexico Press, 1990), 208.

12. Martín Sánchez Jankowski, *City Bound: Urban Life and Political Attitudes among Chicano Youth* (Albuquerque: University of New Mexico Press, 1986), 224.

15

BACKWARDS FROM *AZTLÁN*: POLITICS IN THE AGE OF HISPANICS

IGNACIO M. GARCÍA

The last ten years has seen an explosion in the number of Mexican Americans elected to political office. From the U.S. Congress to the local justice of the peace office, they have sought and gained entrance into a political arena closed to them only twenty years ago.[1] Their victories have come not only in the traditional Southwest, but in places like Kansas, Oregon, Washington, Illinois, and other non-traditional Chicano areas. In areas such as Texas, Arizona, New Mexico, and southern California, Mexican American elected officials, political and community leaders constitute an important political force, and one which tends to remain liberal in its politics while the nation remains in a conservative mood. Mostly Democrat in affiliation, they flaunt their "ethnicity," seek an identification with their community, and they play coalition politics, most having been introduced to the political arena through grassroots political activities. They constitute the most integrated Mexican American generation in history, and potentially the most influential because of their proximity to power, their relatively more affluent economic situation, and because their agendas remain within the liberal wing of the mainstream of American politics.[2]

This generation, which forms part of what is known, along with other Latinos, as the Hispanic Generation, is a hybrid of the two preceding generations: the Mexican American Generation and the Chicano Movement Generation, the two most defined generational groups in the history of the Mexican American community.[3] Because they are a political hybrid, they reflect very defined characteristics of the preceding generations, and their successes and potential "dilemmas" are likely to be influenced by those same characteristics.

This chapter will attempt to define the Hispanic Agenda—as it relates to Mexican Americans—and then trace its origins back to the last two generational groups. This is intended to provide historicity to what I refer to as the Mexican American/Hispanic Generation, and to understand the legacy of the two preceding generations. It will also reveal that there is continuity in the Chicano community's quest for civil rights and economic stability. Finally, this discussion should provide a preliminary prognosis on the future of this generation.

THE HISPANIC POLITICAL AND SOCIAL AGENDA

I will begin by defining the Hispanic political and social agenda. Any attempt, of course, would be an act of simplification of a complex topic. Nonetheless, I have identified several major characteristics that are germaine to most of the largest and most influential Hispanic organizations in the country. First, and above all else, these organizations seek inclusion into the American mainstream. Not satisfied with being a part of the melting pot, these organizations struggle for access to all the national institutions, including the President's Cabinet and the Supreme Court.[4] Second, Hispanic leaders have a minority-issues agenda and emphasize their ethnicity because it allows them participation in the liberal coalition, which for racial and cultural groups in this country is the only way to have a national presence.[5] Third, their agenda is tactically factionalized rather than based on a particular philosophical foundation, because they have no defined national leadership, and because, for all their national aspirations, they do not relate well to American history or Anglo institutions.[6] Fourth, their politics remain regionalized, and nationally weak. They have yet to prove their ability to move Mexican Americans to a particular viewpoint, or to support their issues and candidates against strong mainstream opposition. The Hispanic national leadership to date has been a transcendental leadership rather than an electoral-based one. This means that while they speak for Mexican Americans in a national context, and on major issues, they do not necessarily have the personal influence of national leaders. An exception to this may be politicians like Henry Cisneros and Federico Peña.[7] Only a handful of Hispanic leaders hold statewide elected offices, and of the current group only Cisneros is seen as having the potential to wage a strong national race, though even he is not confident of winning a statewide office.[8]

On the local and regional level, Hispanic politicians may be placed in two categories. One is the veteran legislator or county official who has become part of the local power elite, although he or she still remains seriously dependent on the Mexican American population to stay in office.[9] The other category of Hispanic politicians is the one of younger and newer political office holders who are deeply involved in coalition politics, and remain outside the circle of elites within their communities. They also depend heavily on their Mexican American constituency, but normally speak within the context of their coalition and practice what I call "postmodern" liberal politics. That is, they are sensitive to gender issues, support African American politicians, are environmentalists, and isolationists in foreign affairs.[10]

The first category of politicians was elected in the 1960s and 1970s, or at the end of the heyday of the Mexican American Generation. This group of politicians was bred under the old New Deal coalition of ethnics, Catholics, union workers, and liberal politicians. Their entrance into the public arena occurred during the height of the Civil Rights Movement, though only a few of them played a major role in it, because they objected to the more scathing militancy of the civil rights activists.[11] The second category of politicians may be further divided. Some were elected as reformed activists, while others came in as credentialed politicians, that is, lawyers, party loyalists, educators, and the like. Both groups, however, were elected after the height of the Chicano Movement (1968–1975), and ran as alternative candidates in either one of the major parties. Interspersed in both categories are Hispanic politicians elected during the height of the Chicano Movement by the traditional parties, or who are former militants who switched allegiance to the traditional parties after the decline of Raza politics.[12]

Besides politicians, the Mexican American/Hispanic Generation's leaders are leaders of middle-class organizations such as the Mexican American Legal Defense and Education Fund, the Southwest Voter Registration and Education Project, and numerous chapters of the American G.I. Forum, LULAC, IMAGE, and other more contemporary organizations. They are also bureaucrats in state and federal governments, educators in the public school system, administrators in higher education, and mid-level officials within the major political parties. Whatever their profession or political affiliation, these Mexican Americans share a common historical experience. Many matured politically during a period of ideological transition from the integrationist politics of the Mexican American Generation to the nationalist, often separatist, activism of the Chicano Movement Generation. They saw the issues of immigration, bilingual education, Chicano voting rights, English-only, and other "Latino" issues become part of the national debate on minorities. They have experienced a significant recruitment effort by both political parties, and they have seen a dramatic increase in the Mexican American population. They have also been discovered by the media several times over, which has led to the perception that has been touted since the late 1970s, that Mexican Americans are some kind of political giant awakening to claim its rightful place in American society. The view of this generation's self has been nurtured in the periphery of the nation's spotlight on minorities. Consequently, Mexican American/Hispanic leaders tend to look at issues from the top down. While many of their causes are at the grassroots level, they see solutions coming from national legislation, or through the federal court system. The federal government looms as the friendly political godfather ready to intervene on their behalf—always after a strong nudge. Because of this, political legitimacy for the Mexican American/Hispanic Generation is always in proportion to their number of elected and appointed officials, and to the amount of influence they have on any particular issue. To understand the position of Mexican American/Hispanics, a review of the preceding generations is necessary.

THE MEXICAN AMERICAN GENERATION

The Mexican American Generation, or the G.I. Generation as some call it, grew up two decades into the twentieth century. By this time, the relationship between Mexican Americans and Anglos had solidified into a culture of segregation. The rigidness or fluidity of race relations depended on the economic and political structure. Where Mexican Americans were seen as a potential threat politically or economically, the relationship was tense, and at times hostile. In areas where Mexican Americans posed little threat to the established order, the relationships between groups was distant, but individual Mexican Americans were able to find upward mobility.[13] By the 1930s, according to Mario T. Garcia's research, the majority of Mexicans in the United States were native-born. These individuals had grown up in the states, been educated in American schools—albeit, many in segregated or semi-segregated environments—and had come to see themselves as Americans.[14] A small number had also participated in World War I. Men like Alonso Perales, M.C. Gonzalez, and others had returned from the war anxious to establish organizations that promoted Americanization, yet fought to protect the Mexican American community from abuse.[15] The search for America by this group and the founding of the League of United Latin American Citizens by some of them was based on hard realities.[16]

Mexican Americans, according to the view of these reformers, were locked into poverty as long as they remained isolated in their neighborhoods, and clung emotionally to Mexico. Failure to learn English, go beyond the primary grades, and develop skills in the political and economic arena meant that they were destined to remain outside the country's mainstream. These reformers preached a gospel of collective upward mobility by stressing individual traits such as hard work, English language acquisition, and Americanization. Americanization as a political strategy was based on the need to find a group identity that recognized the importance of American ideals. To accomplish this, Mexican Americans had to seek inclusion rather than separatism, and this could only be possible if their civil rights were respected. And this, they knew, would not come without protest and litigation. The first time this strategy unfolded was in the battles to eliminate segregation, and to upgrade the education Mexican Americans received in the public schools. In legal battle after legal battle, Mexican American lawyers successfully challenged segregation in the schools. They also attacked de jure segregation in public theaters, swimming pools, restaurants, and cemeteries. They appealed to Americans' sense of fair play. And they appealed as loyal Americans who were seeking equal treatment and equal access as guaranteed by the Constitution.[17]

The middle-class leaders of this period were not Anglicized culturally—a charge often made against them. While a number of them were educated professionals, they spoke Spanish well, and were proud to be of Mexican descent. In pursuing an American agenda, they had no intention of disavowing who they were. But these new leaders were quite conscious that politicians and elected officials would ignore the needs of the community if its members did not vote, or litigate. This, however, does not mean that Mexican Americans of this period did not face internal conflicts in dealing with their identities. A large number of Mexican Americans still accepted the view that Mexican culture was backwards, and Americanization was the best option for improving the lot of the barrios of the Southwest.[18]

With the advent of World War II, many Mexican Americans saw a unique opportunity to prove their loyalty and their abilities. Between 375,000 to 500,000 Mexican Americans went off to war.[19] They served in every major theater of war, and came back the most highly decorated ethnic group in the history of the U.S. military.[20]

In the late 1950s and early 1960s, these reformers entered the electoral arena with some success. They elected a mayor in El Paso, congressmen in California and Texas, and they were successful in running slates of candidates for majority control in several communities. They also became an integral part of the John F. Kennedy campaign through the Viva Kennedy Clubs that helped him earn a slim victory in Texas. In coming to the aid of the Kennedy—who was Catholic, had sympathies for Latin America, and whose wife spoke Spanish—the leaders of the Mexican American Generation finally found a national forum through which they could let the nation know of the plight of the Mexican American. In a statement of principle, the Texas Viva Kennedy organizers wrote:

> In moments of bitterness over the sad state of affairs among our people, we might well point out that we did not ask the United States to come here—that we are, in effect, subject peoples for whose well-being the United States has a very special moral obligation, an obligation that has been most pointedly overlooked.[21]

The statement of principle presented a nine-point recommendation "for a brighter tomorrow." Throughout the recommendation it emphasized that there was a "reservoir of talent," that could help in solving the problems of the barrio. And the statement's writers made it clear that "only the mexicanos can speak for the mexicanos."[22]

The Kennedy campaign signalled a more politically active time for Mexican American activists.[23] After the campaign, two new Mexican American organizations were founded by those interested in electoral contests. These were the Mexican American Political Association (MAPA) and the Political Association of Spanish-Speaking Organizations (PASSO). Unlike LULAC and the American G.I. Forum, these two groups endorsed candidates, and led get-out-the-vote campaigns for them.[24]

THE CHICANO MOVEMENT GENERATION

It was at the height of these Mexican Americans' political rise that many Mexican Americans abandoned them to pursue a more radical alternative. The break did not come suddenly or totally unexpectedly. While Mexican Americans were making major inroads in limited areas, the overall conditions of the population remained unchanged. Few attended school beyond the secondary level, and almost twenty percent of them followed the migrant streams. Most lived in substandard housing, and segregation remained a reality for the overwhelming number of Mexican American students. Politically, the Mexican American population remained powerless. Even in communities where they accounted for the overwhelming majority of the population, they were unable to elect their own to school boards, city councils, commissioners' courts, and were even less likely at the regional or state level to have any political success.[25]

The politics of status and traditional civil rights had become class-focused in the eyes of many working class Mexican Americans. That is, the working-class Chicano perceived the middle-class reformers as having little empathy toward issues of culture, race, unionization, police brutality, or blatant racism at the individual level. In creating a greater opening for Mexican American integration, they created a political ambience of rebellion that was much more radical than they. The more scathing criticism by new radical voices of organizations like MAPA and PASSO, combined with the continuing deplorable conditions of the working class barrio, created an environment from whence came a new voice of protest. This voice, unheard before in the public arena, came from those who had not invested their time on civil rights issues or made friends and colleagues outside the barrio.

The activist lexicon changed from that of traditional civil rights rhetoric—discrimination, segregation, paternalism, pluralism, and the like—to one of cultural and racial conflict, from a polemic of equals and unequals to one of oppressor and oppressed. Rather than integration, the new Chicano activists sought cultural respect and a reinterpretation of their historical significance. They rejected middle-class values and promoted a working-class nationalism that stressed a Mexican American communal philosophy.

Leading this new activism were organizations such as the United Farm Workers Union, the Crusade for Justice, La Alianza Federal de Pueblos Libres, and La Raza Unida Party, plus a host of other smaller organizations that were founded from the mid-1960s to the late 1970s.[26] There were also individuals who turned away from the politics of status, and toward a new militancy. These new activists' agendas promoted a rejection of the liberal agenda, a reinterpretation of the Chicano historical experience, and an affirmation of the race and class composition of the *la raza*. Action and reaction provided the refiner's fire to the host of ideologies that were promoted by the numerous activists that appeared in the late 1960s and early 1970s.[27]

Chicanos activist explicitly set out to reject the liberal agenda by pointing out it failures, and its structural weaknesses. Rodolfo "Corky" González, founder of the Crusade for Justice and one of the intellectual precursors of the movement, would condemn the American political system for extracting too heavy a price for those who wanted to improve their lives. Chicanos, he argued, that sought upward mobility through integration suffered "such an immense loss of soul and dignity that the end results are as rewarding as a heart attack."[28] José Angel Gutiérrez, head of La Raza Unida Party, charged that federal and religious programs aimed at social change did not meet the needs of Chicanos, and tended to make matters worse by inflicting cultural genocide that "not only . . . damages our human dignity, but also makes it impossible for la raza to develop . . . self-determination."[29]

In rejecting the liberal agenda, activists made it imperative that Mexican Americans as a whole perceive their historical experience in a contrary fashion. Mexican Americans had to stop blaming themselves for their poverty, illiteracy, delinquency and other cultural deficiencies.[30] The reinterpretation of history brought new heroes. It also brought new theories to the forefront of the discussion on the Mexican American experience. The one that became dominant for a short period was the "internal colony" model, which posited that Mexican Americans shared many of the conditions of people who had been colonized by European powers.[31]

In searching for a new historical interpretation, proponents of the Chicano Movement emphasized the class and racial composition of the Mexican American population. Carlos Munoz refers to it as "a return to the humanistic cultural values of the Mexican working class."[32] Extolling the virtues of the working class meant redefining normative middle class ideologies espoused by organizations such as LULAC and the American G.I. Forum. The adoption of American cultural values, integration as a social strategy, and fidelity to Anglo parties and politicians became antitethical to *Chicanismo*.

By the late 1970s, the Chicano Movement had lost much of its fervency. The stridency of the Movement alienated many Mexican Americans who sought acceptance and legitimacy from the mainstream. Also, those who adhered to the militancy of the Chicano Movement soon found themselves confronted with economic pressures. Students left the universities and had to conform to the labor market demands. Organizations that had depended on federal funds for their existence and activism faced more austere times. Other adherents were attracted away from radicalism by the moderate militancy of groups such as the Mexican American Democrats, and the rejuvenated groups such as LULAC and the American G.I. Forum. Organizations such as the Mexican American Legal Defense and Education Fund (MALDEF) and the Southwest Voter Registration and Education Project (SVREP) attracted young Chicano professionals anxious to politic but not willing to lose their careers in doing so.[33] With the cream of the crop once again joining the mainstream, the politics of nationalism and the participation of the barrio declined significantly. The Chicano community, because of exhaustion and disillusionment over the slowness of change, turned to spokespersons.

THE MEXICAN AMERICAN/HISPANIC GENERATION

These spokespersons, as well as advocacy organizations, and politicians affiliated with powerful mainstream individuals and parties became what I referred to earlier as the Mexican American/Hispanic Generation. Ironically, this generation gained its name not through philosphical contemplation but because of the government's need for a simplified term to use in identifying growing communities of people from Latin America. In 1978, the Office of Management and Budget decided to use the label "Hispanic" to identify "A person of Mexican, Puerto Rican, Cuban, Central or South American . . . culture or origin, regardless of race.[34]

These new advocates and spokespersons arose because of the decline of the Chicano Generation. Both that generation and the one preceding it required wider participation of the Mexican American community. For the Mexican American/Hispanic Generation, however, community activism at the mass level had to subside for new leaders and "reformed" old ones to arise. These new leaders felt that the community could best be served by well-educated, and politically smart, ombudsmen who could best negotiate as individuals rather than representatives of particular groups or organizations.[35]

Many activists returned to the Democratic Party, while some joined the Republican Party.[36] Their new political allies became the liberal and moderate wings of both parties, and the numerous academic and social organizations that now promoted an agenda of cultural diversity. For Mexican Americans it meant subsuming their Chicano ideology for the label "Hispanic," which gained its importance and strength from being a national rather than a regional descriptive term. To be a Hispanic politician or activist meant representing a constituency found almost everywhere in the national territory. This shift toward Hispanization became necessary because of the growing importance of the census as an ideological and rhetorical weapon. More Hispanics, said the new conventional wisdom, translated into potentially more congressional seats, and more federal funds. As Hispanics, Mexican Americans also became more noticeable to businesspeople interested in selling their products. Those who would become the middlemen between the mainstream and the Chicano community stood to gain the leadership role in the community.

Rodolfo Acuña calls Hispanic leaders and activists the new "brokers."[37] These new powerbrokers, nothwithstanding Acuna's less-than-positive evaluation, are not simply a return to the Mexican American Generation as some have argued, nor are they political turncoats who have abandoned all the precepts of the Chicano Movement. Those politics to which we refer to as Hispanic politics may well be the next phase—though not necessarily the only possible or the best—in the struggle for Chicano civil rights. Mexican Americans as a population have reached a crossroad unfamiliar only a few years ago. For the Mexican American Generation, integration into mainstream society, nothwithstanding cultural pluralism, was an act of survival. To learn the language, litigate against segregation, and become patriotic Americans meant a possible acceptability and tolerance by mainstream society. For the Chicano Generation, radicalism and activism meant eliminating internal and external pressures, and self-destructive tendencies often caused by poverty and discrimination that threatened to destroy the barrio from within. It also meant "rediscovering Mexican America" for a forgetful nation.

For Hispanics, still besieged by many of the problems left unresolved by the previous generations, the demographic and political landscape has changed. Mexican American leaders now represent a relatively more culturally integrated community, much more distant from the mother country, more widely distributed geographically, and more politically and socially diverse.[38] It is also a larger community that has more to gain by participating in the mainstream than by staying in its periphery. Yet, it is a community more anxious to flaunt its ethnicity than any before. To represent this community requires a mixture of the two preceding generations' politics.

Much like the reformers of the Mexican American Generation, Hispanic leaders seek inclusion into the mainstream based on their merits. But like Chicano activists, they promote their "uniqueness" and reserve the right to have a viewpoint buttressed by historical experience. Their agenda is geared toward improving the conditions of the working class, albeit in a more conservative fashion. But like the Mexican American reformers, they see individual attainment of a higher education as the panacea for many of the problems in the barrio. Much like their pre-1960s counterparts, these leaders see racism as the principal obstacle facing the community. But like Chicanos, they are more conscious of the unfair economic and social structure that maintains most Mexican Americans locked in low-paying jobs. Mexican American/Hispanics pride themselves in being an ethnic group, one of the fastest growing in fact. In private many call themselves *Chicanos*, and talk the language of cultural militancy. But like premovement Mexican Americans, they are so integrated into American society through their employment and/or political activities that they often subsume their "substantive" nationalism. That is, they talk about cultural pride, but unlike Chicano activists shy away from discussing cultural and historical conflicts that divide Mexican Americans from white America.

Because they are integrated into the liberal mainstream, their civil rights activity depends heavily on the courts and liberal political support. This dependence on the courts is different from that of the Mexican American Generation that often had to convince courts that Mexican Americans should be included in the protective umbrella of the Constitution. The new court dependence seeks mobility and empowerment within the protective umbrella.

Organizations such as MALDEF and the Southwest Voter Registration and Education Project (SVREP) seek to empower Mexican Americans through lawsuits that eliminate obstacles to their wider electoral participation. Organizations such as the National Council of La Raza, LULAC, and the American G.I. Forum lobby for inclusionary national policies, while at the same they seek federal funds to support employment enhancement programs, and economic development initiatives. Politically, Mexican American Democrats, and the few Hispanic Republicans, attempt to influence the writing of political platforms, and the direction of political campaigns. In every instance, however, Mexican Americans/Hispanics depend on the benevolence of the American political and judicial systems. When the system fails to be fair, Mexican Americans/Hispanics revert back to their nationalism, but only to rally mass support for their cause, and to remind the American political mainstream that Mexican Americans are the continually awakening giant whose "potential" strength could tip the balance in favor of any of the major players in American society.

Politically, Hispanics practice a balancing act between integration and cultural distinctiveness. They have learned the American political system, have made powerful allies, understand grassroots activism, and are more than willing to play ethnic politics—or accommodation politics—when it is to their advantage. Philosophically, however, the Mexican American/Hispanic Generation has yet to develop its political ethos. The reason may lie in where they became socialized into their activism and politics. Rather than develop an ethos outside of the mainstream as the preceding generations of activists did, these Mexican American activists have done it at the university, their federal or state jobs, or their Democratic and Republican Party activities. Former activists were often mentored by Mexican Americans and developed their philosophical leanings within Mexican American circles, in proximity to the barrios in which they grew, or in which they became involved politically. Most of the newer Hispanics, and some of the older ones, did not mature philosophically within the confines of the barrio, or simply like Willie Velasquez, late founder of the SVREP, and Raul Yzaguirre of the National Council of La Raza, never gave up the hope of making their barrios part of the American mainstream.

The basic socioeconomic dilemmas confronting Mexican Americans have remained constant or gotten worse for many Chicanos, even as they have gotten better for others. Mexican Americans still drop out of school at a high rate, and few graduates enter institutions of higher education. The number of families living in poverty has grown, and so has the number of female-led families. There is political underrepresentation. Segregation is still a way of life for many Mexican Americans. So is discrimination. Compounding those dilemmas are newer ones that Hispanics have brought on themselves because of their view of the role they play in society. The Hispanic agenda calls for "moving beyond recognition politics to an institutionalization of power."[39] This means that Hispanics want to become an integrated force within American society. They want to serve in government, be selected for important functions, and have accessibility to all the corridors of power and prestige that this country can offer its citizens. But Mexican Americans/Hispanics also want to maintain their cultural distinctiveness.

The ethnicity of the 1990s is different from the nationalism of the 1960s and 1970s. That variation of nationalism promoted separatism. The talk of a Quebec-styled Chicano homeland was common. Mexican American/Hispanic leaders don't talk of segregating themselves or forming a quasi-nation. They talk of transforming this nation from the top down. They see immigration issues in terms of future voters, and they have restructured bilingual education organizations into strong political pressure groups. They have joined coalitions like the Rainbow Coalition to gain status as nation powerbrokers, and they have encouraged the growth of the Spanish-speaking media to create another forum for their agenda.[40]

In politicizing or ethnicizing their activism, they have abandoned both the Mexican American Generation's desire to integrate without accentuating their ethnicity, and the Chicano Generation's yearning for separateness. They have retreated from the politics of Aztlán.[41] While *Chicanismo* failed to build Aztlán, it did make culture a political issue. For Mexican American/Hispanic leaders this culturalization of politics serves both as an opportunity and a dilemma. Without the rise of ethnic pride it is likely that Mexican Americans would have remained an invisible minority, left out of federal funding, and federal civil rights protection. But ethnic politics keep Mexican Americans/Hispanics from acquiring the mainstream acceptance that, like their Mexican American Generation counterparts, they so much desire.

THE FUTURE

For this generation, the future remains uncertain. Since the mid-1980s, Hispanic leaders and politicians have been seen as more liberal than their Mexican American constituency. And the latest survey on Latinos indicates that the ideological difference remains.[42] Many Mexican Americans are uneasy about trading their cultural identity of Mexican or Mexican American for a label that seems to serve the needs of its politicians and middle class leaders, but that translates into very little economically or socially for them. Much like the preceding generations, those in the Mexican American/Hispanic Generation are entering a political and cultural danger zone in which they are separated from their community ideologically at a time when they are maturing politically. Only time will tell whether this generation will succeed in maintaining its constituency even as it evolves and matures in the national arena.

NOTES

1. See the 1992 election coverage in *Hispanic Link Weekly Report*, 10, 44 (9 November 1992); also, see "Number of Latino Elected Officials Passes 5,000," *Hispanic Link Weekly Report*, 11, 38 (27 September 1993).

2. See Mario T. García, *Mexican Americans, Leadership, Ideology, and Identity, 1930–1960* (New Haven: Yale University Press, 1989) for an explanation of his usage of the term "generation." His definition is the one I use in this work. See, in particular, pages 3–22.

3. For works on the Mexican American Generation, see Mario T. García's *Mexican Americans, Leadership, Ideology, and Identity, 1930–1960*; Richard A. García, *Rise of the Mexican American Middle Class: San Antonio, 1929–1941* (College Station: Texas A&M Press, 1991); and Benjamin Marquez, *LULAC: The Evolution of a Mexican American Political Organization* (Austin, University of Texas Press, 1993). On the Chicano Movement, see Juan Gómez-Quiñones, *Chicano Politics: Reality and Promise, 1940–1990* (Albuquerque: University

of New Mexico Press, 1990); Carlos Muñoz, Jr., *Youth, Identity, Power: The Chicano Movement* (London and New York: Verso Press, 1989); and the author's *United We Win: The Rise and Fall of La Raza Unida Party* (Tucson: Mexican American Studies & Research Center, 1989).

4. See "Presidential Appointments and Disappointments," *Hispanic Link Weekly Report*, 11, 41 (18 October 1993). In the same issue, "Clinton Chastized on Appointments." Also, see "Latinas Want Administration Posts," *Hispanic Link Weekly Report*, 11, 7 (15 February 1993); and "Latino Groups Assess Clinton's Court Choice," *Hispanic Link Weekly Report*, 11, 25 (21 June 1993).

5. Liberal coalition is a term I use to describe the groups, both formal and informal, that come together to work for liberal issues. One such group that is minority-oriented is the Rainbow Coalition of the Rev. Jesse Jackson. Another may be the traditional Democratic coalition of unionists, Catholics, minorities,

and middle-class liberals that come together during national elections.

6. While there are several organizations, such the National Association of Latino Elected and Appointed Officials (NALEO), the Hispanic Congressional Caucus, the Hispanic Leadership Council, and the National Council of La Raza, none of them claims to be the voice of the Mexican American community. And a number of Mexican American leaders and politicians belong to several of the aforementioned. As for relating well to American history, none of these organizations are as involved in national holidays and honoring Mexican American war heroes as are the traditional organizations such as the American G.I. Forum and LULAC. And some of the leaders of the newer groups see the patriotism of the aforementioned as archaic.

7. Henry Cisneros is Secretary of Housing and Urban Development; Federico Peña is Secretary of Transportation in the Clinton Administration.

8. See "Cisneros Rules Himself out of Race," *San Antonio Light* (15 December 1992).

9. This category of politicians may best be represented by U.S. Rep. Henry B. Gonzalez of San Antonio. See "Gonzalez of San Antonio: the Politics of Fratricide," *The Texas Observer* (12 December 1980).

10. A good example of this kind of politician is Federico Peña, current Secretary of Transportation, who was elected mayor of Denver through coalition politics. He remains a strong supporter of lesbians/gays, environmentalists, and women. For an analysis of his election to the Denver mayorship, see Rodney E. Hero, "The Elections of Federico Peña," in *Latinos and the U.S. Political System* (Philadelphia: Temple University Press, 1992), 116–130.

11. Former Congressman Edward Roybal of Los Angeles was an example of this kind of politician. So are Esteban Torres, congressman from California, and Tony Anaya, former governor of New Mexico.

12. For a short discussion on circumstances leading to the rise of these politicians, read the chapter entitled "La Raza Unida in Retrospect," in the author's *United We Win*. See also "Postmovement Trends: Fragmentation, Radicalization, Retraditionalization," in Mario Barrera's *Beyond Aztlán: Ethnic Autonomy in Comparative Perspective* (New York, Westport, Connecticut and London: Praeger, 1988), 45–65.

13. For a discussion on this fluidity and rigidity, see David Montejano, *Anglos and Mexicans in the Making of Texas, 1836–1986* (Austin: University of Texas Press, 1987). See in particular "Part Three: Segregation 1920–1940," 157–256.

14. See "The Mexican American Generation," in Mario T. Garcia's *Mexican Americans*, Chapter one, 1–24.

15. For a discussion of Mexican Americans in World War I, see Carole E. Christian, "Joining the American Mainstream: Texas's Mexican Americans during World War I," *Southwestern Historical Quarterly*, XCII (Spring 1989). This is one of the few works that actually deals with this period of time.

16. See Marquez, *LULAC*, 15–38.

17. For a good discussion on this litigation and activism, read chapters 2, 3, and 4 of Mario T. Garcia's *Mexican Americans*; and chapters 3, 4, and 5, in Guadalupe San Miguel, *Let All of Them Take Heed* (Austin, University of Texas Press, 1987).

18. See Muñoz's discussion of the Mexican American Movement in his book *Youth, Identity, Power*, especially pages 31–44. Especially among the young Mexican Americans of the 1940s, there was concern with how society would perceive them. While they fought for the rights of the Mexican American community, it seems they did it with the hope that this community would become similar to those of the Anglo Americans.

19. These figures come from Robin Fitzgerald Scott's dissertation, "The Mexican American in the Los Angeles Area, 1920–1950: From Acquiescence to Activity," (University of Southern California, 1971).

20. See Raúl Morin's *Among the Valiant* (Alhambra, CA: Borden, 1966).

21. "The American of Mexican Descent, A Statement of Principle," p. 1 (undated), Hector P.

Garcia Collection, Texas A&M University at Corpus Christi.

22. Ibid., 4–6.

23. Even today, Hispanics have an ingrained fondness for John F. Kennedy. See "JFK's Inspiration Still on Our Walls and in Our Hearts," *San Antonio Express-News* (22 November 1993).

24. See "Texas Latins Bid for Better Lot with Ballots," *Forth Worth Star-Telegram* (5 April 1964); also, Robert A. Cuellar, "A Social and Political History of the Mexican American Population of Texas, 1929–1963" (Master's Thesis, North Texas State University, 1969), 41–65.

25. See the author's prelude in *United We Win* for an assessment of the state of Mexican America in the mid-1960s, 1–12; also, see Leo Grebler, Joan W. Moore, and Ralph Guzman, *The Mexican American People* (New York: Free Press, 1970), 18–23, for a more extensive view of the Mexican American population's education and economic status.

26. For a good overview of these and other Chicano militant organizations, see "Liberalism: The Chicano Movement and Its Organizations from the 1960s to the 1970s," in Juan Gómez-Quiñones's *Chicano Politics*, 101–153.

27. The author discusses further this agenda in his "The Politics of Aztlán: The Forging of a Militant Ethos among Mexican Americans" Ph.D dissertation, The University of Arizona, forthcoming.

28. See Stan Steiner, *La Raza: The Mexican Americans* (New York: Harpers Brothers, 1969), 383–384.

29. See *Congressional Record* (15 April 1969): 9059. For more of this kind of rhetoric see "MAYO Leader Warns of Violence, Rioting," *San Antonio Express-News*, reprinted in Congressional Record (3 April 1969): 8591.

30. See John C. Hammerback, Richard J. Jensen, and José Angel Gutiérrez, *A War of Words* (Westport, CT: Greenwood Press, 1985), 51.

31. For an indepth explanation of the internal colony model, see Mario Barrera, Carlos Muñoz, Jr., and Charles Ornelas, "The Barrio as Internal Colony," in Harlan H. Hahn (ed.), *Urban Affairs Annual Review*, 6 (1972); also Tomás Almaguer, "Toward the Study of Chicano Colonialism," in *Aztlán*, 2, 1 (Spring 1971): 7–20.

32. See Muñoz, *Youth, Identity, Power*, 15.

33. For general article on the "new" type of activist, see "Watch Out For Willie Velásquez," *Nuestro*, March 1979. This article discusses the work of Willie Velásquez, founder of the Southwest Voter Registration and Education Project. He was the first real hero of the Hispanic Generation, even though his roots were in the Chicano Movement.

34. See Gerardo Marin and Barbara VanOss Marin, "Research with Hispanic Populations," *Applied Social Research Methods Series*, 23 (Newbury Park and London: Sage Publications, 1991), 20–23. See Federal Register (4 May 1978): 19269.

35. Leodoro Martínez, interview with author, Cotulla, Texas, Summer 1985. Martínez, who had been a La Raza Unida Party activist but was then judge of Dimmit County, indicated that the time of mass participation in decision making was over. Chicanos, he argued, now needed politically astute leaders to make decisions for them. The working class, he concluded, did not always know what was good for it. Organizations such as COPS (San Antonio), UNO (Los Angeles), and other similar grassroots entities do not endorse candidates and do not support their members in quests for political office. Consequently, they are pressure groups rather than decision-making groups. Henry Cisneros as mayor of San Antonio, and Albert Bustamante as county judge of Bexar County, often went against the wishes of COPS and still gained a large percentage of the organization's membership's vote.

36. For a discussion on Mexican Americans and the Republican Party, see "The Browning of Presidential Politics," *Hispanic Link Weekly Report*, 10, 31, beginning on 3 August 1992 and running for thirteen weeks.

37. See Rodolfo Acuña, *Occupied America* (New York: Harper & Row, 1988), 363–412.

38. There is no attempt to ignore the large number of Mexican resident aliens and undocumented workers in this country, and the kind of impact they have on the political culture of

Mexican Americans/Hispanics. That is simply a topic for further study.

39. See Christine Marie Sierra, "Chicano Politics—After 1984."

40. This, of course, they have done in conjunction with other Hispanic groups. And, in all fairness, it must be said that their own regional agendas have been influenced by the other Latino groups.

41. By politics of Aztlán, I mean the political goals of the Chicano Movement. Aztlán was a term used to signify a nation-within-a-nation concept that was popular early in the Movement. Later, Aztlán simply referred to the concept of Chicano empowerment. See Rudolfo A. Anaya's and Francisco Lomeli's *Aztlán Essays on the Chicano Homeland*.

42. See Rodolfo O. de la Garza, Louis DeSipio, F. Chris García, John García, and Angelo Falcon (eds.), *Latino Voices: Mexican, Puerto Rican, and Cuban Perspectives* (Boulder, CO: Westiview Press, 1992).

INDEX

Acculturation
   bilingual education and, 162, 171–172
   reversing process of, 161
Acuña, Rodolfo, 198, 203
Aguila, Pancho, 122, 125
A Nation at Risk, 168
   See also Human capital
American G.I. Forum, 193, 195, 197, 199
Assimilation
   and social class, 183–185
   mass media and cultural, 128
   mass media and structural, 128
Austin, Texas, 128, 130, 132, 152
Aztlán
   and new world view in schools, 175
   as political goal, 200, 204

Barrera, Mario, 158, 174, 189, 203
Bean, Frank, 21, 23, 49, 94–95
Becerra, Rosina M., 87, 88, 90, 94
Bilingual/bicultural education
   changes in structure of, 169–173
   Chicano Movement advocates, 161
   emergence of, 161
   parents' attitudes toward, 171
   rationale for maintenance, 162
   rationale for transitional, 162
   students disadvantaged taking achievement tests, 170
Bluestone, Barry, 28, 37, 39
Bourdieu, Pierre, 76, 86
Brisco, Dolph, 163
Brody, Elaine M., 88, 94

Cadena, Gilbert R., 101, 110
California Test of Basic Skills (CTBS), 169, 170
Calpulli
   activities in Southern California, 106–108
   philosophy of, 107
   stress on social change, 107
   See also Comunidades de base
Cantor, Marjorie H., 88, 93, 94
Chávez, César, 104
Chicana sisters
   and pipeline issues, 100
   influenced by liberation theology, 104
Chicano gang
   and rehabilitation, 144, 149–152
   and retribution, 144, 149–152
   as "problem people" news frame, 146–149, 151
   associated with criminal behavior, 144–148
   operationalization of, 148
   promoted by police and mass media as "moral panic," 146
Chicano homeland: *See* Aztlán
Chicano Movement
   emphasis on class and race, 197
   goals and bilingual education, 173
   politicians elected during height of, 193
Chicano Movement Generation, 195–197, 198
Chicano population
   age structure of, 19, *20*
   family characteristics of, 17, 19–22
   geographic distribution of, 12–17
   growth from 1910 to 1990 of, 9
   increase between 1980 and 1990, 12–13, *14*
   residence patterns of, 17–19

Chicano priests
    and pipeline issues, 100
    beliefs about discrimination in Church, 101
Cholos, 144
Cinco de Mayo, 161, 171
Cisneros, Henry, 192, 202
Ciudadanos Unidos (United Citizens), 160,
    163–164
Class/structural theories
    research utilizing, 26–28
Comité de Nueve (Committee of Nine), 164
Comunidades de base (base communities)
    defined, 106–107
    inspired by liberation theology, 107
    See also Calpulli
Contradictory class locations, 181
Corporate restructuring
    and earnings inequality, 34
    and involuntary part-time employment, 28
    impact on young Latino workers, 29–36
Corrido
    accounts of the prison experience, 118
    ascendancy, 114
    poetics of intercultural conflict, 116
    social conflict and, 115
Cortez, Gregorio, 114, 116–117
Crusade for Justice, 196
Crystal City, Texas, 157, 160, 163, 166
Cuellar, José, 89, 94
Cultural nationalism
    as alternative ideology, 157
    defined, 174
    RUP disbanding weakens, 166

De Anda, Roberto M., 37–38, 48, 49
DeFreitas, Gregory, 25, 37, 49
Democratic Party, 198, 200
Demography
    of Chicanos in Catholic Church, 100–102
Díaz, José, 117
Diez y Seis de Septiembre, 161, 171
Downing, John D., 143, 153

"El Contrabando de El Paso," 119
Elizondo, Virgilio, 104, 105, 111
Ell, K., 88, 94
"El Plan de San Diego," 124
Enculturation
    defined, 76

English Only, 186, 187
Extended family
    defined, 87
    myth of, 87, 90
    unable to provide for elders, 87, 89–91
    urbanization and, 92
    See also Mexican American elderly; Social
      support system

Falbo, Tony, 150
Families in poverty
    headed by single Chicanas, 21
    Latino youth living with, 29
    profile of Latino and Chicano, 65–66
Familism
    and academic achievement, 53
    attitudes on, 53, 56, 58
    defined, 53
    dimensions of, 53
    effect of acculturation on, 53–54, 58, 60–61
    generational status and, 53, 56–58
    influence of structural factors on, 54, 56, 58
    socioeconomic mobility and, 53, 57
    See also Extended family
Fanon, Frantz, 113, 123, 124, 125
Fishman, Mark, 143, 153
Flores, Patricio Fr., 100
Fort Worth, Texas, 88

Gamba, Raymond J., 101, 110
García, Mario T., 188, 194, 201, 202
García, Rito, 114–116, 118, 121
Garza de León, Manuel, 119
Gómez-Quiñonez, Juan, 185, 189
González, Henry B., 162, 175, 202
González, Roberto O., 101, 110
González, Rodolfo "Corky," 196
Gramsci, Antonio, 102, 110
Guillen, Patricio Fr., 106, 107
Gutiérrez, Gustavo, 103, 111
Gutiérrez, José Angel, 160–161, 174, 175, 203
    leadership style, 163–167
    on self-determination, 196–197
    ousted as county judge, 166–167

Hansen, Niles, 158, 174
Harrison, Bennett, 28, 37, 39
Hatch, Barry, 186–187

Hegemony
  and Latino counter-, 109
  defined, 102
  in Catholic Church, 102
Hispanic agenda, 192–193, 200
Hispanic politicians, 192–193, 198
Household cluster
  economic and social exchanges in, 77–78, 80, 85
  defined, 77
  partial, 83
Human capital
  and earnings inequality, 36
  defined, 26
  development in Texas, 168
  returns to, 29

Immigration of Mexicans to U.S., 10–12
Immigration Reform and Control Act (IRCA), 11
Income inequality
  and occupational distribution, 25, 29, 34–36
  between Latinos and Anglos, 25–26, 32
Intercultural conflict, 120
Intermittent employment
  defined, 44
  distribution by race and gender, 46
  distribution by schooling, 47
Internal colonialism, 159
Internal labor market
  and economic sectors, 30
  defined, 38
Involuntary part-time work
  and women, 28
  defined, 37, 44
  distribution by race and gender, 46
  distribution by schooling and gender, 47
Isasi-Díaz, Ada Maria, 102, 105–106, 110–111

Job deskilling, 27
  defined, 37
  teachers in Texas, 168
Joblessness
  and labor force marginality, 44
  level of, 41, 42

Keefe, Susan E., 54, 61, 62

La Alianza Federal de Pueblos Libres, 196
Labor force
  in South Texas, 158–159

integration
  defined, 42
participation
  defined, 42
Lacayo, Carmela G., 87, 94
Latina theologians
  challenge patriarchy, 105
  contributions by feminist, 104
  struggle towards liberation, 103, 105
Latina/o theology
  and group empowerment, 104
  example of religious cultural resistance, 103
Latino youth
  in competitive sector, 30–31
  in monopoly sector, 31
  in state sector, 31–32
Latino identity
  situational character of, 181–182
La Raza Unida (Raza Unida Party–RUP)
  and schooling reform, 160–161
  factionalization within, 163–167
  in Crystal City, 157–158
La Velle, Michael, 101, 110
La vida loca, 113
League of United Latin American Citizens
    (LULAC), 193, 195, 197, 199
Liberation theology
  Latin America, 103–104
  influence on U.S. Latina/o theology, 103–104
Lockery, Shirley A., 88, 94
Los Angeles, 15, 76, 78, 79, 82
Los Angeles County, California, 179
Lubben, James E., 88, 94

Maduro, Otto, 102, 110, 111
Marginal jobs, 41, 44
  See also Underemployment
Marin, Gerardo, 101, 110
Markides, Kyriakos S., 87, 88, 94
Martínez, Lorrie, 118, 125
Mass media
  and linguistic acculturation, 132–133
  "hypodermic needle" approach to, 145
  "magic bullet" approach to, 127
  uses and gratifications approach to, 129–130
Marxism, 104
McLemore, Dale S., 144, 153
Mestizaje
  Virgilio Elizondo on, 104–105

Mexican American elderly
  access to social services, 92–93
  and independent living, 87, 92
  projected growth, 88
  underutilization of social services, 87–88,
    92–93
  See also Extended family; Social support
    system
Mexican American Generation
  advocates Americanization, 194–195
  attacks segregation, 194
  political ambivalence of, 185
Mexican American/Hispanic Generation
  compared to previous generations, 198–201
  leaders of middle-class organizations, 193
  origins of, 197–198
Mexican American Legal Defense and Education
    Fund (MALDEF), 193, 197, 199
Mexican American Political Association
    (MAPA), 195, 196
Mexican American War, 10, 115
Mexican American Youth Organization (MAYO)
  and school walkouts, 159
  criticized by Henry B. Gonzáles, 162
  See also Winter Garden Project
Mexican immigrant households: *See* U.S.
    Mexican households
Mirandé, Alfredo, 117, 124
Monterey Park, California
  basis of political organizing in, 184–185
  demography of Mexican Americans and
    Latinos in, 180–181
  characteristics of elected officials in, 185–188
Moore, Joan W., 144, 146, 153
Mujerista theology
  defined, 106
  See also Latina theologians
Muñoz, Carlos Jr., 185, 189, 197, 201, 202, 203
Mutran, Elizabeth, 89, 93, 94

National Council of La Raza, 199, 200
Newspapers
  used for cultural maintenance and
    assimilation by Chicanos, 138–140
Now and Then in Zavala County, 167

O'Connor, James, 30, 31, 38
Occupational distribution
  of Mexican-origin and white workers by
    gender, 43–44
  of young Latino and white workers by gender,
    31, 32–33

Pachucos, 144
Padilla, Amado, 54, 61, 62, 63
Padilla, Felix, 181, 188
Paredes, Américo, 114–115, 117–118, 124
Parsons, Talcott, 53
Patriarchy
  defined, 106
  justified by Catholic Church, 105
Peña, Federico, 192, 202
Perot, Ross, 168
Phoenix, Arizona, 145–146, 15
Pinto (Chicano prisoner)
  contestative tradition, 123
  institutional violation against, 118
  poets, 116
  poetics, 117
Pizaña, Aniceto, 114, 124
Political Association of Spanish-Speaking
    Organizations (PASSO) 195, 196
Pope Paul VI, 102, 107
Popol Vuh, 109
Posada, 84
Praxis
  as "doing theology," 105
  and Latina liberation, 105

Quinceañera, 84

Radio
  used for entertainment and cultural
    maintenance by Chicanos, 137
Rainbow Coalition, 200
Reagan administration
  educational policy shifts during, 167–168
Religion
  as source of social change, 102–103
Rinches (Texas Rangers), 115–116, 119
Republican Party, 198, 200
Ríos, Diana I., 130, 141
Romo, Harriet, 150
Romo, Ricardo, 144, 153

Saldivar, José D., 123, 125
Salinas, Raúl, 116–118, 120–123, 124, 125
San Antonio, Texas, 15, 137, 159
Sánchez Jankowski, Martín, 185, 189
Sánchez, Ricardo, 119, 125

San Francisco Bay Area, 55
Sediciosos (seditionists), 114
Sexism
  in Catholic Church, 105
Shaw, David, 90, 94
Sleepy Lagoon
  case of, 117
  Defense Committee, 117
Social support system
  components
    formal, 88
    informal, 88
      affective, 89, 91
      instrumental, 88–89, 91–92
  defined, 88
  See also Extended family; Mexican American
    elderly
Socioeconomic integration
  of Mexican-origin population, 41
Southwest Voter Registration and Education
    Project (SVREP)
  Chicano professionals and, 197
  seeks to empower Mexican Americans,
    199–200
  voter registration in San Gabriel Valley, 180
Surace, Samuel J., 144, 145, 150, 153, 154

Talamántez, Luis, 120–121, 125
Tapia, Javier, 77, 81, 86
Tarango, Yolanda, 105, 106, 110–111
Tarrant County, Texas, 89
Telenovelas, 135–136
Television
  used for entertainment by Chicanos, 134–136
  used for surveillance and assimilation by
    Chicanos, 133–134
Texas Educational Assessment of Minimal Skills
    (TEAMS), 169, 170, 171
Tienda, Marta, 21, 23, 49
Tonantzin (Cihuacoatl), 108
Treaty of Guadalupe Hidalgo, 10
Treviño, Jacinto, 114
Treviño, Margarita C., 93, 95
Tuchman, Gaye, 143, 153, 154
  on news frame construction, 146–147
Tucson, Arizona, 145–146
Turner, Ralph, 144, 145, 150, 153, 154

Underemployment
  components, 44–47
    defined, 44
    distribution by race and gender, 46–47
    distribution by schooling, 47–48
  defined, 44
  levels of, 44, *45*
Undocumented Mexican immigration, 11
Unemployment: *See* Joblessness
United Farm Workers Union, 196
U.S. dominant discourse, 123
U.S. Mexican households
  ceremonial activities, 83–84
  composition, 78
  division of labor based on gender, 80
  recreational activities, 81–82, 84
  reproduction of based on gender, 84–85
  social and cultural reproduction of, 75–77
  survival strategies of, 80

Velasquez, Willie, 200, 203
Vélez-Ibáñez, Carlos, 77, 81, 86
Vigil, James Diego, 146, 153
Villa, Pancho, 182
Viva Kennedy Clubs, 195

Weeks, John R., 89, 94
"White Latinos," 184
White, Mark, 168
Winter Garden Project
  and Chicano self-determination, 160
  goals of, 160
Winter Garden Region
  description of, 158–160
Working poor
  defined, 44, 49
  distribution by race and gender, 46
Wright, Erik Olin, 181, 189

Youth, Identity, Power (Muñoz), 185
Yzaguirre, Raúl, 200

Zárate Macías, Rosa Marta Sr., 106, 107, 108,
  110, 111
Zatz, Margorie S., 145–146, 153
Zoot-suiter, 144–145